Also by Henry Louis Gates, Jr.

*The Future of the Race*, with Cornel West

*Identities*, with Anthony Appiah

*Colored People*

*Loose Canons*

*Figures in Black*

*The Signifying Monkey*

General Editor, *The Schomburg Library of
Nineteenth-Century Black Women Writers*
(in forty volumes)

# Thirteen Ways of Looking at a Black Man

# Thirteen Ways
# of Looking
# at a
# Black Man

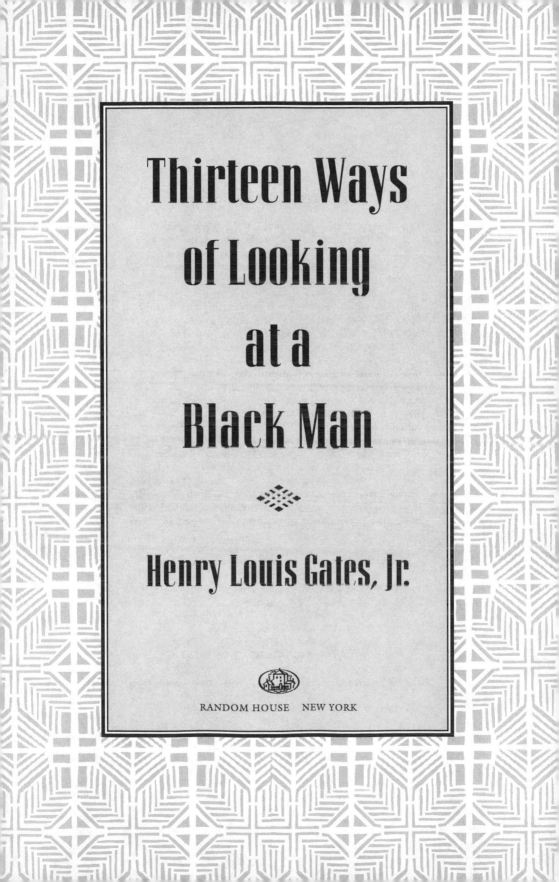

## Henry Louis Gates, Jr.

RANDOM HOUSE    NEW YORK

All rights under International and Pan-American
Copyright Conventions. Published in the
United States by Random House, Inc., New York,
and simultaneously in Canada by Random House
of Canada Limited, Toronto.

All of the essays that appear in this work were originally published
in *The New Yorker,* except for "The Welcome Table," which was
originally published as "The Fire Last Time: What James Baldwin Can and Can't Teach America" in *The New Republic.*

Grateful acknowledgment is made to the following for permis-
sion to reprint previously published material:
Amiri Baraka: Three-line poem. Copyright © Amiri Baraka.
Reprinted by permission of Amiri Baraka.
Alfred A. Knopf, Inc.: Seven lines from "Thirteen Ways of Look-
ing at a Blackbird" from *Collected Poems* by Wallace Stevens.
Copyright © 1923 and renewed 1951 by Wallace Stevens.
Reprinted by permission of Alfred A. Knopf, Inc.
University Press of Virginia: Six lines from "Omni-Albert
Murray" from *The Venus Hottentot* by Elizabeth Alexander.
Copyright © 1990 by the Rector and Visitors of the University
of Virginia. Reprinted with permission of the University Press of
Virginia.

Library of Congress Cataloging-in-Publication Data
Gates, Henry Louis.
Thirteen ways of looking at a black man / Henry Louis Gates, Jr. — 1st ed.
p.    cm.
ISBN 0-679-45713-5
1. Afro-American men.   I. Title.
E185.86.G375   1997
920.71'089'96073—dc20        96-33138

Random House website address: http://www.randomhouse.com/

Printed in the United States of America on acid-free paper
23456789
First Edition
Book design by Tanya M. Pérez-Rock

For
Henry Rosovsky

When the blackbird flew out of sight,
It marked the edge
Of one of many circles.

—Wallace Stevens,
from "Thirteen Ways of Looking at a Blackbird"

# Contents

# Introduction: Ways of Looking

## 1.

Liggett's Drug Store was at the epicenter of the cultural revolution that overtook New Haven in 1969. It was situated at the north corner of Yale's campus, where, at a rotary, five streets met helter-skelter, despite a full battery of traffic lights and pedestrian islands. Like a fortress, it seemed to hold at bay the chaos that lay just a block or so "up Dixwell," where the ghetto began. In one direction lay Yale University and all that we black students so ardently (and so guiltily) sought to become. In the other direction lay Dixwell Avenue and all that we sought to flee. Liggett's corner was seized by black revolutionaries of every kind, who recognized it as prime real estate for hawking their wares. As a result, making your way to Liggett's—which was as big as a Wal-Mart today—involved what we called "running the gauntlet," at least if you were black.

You might think you needed to pick up a roll of film, some Gummi Bears, a jar of Afro-Sheen, a prescription of penicillin. But they knew what really ailed you, and had their prescriptions at the ready: there was much wisdom about "offing the pigs," "freeing your mind," and liberating "our people." And they really did have something on the ball, to have planted themselves so strategically at points along the route that connected New Haven's largest drug-store with its best record shop, Cutler's, twenty yards farther down the street, and, another twenty yards along, the Yale Co-op.

"Already got it, my brother," I soon learned to say to the clean-

shaven, close-cropped Black Muslim pushing *Muhammad Speaks*. To
avoid his amused eyes, I'd stare at his bow tie and try to determine if
it was a clip-on or if he and his co-religionists were taught to knot their
ties by hand, perhaps (as I liked to imagine) in special classes. If you
thought ahead, you could start the day's shopping down at the Co-
op, working backwards up the street toward campus, and slip by the
Muslim as he worked the new arrivals heading in the opposite direction. But the Panthers were parked squarely in front of Cutler's
Record Shop and there was no way to avoid them. Since they knew
you were headed to buy the latest Coltrane album, you couldn't deny
that you had any money. Then, too, the Panthers had a secret weapon
for arresting your gaze, making you pause just a moment too long to
be able to avoid an exchange: they were, you see, the fashion plates
of black insurrection. They had the kind of long black leather coat
that is now sold by J. Peterman, which they wore with matching
pants and gleaming black boots; and their jaunty black berets were
pushed down so that their carefully coifed Afros would poke out just
over the ears. If the Muslim brother, with his starched white shirt and
dark suit, looked like the local colored undertaker, the Panthers were,
in their aggressively haute couture way, the revolution made visible,
right down to the ankle length of their leather overcoats.

"Today's Pig is tomorrow's pork chop!" they would shout. You
handed them money because they were working for a better tomorrow; because they were strong, proud, and black; because they
had a wardrobe you could only dream about; because if you dared
to walk past them, they'd demand, "Where *you* gonna be when the
revolution comes, handkerchief-head?" and images of the tumbrel
would pass before your eyes. "Power to the People," you'd murmur
sympathetically, and then both of you, almost in unison: "Right
On." Assume the position: right fist clenched, swinging deliberately
toward the heart.

You handed them money because there was a revolution going
on, and you were preoccupied with next week's exam in cell biol-
ogy. True, the unit on Blackness wasn't going to be on the final; but
you still were responsible for it, responsible in a big way. Were we
going to sell out or keep the faith? Were we being trained to be

"race men," like Thurgood Marshall, or soul-less, colorless opportunists whose success would be engineered by racists who wanted to use it as a bludgeon against our disadvantaged brethren: *They made it—why can't you?* Where *would* we be when the revolution came? It was a protracted battle for the souls of the race, and that battle rages still.

2.

Freshly transplanted from the Appalachian village where I grew up, I felt ill-prepared to deal with any of this. I remember attending my first meeting of the Black Student Association, being in the company of these largely urban New Negroes—black and smart and elegant and from Elsewhere—a group with a definite sense of what was and was not authentically black, jockeying for position by being blacker than thou. As we filed out, I asked a friend, Linwood, from North Carolina, whether he'd found it hard to fit in. "Skip," he said, shaking his head sadly at all the posturing, "I been black my whole life." I can't tell you how great was the sense of relief his words inspired.

Or how short-lived. As with falling in love, or having a child, everyone imagines that he is unique—that these torturous pathways have never been trodden by anyone else, not the same way. Indeed, how mortifying to recognize that our innermost religion was the very one that Ellison spoofed in *Invisible Man:*

> "Brothers and sisters, my text this morning is the 'Blackness of Blackness.' "
> And a congregation of voices answered: "That blackness is most black, brother, most black . . ."
> "In the beginning . . ."
> "At the very start," they cried.
> ". . . there was blackness . . ."
> "Preach it "

Whatever else we were, we knew we were black men. And there in all its glory, that was our weird double confinement: we were to be black—and what did it mean to be black? We were to be men—and what did it mean to be men? At the overlap of the two categories, black and male, wasn't there an amalgamation-effect that was more than simply additive?

My generational cohorts and I may have experienced the conflicts and struggles attendant on being defined as black and male in a particularly flamboyant form, but black men of every age have experienced these as well. The cultural critic Stuart Hall puts it nicely: "Identities are the names we give to the different ways we are positioned by, and position ourselves in, the narratives of the past." Every black man, then, has had his own gauntlet to run. Each has been asked to assume the position.

## 3.

This is a book of stories about black men, stories that tell you (they told me, anyway) something about the perplexities of race and gender so near the end of this century. All these stories might be described as what the literary critic Robert Stepto has dubbed "narratives of ascent." The men you will encounter in this book came from modest circumstances—in Roxbury, an Alabama hamlet, a Bronx or Harlem tenement, a hardscrabble upstate New York farm—and all have achieved preeminence of one variety or another: these are people who have shaped the world as much as they were shaped by it, who gave as good as they got. Three of these men—James Baldwin, Albert Murray, and Anatole Broyard—are writers. Then there is a dancer-choreographer, Bill T. Jones; a religious leader, Louis Farrakhan; a general-turned-political-figure, Colin Powell; an entertainer, Harry Belafonte.

One could inscribe their lives in a larger narrative of ascent. There's a sense in which the American century might be thought of as the African-American century—culturally speaking. As the writer Albert Murray would insist, the cultural differentia that would elevate America—in an aesthetics of modernism otherwise dominated by Europe—was indelibly black: It's also true that most of the American culture that has gone global (pop music, Motown, rap;

some of it junk, some of it sublime) is at least partly of black parentage. Of course, the paradox is that the cultural centrality of the African-American—this is a country where Michael Jordan and Shaquille O'Neal look down from every billboard—coexists with the economic and political marginality of the African-American, most especially of the African American male.

## 4.

The facts are familiar but retain their power to appall. If you're a black man, you're a hundred times more likely to be sent to jail than to college. If you're a black man in your twenties and thirties, you're more likely than not to be unemployed or, in the gingerly euphemism, "underemployed." Even black women, despite shouldering the burdens of sexism and racism—and, so often, family rearing—have created for themselves a more hopeful prospect. Black men's very rate of survival is dramatically lower: they are far more likely to fall victim to AIDS and homicide, usually at the hands of other black men. (And young black men are fifteen times more likely to skip the middleman and commit suicide than are their female counterparts.) Their rates of dropping out of school, of incarceration, of drug abuse, also far exceed those of black women. In a country that increasingly places a premium on a high level of education, the gender gap in education is particularly worthy of note. Black men do worse in school than black women, and are far less likely to graduate from college; and the compounding effect down the pike is such that there are roughly eighty percent more black women than black men in graduate programs. (Indeed, black women with four years of college education earn slightly more than their white counterparts.) Despite the familiar syndrome of the "feminization of poverty," black men are dramatically less likely than black women to achieve middle-class status. (Yes, America, this *will* be on the final; just wait.)

"How does it feel to be a 'problem'?" is the question Du Bois liked to pose, with due sardonicism, to his black brethren, constituents all of the venerable Negro Problem. The passing years have not made the problem less acute. "Reduced to its most fundamental truth," the playwright August Wilson has written, "black men are a commodity of flesh and muscle which has lost its value in the marketplace. We are left over from history."

## 5.

I distrust the rhetoric of crisis. It's at once too gloomy and too hopeful: the Hippocratic trope of "crisis" invokes a turning point, beyond which lies recovery or death, and neither one seems in the cards for us. I have my doubts, too, about the way the ostensible subject of the crisis, the black male, has been conceptualized. It's a conversation that still bears traces (though fading ones) of a rivalry over victim status: the sort of Oppression Sweepstakes that ran through so much harebrained attitudinizing of the seventies and eighties. The remarkable cultural efflorescence of black women in the past couple of decades, by a sort of paradox, almost underlined the supposed crisis of the black man. The conversation has sometimes also been marred by a desire to look at racial politics in isolation from gender politics, at men in isolation from women, at blacks in isolation from whites, at Us in isolation from Them.

Consider the cultural contradictions of the Million Man March of 1995. The black man was represented as singularly prone to wickedness, thus singularly in need of rehabilitation, and at the same time distinctively suited for the role of racial uplift: he was reprobate and redeemer in one. How does it feel to be a paradox?

## 6.

Are the men in this book representative of black men generally? No, not in the ordinary sense of "representative"—that they exemplify some imaginary median or mean. Rather, they are extraordinary men who may be taken as Representative in an Emersonian rather than a statistical sense. (Thus Frederick Douglass was known as the "Representative Negro" of his era; yet what Negro was more anomalous?) Yet for all that, how can these men *not* be representative? The cultural script of being a black man doesn't tell you what he might have come to cherish or revile: but it gives you a good idea of the issues history has presented him with. And so it is with the men in this book. In them, the contradictions and anxieties of the moment and milieu are writ large. They resonate to those lower frequencies that Ralph Ellison wrote about, and sometimes they produce them.

We can agree that the notion of a unitary black man is as imaginary (and as real) as Wallace Stevens's blackbirds are; and yet to be a black man in twentieth-century America is to be heir to a set of anxieties: beginning with what it means to *be* a black man. All of the protagonists of this book confront the "burden of representation," the homely notion that you represent your race, thus that your actions can betray your race or honor it. I don't much believe in exemplary lives—and what a hateful thing, to be compelled to live one!—and the characters in this book share with the rest of us the ways in which they are both perfectly unrepresentative and perfectly representative. Each, in his own way, rages against the dread requirement *to represent;* against the demands of "authenticity." By no stretch of the imagination do the men portrayed in this book present a cross section of black males. But all are people who have borne some freight of being iconic: people who have been vested with meaning, allegorized; and who have defined themselves by struggling against other meanings, other allegories. (It's no trivial predicament to be cast as a Genus with genitals, a Lesson with legs.) Then again, railing against something doesn't mean you've escaped from it. The grand theme of your career may be that the burden of representation is an illusion—a paradigm, par excellence, of ideological *mauvaise foi*—but that will only heighten your chagrin when you realize that it follows you everywhere like your own shadow. It isn't a thing of your making, and it won't succumb to your powers of unmaking—not yet, anyway.

So here is a portfolio of black American men—yes, Representative Negroes, which is to say, most unrepresentative ones indeed. If

you find that the idea of such a burden recurs throughout, I submit
that this reflects not my own preoccupations merely, but those of a
larger culture as well.

### 7.

"One is not born a woman," Beauvoir famously wrote; and neither are you born a man, or a black, or the conjunction of the two.
But what good does *that* do you? You can rebel against the content
of an identity you didn't get to choose—and yet badly stitched vest-
ments are not easily cast off. It's a version of the predicament faced
by the wolf who would have to gnaw off a limb to escape from a
trap. Hence the appeal of that comforting old lie: I'm not a black $x$
(poet, president, whatever), I'm an $x$ who happens to be black. Alas,
circumstance won't have it so. Nobody happens to be black: this is
a definitional truth. For a world in which blackness is elective or in-
cidental—a world where you can "happen to be" black—is a world
without blackness, a world, that is, where the concept has been dis-
mantled or transfigured beyond recognition.

So you might inveigh against, say, the ideology of authenticity,
but in some measure you participate in it all the same. It's like the
child's game of *fort-da* that Freud wrote about: with a jerk of a
string, the toys we've hidden from view come tumbling out again.
And surely our seeming contradictions, our own versions of *fort-da*,
are what make us interesting.

Consider Bill T. Jones, who has become, by turns, the whipping
boy and poster child of postmodernism; a man who makes a fetish-
object of his own demonized and desired flesh, by way of a critique
of fetishism. Or Colin Powell, who made history by making the idea
of a black president seem utterly plausible—without troubling to
run for the office. Or Louis Farrakhan, who attracts love and
loathing in equal measure and is sustained by the tension between
those poles. Or Al Murray, a putative integrationist who wars
against black nationalists, not because their demands are outrageous, but because their demands are all too modest. Or Harry Belafonte, packaged as everything he was not, who so suited a culture

industry he so distrusted. Or James Baldwin, who sought to defend his integrity by lashing himself to the mast of black radicalism, with contrary results. Or Anatole Broyard, who loved possibilities too much to want to realize his own; and who, like a guilt-ridden fugitive, became curiously tethered to the one subject he couldn't address with candor. Somehow the choice is always between alternate inauthenticities, competing impostures. Another approach toward the question: How does it feel to be a paradox?

## 8.

I said before that all of these stories could be taken as narratives of ascent. To be sure, no one shares precisely the same notion of what "ascent" consists of. One may build institutions; another will subject their foundations to close scrutiny. Thus, in this book, you will meet followers of Booker T. Washington—a tradition in which Colin Powell and Louis Farrakhan alike are secret sharers; disciples of Washington's great antagonist, W. E. B. Du Bois—like the activist-entertainer Harry Belafonte or that tortured sage James Baldwin. (In a forty-year career, Belafonte knew what it was like to be too black and too "white"; for a few years, he also experienced the astonishing grace of being just black enough, and you would have to have a heart of stone to begrudge him that.) Colin Powell's rise, in the highly rule-bound environment of the American military, is probably more typical, demographically, than most: the military is, in no small part, a black institution, and its procedural formality has proven reassuring to a people for whom informality hasn't always worked to their advantage. Others trod the path of *la vie de bohème,* or, anyway, the grungy North American version of it. You might say that Anatole Broyard's story takes the narrative of ascent to its next logical step, his life being a testing ground for the question of how much you can leave behind before the past rears up and strikes back—a cottonmouth in the swamps of biography. Broyard was not the invisible man but the liminal man. Ellison's great conceit was that the black man was someone you couldn't see; what Broyard understood was that sometimes the problem was that people could see him all too well, or, more to the point, that they could see what he was too clearly to be able to see *who* he was. As a trickster, however, Broyard would not be stopped, would not stop himself, from turning racial identity into an elaborately subtle game of peekaboo.

### 9.

At the opposite extreme is Louis Farrakhan, who turned blackness into a cult, and something of a masculinist cult at that. ("The colored races are highly susceptible of religion," the eminent nineteenth-century black social reformer Martin Delany once remarked. "It is a constituent principle of their nature and an excellent trait in their character, but unfortunately they carry it too far.") Those curious mythologies he purveys fill a social vacuum: he offers the imaginative reconstitution of a disintegrating community. But do not suppose that our uncertainties about our identity—and the corresponding desire to stabilize something that is by its nature labile and ambiguous—are a new development, a backlash aspect of modernity. Such mythologizing is, historically considered, far from anomalous; attempts to clarify the vexed identity of the African-American have a long and various history.

Consider Timothy Drew, a North Carolina man who, at age forty-seven, renamed himself Noble Drew Ali and founded the Moorish Science Temple, in 1913. The tens of thousands of black followers he soon attracted were taught to know themselves as "Moors," of Asiatic ancestry, and were given self-ascription cards that they treated as amulets. On each were printed these reassuring words:

This is your Nationality and Identification Card for the Moorish Science Temple of America, and Birthrights for the Moorish Americans, etc. We honor all the Divine Prophets, Jesus, Mohammed, Buddha, and Confucius. May the blessings of the God of our Father Allah be upon you that carry this card. I do hereby declare that you are a Moslem under the Divine Laws of the Holy Koran of Mecca, Love, Truth Peace Freedom and Justice.

"I AM A CITIZEN OF THE U.S.A."

These "Nationality and Identification Cards" had a remarkable and unsettling effect upon Drew's Moorish men; they started to behave contemptuously toward whites, to the point that Prophet Drew Ali had to issue an order: "Stop flashing your cards before Europeans as this only causes confusion." Far more distinguishing, you might have thought, were the red fezzes that Ali required men to wear. But somehow the red fezzes did not embolden them to misbehave; it really was the identity cards that did it. Today, we mostly think we know better than to believe our identity might be reduced to a few words of print on a cardboard rectangle (or that the gods we honor might be listed like the credit cards recognized by a dining establishment); but at times the concept remains oddly alluring.

## 10.

The manifold ambiguities of black masculinity and its social valence have led, inevitably, to an outpouring of books with titles like *The Conspiracy to Destroy Black Men*. Talk of conspiracy is a nearly irresistible labor-saving device in the face of recalcitrant complexity. One of the reassuring things about talk of conspiracy is that it posits a bright line between victims and victimizers. Of course, it is all too simple.

Consider those terrible myths about the extraordinary sexual prowess of the black man: How badly they serve us! We wring our hands and furrow our brows at the way that black teens have been saddled with such imagery. But what American male adolescent would willingly renounce such a mythology, were it offered to him? This is to point not to a feature of black culture but to a feature of American (and, I suspect, not just American) youth culture. Such imagery does harm us. But we're not rag dolls, passively tossed around by a malign cultural sea. We participate in that culture: we interpret it, shape it, subvert it, remold it. Bill T. Jones—among the most brilliantly self-aware of performing artists—deconstructs certain ideas of black male sexuality, but, equally, he plays with them, uses them, turns them this way and that.

For cultural critique never results in a clean-wiped blackboard. Hip-hop culture energized the eighties, establishing a counterreality to the administrations of Reagan and Bush; and the way it deploys those tropes of authenticity, sexual aggression, and the warrior code by turns underlines and undermines them. In nineties America, the B-Boy stands for untrammeled masculinity (the image-effluent of Madison Avenue will confirm this) precisely as the Marlboro Man did a few decades ago. Here is the postmodern cowboy, untamed, unruly, and unbelted. He is vilified, yes; but this frontier culture has always had an ambivalent attitude toward its villains, possessed by a sense of their dangerous glamour. Wyatt Earp is a hero of the American frontier, but so is the outlaw Jesse James.

The African-American historian Robin D. G. Kelley has written, with a candor both unusual and uncomfortable, about the experience of being mistaken for a criminal. Late for a movie, the youthful professor—braving freezing winter winds with a baseball cap, and a scarf around his nose and mouth—rushes over to the ticket counter. The young white woman behind the counter, terrified, blurts that she doesn't have anything in the cash register, and is humiliated to discover that this black man just wants a ticket to join his wife and daughter at a screening of *Little Women*. The encounter would join a long litany of such incidents—I don't know a black man who doesn't have at least one to tell—except that Professor Kelley admits his own complicated feelings about what happened. He is, he admits, a hopelessly unintimidating man. (He laments that his "inability to employ black-maleness as a weapon"—this despite his relative youth and ghetto upbringing—"is the story of my life.") Earlier that day, he has failed even to intimidate his four-year-old daughter into putting her toys away.

So those five seconds as a media-made black man felt kind of good. I know it's a product of racism. I know the myth of black male violence has resulted in the deaths of many innocent boys and men of darker hue. I know that the power to scare is not real power. I know all that—after all, I study this stuff for a living! For the moment, though, it felt good.

Again, you may well ask: How does it feel to be a paradox?

## 11.

I have referred to the problem of representation, but the problem of representation is involved here in another, and very simple, sense. This book is not a collection of black men but of my (necessarily partial and personal) representations of them. Writing this book involved making new acquaintances and renewing old ones. Murray and Baldwin, of course, were people I'd known through the years, people who helped shape who I wanted to become, to be. Albert Murray, foremost cultural explicant of black modernism—the modernism of Ellington and Ellison—came to prominence, ironically, only after such modernism was besieged by the simplifying insurgence of black nationalism; which was when I myself needed him. Belafonte was someone I met only in the process of writing about him, though I was in touch with him on and off over the course of a year; and my acquaintance with Powell and Jones and Farrakhan was similarly circumscribed. Broyard presented the challenge of writing about someone I could never meet, a circumstance that turned out to have advantages as well as disadvantages. Every subject had something to teach. But because profiles represent human encounters, they aren't simply a matter of downloading information, as from a dataport.

So I'd find myself scampering after Belafonte's road show or meeting up with him outside his rehearsal studio in midtown Manhattan. I'd realize that his friends have been analyzing him for decades—it is one of their favorite pursuits—and that there was much to catch up with. So I'd find myself talking about collage technique with Al Murray over lunch at his beloved Century Club. And remembering lunches with him in less elevated settings many years earlier. So I'd watch Bill T. Jones get the kinks worked out of a dance piece at an unfamiliar regional theater. And realize, at a performance later that day, that the audience itself had become part of the show, and that I had become part of the audience, the show, too.

There's a difference between "interviewing" subjects and conversing with people. The former posture is one that I'm not cut out for and that I try always to avoid. Once in a while, there is an abrupt shift from "interview" to conversation. I recall the frustration of sitting with a cautious, media-savvy Colin Powell, asking sensible questions and getting sensible answers. Finally, scanning the pictures of recent presidents, hanging on the wall behind him, I asked him to rate them as military commanders. The anodyne, deflective mode suddenly evaporated as he got up from his seat and, for the first time, grew excited. If I really wanted to talk military strategy, he really wanted to tell me about it.

I doubt I could write a decent profile of someone I had no respect for, because I'm not good at concealing my feelings. Louis Farrakhan, for whom my respect was not unmixed with mistrust, was an interesting encounter, of the labor-and-management variety: he knew that I disapproved of him from the outset, and he greeted me as a worthy opponent. To be honest, I'd experienced greater hostility at meetings of the Modern Language Association than I did at his residence on Woodlawn Avenue in Chicago. If he hoped to complicate my sense of him, he succeeded; if (as I doubt) he hoped to overcome my reservations, he did not. I thought he was a crackpot, who trafficked in the poisonous currency of paranoia; oh, and another thing—I really liked the guy. Who knew the scarily messianic demagogue turned into Dr. Cliff Huxtable when he was at home?

Actually, what struck me most about visiting him was the aura of a Sunday parlor respectability, an aura that evoked a figure known in the Negro world as the "elocutionist." The "elocutionist," I should explain, traveled through colored society, visiting the homes and churches of the black genteel, delivering uplifting homilies and reciting the "race poetry" of Paul Laurence Dunbar and Frances

Ellen Watkins Harper. It was the *sound* of culture that mattered: noble thoughts and noble words, but a noble voice and bearing most of all. Before, I had seen only the fiery demagogue; now I caught a glimpse of the stocking-capped mind of the fifties, and the vision of striving cultivation that the Sunday elocutionist represented.

But then the point about Farrakhan—né Louis Eugene Walcott—is that he really did represent the best and the brightest, and had he grown up in a meritocracy, he would have been rewarded for it. He didn't, and, as it is, he and the direction of his career stand as a reproach to a country that failed so utterly, and for so long, to honor black talent.

It isn't surprising that Farrakhan succumbed to a dark hermeneutics, the effort to "peep" the hidden archives of history. W. D. Fard, founder of Farrakhan's creed, was a great believer in covert meanings: like Leo Strauss, like Paul De Man, he believed in educing hidden significance from texts, though he was not so gingerly in how he went about it. Fard believed that "the words of whites were not to be taken literally," as the scholar C. Eric Lincoln notes, "for they were incapable of telling the truth. Their writings were symbolic and needed interpretation."

## 12.

"There's shit so heavy about us," I recently overheard a porter at Kennedy Airport say, "that the Man won't *never* let that stuff even be published." Farrakhan's two-hour address at the Million Man March of 1995 about the number nineteen and its Masonic implications was only a particularly well-publicized instance of a discourse in black letters that goes back (at least) to Prince Hall and his black Masonic order at the end of the eighteenth century. I recall from my own youth that at the height of the black nationalist/Black Arts movements, Amiri Baraka and Maulana Karenga (whom Eldridge Cleaver used to refer to, unkindly, as "the Mama Llama") well understood this thirst for underground knowledge: from time to time, at well-spaced intervals, they would publish an excerpt billed as "From *The Book of Life,*" like unveiled chapters of Revelations, the Dead Sea Scrolls in black face. ("This shit is so deep that we can only release it in bits and pieces," I'd hear Baraka say, "because the black man just ain't ready for its full revelation.") "From *The Book of Life.*" Always *from.* (There was power in that synecdoche.) As young men, we'd read it with great trepidation; it was like seeing the unpronounceable name of God, while listening to the scarily advanced chromaticisms of Coltrane's *A Love Supreme.*

The O. J. Simpson controversy wasn't unusual in the way epistemic authority played out differently for different groups. What was unusual was only that, under the glare of relentless scrutiny, white America caught a glimpse of this. Those more attentive to such matters had seen it happen again and again. In the wake of the Los Angeles riots, white Americans grew misty-eyed over a befuddled Rodney King's appeal, "People, can we all get along?"; at the same time, the reaction of many black youth was captured in Willie D's hit rap single entitled "Fuck Rodney K." (Sample lyrics: "Fuck that motherfuckin' sellout ho/They need to beat his ass some mo'.") I'm no relativist: counternarrative can at times involve interpretation, and interpretation admits of pluralism; yet it's also the case that some counternarratives are true and some are false. That a given counternarrative is false, however, is not likely to be the most interesting thing about it. For me, an ethnography of the *Kulturkampf* over O. J. Simpson—however sketchy and roughed-out—had a greater interest than the reasonably straightforward forensics of the case.

### 13.

Woven through this book are issues I've thought about for most of my life, and so there may be distorting effects of the partiality and perspective I bring. Always I hope that the sympathetic intimations I think I hear aren't echoes of my own rumblings. There's a strong temptation simply to elicit a meaning you know in advance, as when you hide an Easter egg and then discover it with a startled cry. Avoiding this pitfall is the thing I struggle for hardest, and sometimes I imagine that I succeed. If the saints and sinners of this book have nothing to teach me, then I am a poor student. I think they do, and I think there are lessons here of more general import, as well. Like my friend Linwood, I've been black my whole life, also a man; but I've come to suspect that this isn't the whole story.

You can read this book as being about the invention of the modern black man, given that its subjects are the sorts of men—Bill T. Jones, Albert Murray, Louis Farrakhan, James Baldwin, Colin Powell, Harry Belafonte, Anatole Broyard—who helped create our crazy-quilt culture, especially as it responds to the issues of race and sex and art and power. But what follows isn't so much a portrait gallery as a series of conversations, unresolved and unconcluded. Listen, and you will hear all the tensions and uncertainties and ambivalences that shaped them, that shaped me, and that—just maybe—shaped you, too.

—Henry Louis Gates, Jr.
Cambridge, Massachusetts

# Thirteen Ways of Looking at a Black Man

# The Welcome Table

Take one young, eager, black American journalist—that was me. One aging actress-singer/star—that was Josephine Baker. And one luminary of black letters: James Baldwin. I was twenty-two, a London-based correspondent for *Time* magazine, and I felt like a mortal invited to dine at his personal Mount Olympus.

My story, for which the magazine had sent me to France, was on "The Black Expatriate." One of my principal subjects was Baldwin. Another was Josephine Baker, who, being a scenarist to her very heart, put a condition on her meeting with me. I was to arrange her reunion with Baldwin, whom she hadn't seen since she left France many years ago to live in Monte Carlo.

Well into her sixties in 1973, Josephine Baker still had a lean dancer's body. One expected that. She was planning a return to the stage, after all. What was most surprising was her skin, smooth and soft as a child's. The French had called it "café au lait," but that says nothing of its translucency or the delicate shading of her face. Her makeup was limited to those kohl-rimmed eyes, elaborately lined and lashed, as if for the stage. She flirted continually with those eyes, telling her stories with almost as many facial expressions as words.

I do not know what she made of me, with my gold-rimmed cool-blue shades and my bodacious Afro, but I was received like a dignitary of a foreign land who might just be a long-lost son. And so we set off, in my rented Ford, bearing precious cargo from Monte Carlo to Saint-Paul-de-Vence, Provence, *chez* Baldwin. In case I was in any danger of forgetting that a living legend was my passenger, her fans mobbed our car at regular intervals. Invariably, she responded with elaborate grace, partly the star who expects to be adored, partly the aging performer who was simply grateful to be recognized.

Baldwin made his home just outside the tiny ancient walled town of Saint-Paul-de-Vence, nestled in the Alpine foothills that rise from the Mediterranean Sea. The air carries the smells of wild thyme, pine, and centuries-old olive trees. The light of the region, prized by painters and vacationers, at once intensifies and subdues colors, so that the terra-cotta tile roofs of the buildings are by turns rosy pink, rust brown, or deep red.

His house—situated among shoulder-high rosemary hedges, grape arbors, acres of peach and almond orchards, and fields of wild asparagus and strawberries—was built in the eighteenth century and retained its original frescoed walls and rough-hewn beams. And yet he had made of it, somehow, his own Greenwich Village café. Always there were guests, a changing entourage of friends and hangers-on. Always there was drinking and conviviality. "I am *not* in paradise," he assured readers of the *Black Scholar* that year, 1973. "It rains down here too." Maybe it did. But it seemed like paradise to me. And if the august company of Jo Baker and James Baldwin wasn't enough, Cecil Brown was a guest at Saint-Paul, too: Cecil Brown, author of the campus cult classic *The Life and Loves of Mister Jiveass Nigger* and widely esteemed as one of the great black hopes of contemporary fiction.

The grape arbors sheltered tables, and it was under one such grape arbor, at one of the long harvest tables, that we dined. Perhaps there was no ambrosia, but several bottles of Cantenac Braun provided quite an adequate substitute. The line from the old gospel song, a line Baldwin had quoted toward the end of his then latest novel, inevitably suggested itself: *"I'm going to feast at the welcome table."* And we did.

I wondered why these famous expatriates had not communicated in so long, since Saint-Paul was not far from Monte Carlo. I wondered what the evening would reveal about them, and I wondered what my role in this drama would be. It was the first time Jo and Jimmy had seen each other in years; it would prove the last.

At that long welcome table under the arbor, the wine flowed, food was served and taken away, and James Baldwin and Josephine Baker traded stories, gossiped about everyone they knew and many people they didn't, and remembered their lives. They had both been hurt and disillusioned by the United States and had chosen to live in France. They never forgot, or forgave. At the table that long, warm night, they recollected the events that led to their decisions to leave their country of birth, and the consequences of those decisions: the difficulty of living away from home and family, of always feeling apart in their chosen homes; the pleasure of choosing a new life, the possibilities of the untried. A sense of nostalgia pervaded the evening; for all their misgivings, they shared a sense, curiously, of being on the winning side of history.

And with nostalgia, anticipation. Both were preparing for a comeback. Baker would return to the stage in a month or so; and it was onstage that she would die. Baldwin, whose career had begun so brilliantly, was now struggling to regain his voice. The best was yet to come, we were given to understand.

People said Baldwin was ugly; he himself said so. But he was not ugly to me. There are, of course, faces that we cannot see simply as faces because they are so familiar that they have become icons to us, and Jimmy's visage was one such. And as I sat there, in a growing haze of awe and alcohol, studying his lined face, I realized that neither the Jimmy I had met—mischievous, alert, and impishly funny—nor even the Jimmy I might come to know could ever mean as much to me as James Baldwin, my own personal oracle, that gimlet-eyed figure who had stared at me out of a fuzzy dust-jacket photograph when I was fourteen. For that was when I met Baldwin first and discovered that black people, too, wrote books. You see, that was *my* Baldwin. And it was strictly Private Property. No trespassing allowed.

I was attending an Episcopal church camp in eastern West Virginia, high in the Allegheny Mountains overlooking the South Branch of the Potomac River. It was August 1965, a month shy of my fifteenth birthday. This, I should say at the outset, was no ordinary church camp. Our themes that year were "Is God dead?" and "Can you love two people at once?" (*Doctor Zhivago* was big that summer, and Episcopalians were never ones to let grass grow under their feet.) After a solid week of complete isolation, a delivery man, bringing milk and bread to the camp, told the head counselor that "all hell had broken loose in Los Angeles," and that the "colored people had gone crazy." Then he handed him a Sunday paper, screaming the news that Negroes were rioting in some place called Watts.

I, for one, was bewildered. I didn't understand what a riot was. Were colored people being killed by white people, or were they killing white people? Watching myself being watched by all of the white campers—there were only three black kids among hundreds of campers—I experienced that strange combination of power and powerlessness that you feel when the actions of another black person affect your own life, simply because you both are black. For I knew that the actions of people I did not know had become my responsibility as surely as if the black folk in Watts had been my relatives in the village of Piedmont, just twenty or so miles away.

Sensing my mixture of pride and discomfiture, an Episcopal priest from New England handed me a book later that day. From the cover, the wide-spaced eyes of a black man transfixed me. *Notes of a Native Son* the book was called, by one James Baldwin. Was this man the *author*, I wondered to myself, this man with a closely cropped "natural," brown skin, splayed nostrils, and wide lips, so very Negro, so comfortable to be so?

It was the first time I had heard a voice capturing the terrible exhilaration and anxiety of being a person of African descent in this
country. From the book's first few sentences, I was caught up thoroughly in the sensibility of another person—a black person. The
book performed for me the Adamic function of naming the complex racial dynamic of the American cultural imagination. Coming
from a tiny, segregated black community in a white village, I knew
both that "black culture" had a texture, a logic, of its own *and* that
it was inextricable from "white culture." That was the paradox that
Baldwin identified and negotiated, and that is why I say his prose
shaped my identity as an Afro-American, as much by the questions
he raised as by the answers he provided. If blackness was a labyrinth,
Baldwin would be my cicerone, my Virgil, my guide. I could not
put the book down.

I raced through this book, then others, filling my commonplace
book with his marvelously long sentences, bristling with commas and
qualifications. Of course, the biblical cadences spoke to me with a
special immediacy, for I, too, was to be a minister, having been
"saved" in a small black evangelical church at the age of twelve.
(From this fate as well, the Episcopalians—and, yes, James Baldwin—
diverted me.) I devoured his books: first *Notes,* then *Nobody Knows
My Name, The Fire Next Time,* and then *Another Country.* I began to
imitate his style of writing, using dependent clauses whenever and
wherever I could—much to my English teacher's chagrin. Consider:

> And a really cohesive society, one of the attributes, perhaps, of what
> is taken to be a "healthy" culture, has, generally, and I suspect, nec-
> essarily, a much lower level of tolerance for the maverick, the dis-
> senter, the man who steals the fire, than have societies in which, the
> common ground of belief having all but vanished, each man, in awful
> and brutal isolation, is for himself, to flower or to perish.

There are sixteen commas in that sentence; in my essays at school
I was busy trying to cram as many commas into my sentences as I
could—until Mrs. Iverson, my high school English teacher, forbade
me to use them "unless absolutely necessary!"

. . .

Poring over his essays, I found that the oddest passages stirred my imagination. There were, for example, those moments of the most un-Negro knowingness, a cosmopolitanism that moved me to awe: such as his observation that, unlike Americans,

> Europeans have lived with the idea of status for a long time. A man can be as proud of being a good waiter as of being a good actor, and in neither case feel threatened. And this means that the actor and the waiter can have a freer and more genuinely friendly relationship in Europe that they are likely to have here. The waiter does not feel, with obscure resentment, that the actor has "made it," and the actor is not tormented by the fear that he may find himself, tomorrow, once again a waiter.

I remember the confident authority with which I explained this insight (uncredited, I suspect) about French and American waiters to a schoolmate. It hardly mattered that there were no waiters in Piedmont, W.Va., unless you counted the Westvaco Club, which catered to the management of our one industry, a paper mill. It mattered less that there were no actors. How far was Paris, really? Baldwin wrote about an epiphany experienced before the cathedral in Chartres. In Piedmont, true enough, we had no such imposing monuments, but I struggled to collect his noble sentiments as I stood before our small wooden church, in need though it was of a fresh coat of white paint.

I, of course, was not alone in my enthrallment and, much as it vexed me, Baldwin was *not* my private property. When James Baldwin wrote *The Fire Next Time* in 1963, he was exalted as *the* voice of black America. The success of *Fire* led directly to a cover story in *Time* in May of 1963; soon he was spoken of as a contender for the Nobel Prize. ("Opportunity and duty are sometimes born together," Baldwin wrote later.) Perhaps not since Frederick Douglass a century earlier had one man been taken to embody the voice of "the Negro." By the early sixties, his authority seemed nearly un-challengeable. What did the Negro want? Ask James Baldwin.

The puzzle was—as anyone who read him should have recognized—that his arguments, richly nuanced and self-consciously ambivalent, were far too complex to serve straightforwardly political ends. Thus he would argue in *Notes from a Native Son* that

> the question of color, especially in this country, operates to hide the graver question of the self. That is precisely why what we like to call "the Negro problem" is so tenacious in American life, and so dangerous. But my own experience proves to me that the connection between American whites and blacks is far deeper and more passionate than any of us like to think. . . . The questions which one asks oneself begin, at last, to illuminate the world, and become one's key to the experience of others. One can only face in others what one can face in oneself. On this confrontation depends the measure of our wisdom and compassion. This energy is all that one finds in the rubble of vanished civilizations, and the only hope for ours.

One reads a passage like this one with a certain double take. By proclaiming that the color question conceals the graver questions of the self, Baldwin leads us to expect a transcendence of the contingencies of race, in the name of a deeper artistic or psychological truth. Instead, with an abrupt swerve, Baldwin returns us to them.

> In America, the color of my skin had stood between myself and me; in Europe, that barrier was down. Nothing is more desirable than to be released from an affliction, but nothing is more frightening than to be divested of a crutch. It turned out that the question of who I was was not solved because I had removed myself from the social forces which menaced me—anyway, these forces had become interior, and I had dragged them across the ocean with me. The question of who I was had at last become a personal question, and the answer was to be found in me.
>
> I think that there is always something frightening about this realization. I know it frightened me.

Again, these words are easily misread. The day had passed when a serious novelist could, as had Thomas Mann at thirty-seven, compose his *Betrachtungen eines Unpolitischen (Reflections of an Unpolitical Man)*. Baldwin proposes not that politics is merely a projection of private neuroses, but that our private neuroses are shaped by quite public ones. The retreat to subjectivity, the "graver questions of the self," would lead not to an escape from the "racial drama," but—and this was the alarming prospect Baldwin wanted to announce—a rediscovery of it. That traditional liberal dream of a nonracial self, unconstrained by epidermal contingencies, was hopefully entertained and, for him, at least, reluctantly dismissed. "There are," he observed,

> few things on earth more attractive than the idea of the unspeakable liberty which is allowed the unredeemed. When, beneath the black mask, a human being begins to make himself felt one cannot escape a certain awful wonder as to what kind of human being it is. What one's imagination makes of other people is dictated, of course, by the laws of one's own personality and it is one of the ironies of black-white relations that, by means of what the white man imagines the black man to be, the black man is enabled to know who the white man is.

This is not a call for "racial understanding": on the contrary, we understand each other all too well, for we have invented one another, derived our identities from the ghostly projections of our alter egos. If Baldwin had a central political argument, then, it was that the destinies of black America and white were profoundly and irreversibly intertwined. Each created the other, each defined itself in relation to the other, and each could destroy the other.

For Baldwin, then, America's "interracial drama" had "not only created a new black man, it has created a new white man, too." In that sense, he could argue, "the history of the America Negro problem is not merely shameful, it is also something of an achievement. For even when the worst has been said, it must also be added that the perpetual challenge posed by this problem was always, somehow, perpetually met."

These were not words to speed along a cause. They did not mesh with the rhetoric of self-affirmation that liberation movements require. Yet couldn't his sense of the vagaries of identity serve the ends of a still broader, braver politics?

As an intellectual, Baldwin was at his best when exploring his own equivocal sympathies and clashing allegiances. He was here to "bear witness," he insisted, not to be spokesman. And he was right to insist on the distinction. But who had time for such niceties? The spokesman role was assigned him willy-nilly.

The result was to complicate further his curious position as an Afro-American intellectual. On the populist Left, the then favored model of the oppositional spokesman was what the Italian political theoretician Antonio Gramsci called the "organic intellectual": someone who participated in and was part of the community he would uplift. And yet Baldwin's basic conception of himself was formed by the familiar, and still well-entrenched, idea of the alienated artist or intellectual, whose advanced sensibility entailed his estrangement from the very people he would represent. Baldwin could dramatize the tension between these two models—he would do so in his fiction—but he was never to resolve it.

A spokesman must have a firm grasp on his role, and an unambiguous message to articulate. Baldwin had neither, and when this was discovered a few short years later, he was relieved of his duties, shunted aside as an elder, and retired, statesman. The irony is that he may never fully have recovered from this demotion from a status he had always disavowed.

And if I had any doubts about that demotion, I was set straight by my editor at *Time* once I returned to London. They were not pleased by my choice of principal subjects. Josephine Baker, I was told, was a period piece, a quaint memory of the twenties and thirties. And as for Baldwin, well, wasn't he passé now? Hadn't he been for several years?

Baldwin, *passé*? In fact, the editor, holding a wet finger to the wind, was absolutely correct, and on some level I knew it. If Baldwin had once served as a shadow delegate for black America in the congress of culture, his term had expired. Besides, soldiers, not delegates, were what was wanted these days. "Pulling rank," Eldridge Cleaver wrote in his essay on Baldwin, "is a very dangerous business, especially when the troops have mutinied and the basis of one's authority, or rank, is devoid of that interdictive power and has become suspect."

Baldwin, who once defined the cutting edge, was now a favorite target for the *new* cutting edge. Anyone who was aware of the ferment in black America was familiar with the attacks. And nothing ages a young Turk faster than still younger Turks.

Baldwin was "Joan of Arc of the cocktail party," according to the new star of the Black Arts movement, Amiri Baraka. His "spavined whine and plea" was "sickening beyond belief." He was—according to a youthful Ishmael Reed—"a hustler who comes on like Job."

Eldridge Cleaver, the Black Panthers' Minister of Information, found in Baldwin's work "the most gruelling agonizing, total hatred of the blacks, particularly of himself, and the most shameful, fanatical, fawning sycophantic love of the whites that one can find in any black American writer of note in our time." Above all, Baldwin's sexuality represented treason: "Many Negro homosexuals, acquiescing in this racial death-wish, are outraged because in their sickness they are unable to have a baby by a white man." Baldwin was thus engaged in "a despicable underground guerrilla war, waged on paper, against black masculinity." Young militants referred to him, unsmilingly, as Martin Luther Queen.

Baldwin was, of course, hardly a stranger to the sexual battlefield. "On every street corner," Baldwin would later recall of his early days in Greenwich Village, "I was called a faggot." What was different this time was a newly sexualized black nationalism that could stigmatize homosexuality as a capitulation to alien white norms, and correspondingly accredit homophobia—a powerful means of policing the sexual arena—as a progressive political act.

A new generation, so it seemed, was determined to define itself by everything Baldwin was *not*. By the late sixties, Baldwin-bashing was almost a rite of initiation. And yet Baldwin would not return fire, at least not in public. He responded with a pose of wounded passivity. If a new and newly militant generation sought to abandon him, Baldwin would not abandon them.

In the end, the shift of political climate forced Baldwin to simplify his rhetoric or else risk internal exile. As his old admirers saw it, Baldwin was now chasing, with unseemly alacrity, after a new vanguard, one that esteemed rage, not compassion, as our noblest emotion. "It is not necessary for a black man to hate a white man, or to have particular feelings about him at all, in order to realize that he must kill him," he wrote in *No Name in the Street,* a book he started writing in 1967 but did not publish until 1972. "Yes, we have come, or are coming, to this, and there is no point in flinching before the prospect of this exceedingly cool species of fratricide." That year he told *The New York Times* of his belated realization that "our destinies are in our hands, black hands, and no one else's." A stirring if commonplace sentiment, this, which an earlier Baldwin would have been the first to see through.

How far we had come from the author of *The Fire Next Time,* who had forecast the rise of Black Power and yet was certain that "we, the black and the white, deeply need each other here if we are really to become a nation—if we are really, that is, to achieve our identity, our maturity, as men and women. To create one nation has proved to be a hideously difficult task; there is certainly no need now to create two, one black, and one white." All such qualms were irrelevant now. In an offhanded but calculated manner, Baldwin affected to dismiss his earlier positions: "I was, in some way, in those years, without entirely realizing it, the Great Black Hope of the Great White Father." Now he knew better.

In an impossible gambit, the author of *No Name in the Street* sought to reclaim his lost authority by signaling his willingness to be instructed by those who had inherited it: this was Baldwin and the new power generation. He borrowed the populist slogans of the day and returned them with a Baldwinian polish. "The powerless, by definition, can never be 'racists,' " he writes, "for they can never make the world pay for what they feel or fear except by the suicidal endeavor that makes them fanatics or revolutionaries, or both;

whereas those in power can be urbane and charming and invite you to those homes which they know you will never own." The sentiment in its unadorned rendering—that blacks cannot be racist—is now a familiar one, and is often dismissed as an absurdity; but the key phrase here is "by definition." For this is not a new factual claim but a rhetorical move. The term "racism" is redefined to refer to systemic power relations, a social order in which one race is subordinated to another. (A parallel move is common in much feminist theory, where "patriarchy"—naming a social order to which Man and Woman have a fixed and opposed relation—contrasts with "sexism," which characterizes the particular acts of particular people.) It cannot, therefore, by dismissed as a factual error. And it does formulate a widely accepted truth: the asymmetries of power mean that not all racial insult is equal. (Not even a Florida jury is much concerned when a black captive calls his arresting officer a "cracker.")

Nonetheless, it is a grave political error, for black America needs allies more than it needs absolution. And the slogan—a definition masquerading as an insight—would all too quickly serve as blanket amnesty for our dankest suspicions and bigotries. It is a slogan Baldwin once would have repudiated, not for the sake of white America— for them, he would have argued, the display of black prejudice could only provide a reassuring confirmation of their own—but for the sake of black America. The Baldwin who knew that the fates of black and white America were one knew that if racism was to be deplored, it was to be deplored *tout court,* and without exemption clauses for the oppressed. Wasn't it this conviction, above all, that explained his repudiation of Malcolm X?

I should be clear. Baldwin's reverence for Malcolm was real, but posthumous. In a conversation with the psychologist Kenneth Clark, recorded a year and a half before the assassination, Baldwin ventured that by preaching black supremacy, "what [Malcolm] does is destroy a truth and invent a myth." Compared with King's appeal, Malcolm's was "much more sinister because it is much more effective. It is much more effective, because it is, after all, comparatively easy to invest a population with false morale by giving them a false sense of superiority, and it will always break down in a crisis.

That is the history of Europe simply—it's one of the reasons that we are in this terrible place." But, he cautioned, the country "shouldn't be worried about the Muslim movement, that's not the problem. The problem is to eliminate the conditions which breed the Muslim movement." (Five years later, under contract with Columbia Pictures, Baldwin began the task of adapting Malcolm to the silver screen.)

That ethnic scapegoating was an unaffordable luxury had been another of Baldwin's lessons to us. "Georgia has the Negro," he once pithily wrote, slicing through thickets of rationalization, "and Harlem has the Jew." We have seen where the failure of this vision has led: the well-nigh surreal spectacle of urban activists who would rather picket Korean grocery stores than crack houses, presumably on the assumption that sullen shopkeepers with their pricey tomatoes—not smiley drug dealers and their discount glass vials—are the true threat to black dignity.

The sad truth is that as the sixties wore on, Baldwin, for all his efforts, would never be allowed to reclaim the cultural authority he once enjoyed. To give credit where credit is due, the media can usually tell the difference between a trend-maker and a trend follower. What did the Negro *really* want? Ask Eldridge Cleaver.

I did. Several months after my visit to Saint-Paul-de-Vence, I returned to France to interview the exiled revolutionary. We had moved with the times from cosmopolitan expatriates to international fugitives. ("How do I know you're not a C.I.A. agent?" he had demanded when we first talked.) This was not a soirée on the Riviera. It was an apartment on the Left Bank, where Eldridge and Kathleen lived, and where he put me up in his study for a couple of weeks; here, ostensibly, was the radical edge that Baldwin now affected to covet.

Between Cleaver and Baldwin, naturally, no love was lost. Eldridge complained to me that Baldwin was circulating a story about him impugning his manhood. He wanted me to know it was untrue. He also wanted me to know that he would soon be returning and would take up where he had left off. The talk was heady, navigating the dialectical turns of Fanon and Marx and Mao and Che.

(Jesus would be added a few months later.) His shelves were lined with all the revolutionary classics, but also W. E. B. Du Bois, Richard Wright, and, yes, James Baldwin. Young Baldwin may have warned of "the fire next time," but Cleaver, determined to learn from the failures of his revolutionary forebears, was busily designing the incendiary devices.

What came as a gradual revelation to me was that Cleaver really wanted to be a writer, and that Baldwin was, perforce, his blueprint of what a black writer could be. He was at work, he told me, on a memoir, to be entitled "Over My Shoulder"; on a novel, to be called "Ahmad's Jacket." But commitment, to be genuine, had to spill over the page. And in case I forgot our parlous position in the nether zone of the law, there was that hijacker—armed, dangerous, and definitely deranged—who had insisted on staying with them too. Eldridge, who had adopted me as a younger brother for the nonce, handed me a butcher's knife to keep under my pillow and made sure I propped a filing cabinet in front of the door before I went to sleep at night.

Times had changed all right. That, I suppose, was our problem. But Jimmy wanted to change with them, and that was his.

We lost his skepticism, his critical independence. Baldwin's belated public response to Cleaver's charges was all too symptomatic. Now, with slightly disingenuous forbearance, he would turn the other cheek and insist, in *No Name in the Street,* that he actually admired Cleaver's *Soul on Ice.* Cleaver's attack on him was explained away as a regrettable if naïve misunderstanding: the revolutionary had simply been misled by Baldwin's public reputation. Beyond that, he wrote,

> I also felt that I was confused in his mind with the unutterable debasement of the male—with all those faggots, punks, and sissies, the sight and sound of whom, in prison, must have made him vomit more than once. Well, I certainly hope I know more about myself, and the intention of my work than that, but I *am* an odd quantity. So is Eldridge, so are we all. It is a pity that we won't, probably, ever have the time to attempt to define once more the relationship of the

odd and disreputable artist to the odd and disreputable revolutionary . . . And I think we need each other, and have much to learn from
each other, and, more than ever, now.

It was an exercise in perversely *willed* magnanimity, meant, no
doubt, to assure us that he was with the program; and to suggest,
by its serenity, unruffled strength. Instead, it read as weakness, the
ill-disguised appeasement of a creature whose day had come and
gone.

Did he know what was happening to him? His essays give no clue,
but, then, they wouldn't. Increasingly, they came to represent his
official voice, the carefully crafted expression of the public intellectual James Baldwin. His fiction became the refuge of his growing
self-doubts.

In 1968, he published *Tell Me How Long the Train's Been Gone*.
Formally, it was his least successful work. But in its protagonist, Leo
Proudhammer, Baldwin created a perfectly Baldwinian alter ego, a
celebrated black artist who, in diction that matched that of Baldwin's essays, could express the quandaries that came increasingly to
trouble his creator. "The day came," he reflects at one point, "when
I wished to break my silence and found that I could not speak: the
actor could no longer be distinguished from his role." Thus did
Baldwin, our elder statesman, who knew better than anyone how a
mask could deform the face beneath, chafe beneath his own.

Called to speak before a civil-rights rally, Proudhammer rumi-
nates upon the contradictions of his position. "I did not want others to endure my estrangement, that was why I was on the platform;
yet was it not, at the least, paradoxical that it was only my estrangement which had placed me there? . . . [I]t was our privilege, to say
nothing of our hope, to attempt to make the world a human
dwellingplace for us all; and yet—yet—was it not possible that the
mighty gentlemen, my honorable and invaluable confreres, by
being unable to imagine such a journey as my own, were leaving
something of the utmost importance out of their aspirations?"

These are not unpolitical reflections, but they are not the reflections of a politician. Contrast LeRoi Jones's unflappable conviction,

in an essay published in 1963: "A writer must have a point of view, or he cannot be a good writer. He must be standing somewhere in the world, or else he is not one of *us*, and his commentary then is of little value." It was a carefully aimed arrow and it would pierce Baldwin's heart.

The threat of being deemed "not one of *us*" is a fearful thing. *Tell Me How Long* depicts a black artist's growing sense that (in a recurrent phrase) he no longer belongs to himself. That his public role may have depleted the rest of him. There is a constituency he must honor, a cause he must respect; and when others protect him, it is not for who he is but what he stands for.

To be sure, what Baldwin once termed "the burden of representation" is a common malady in Afro-American literature; but few have measured its costs—the price of that ticket to ride—as trenchantly as he. Baldwin risked the fate that Leo Proudhammer most feared: which was to be "a Jeremiah without convictions." Desperate to be "one of us," to be loved by us, Baldwin allowed himself to mouth a script that was not his own. The connoisseur of complexity tried to become an ideologue. And with the roaring void left by the murders of Malcolm X and Martin Luther King, he must have felt the obligation ever more strongly.

However erratic some of his later writing might have been, I believe he could still have done anything he wanted with the English essay. The problem was, he no longer knew what he wanted . . . or even what we wanted from him. Meanwhile, a generation had arrived that didn't want anything from him—except, perhaps, that he lie down and die. And this, too, has been a consistent dynamic of race and representation in Afro-America. If someone has anointed a black intellectual, rest assured that others are busily constructing his tumbrel.

In an essay he published in 1980, he reflected on his role as an elder statesman: "It is of the utmost importance, for example, that I, the elder, do not allow myself to be put on the defensive. The young, no matter how loud they get, have no real desire to humiliate their elders and, if and when they succeed in doing so, are lonely, crushed, and miserable, as only the young can be." The passage is eloquent, admirable . . . and utterly, utterly unpersuasive.


We stayed in touch, on and off, through the intervening years, often dining at the Ginger Man when he was in New York. Sometimes he would introduce me to his current lover, or speak of his upcoming projects. But I did not return to Saint Paul de Vence until shortly after his death three years ago, when my wife and I came to meet Jimmy's brother, David.

Saint-Paul had changed remarkably in the twenty or so years since he settled there. The demand for vacation homes and rental property has claimed much of the farmland that once supported the city and supplied its needs. Luxury homes dot the landscape on quarter-acre plots, and in the midst of this congestion stood Baldwin's ten-acre oasis, the only undivided farm acreage left in Saint-Paul. Only, now the grape arbors are strung with electric lights.

There we had a reunion with Bernard Hassell, Jimmy's loving friend of so many decades, and met Lucien Happersberger, the friend to whom *Giovanni's Room* is dedicated. After a week of drinking and reminiscing, David Baldwin asked me just when I had met Jimmy for the first time. As I recounted the events of our visit in 1973, David's wide eyes grew wider. He rose from the table, went downstairs into Jimmy's study—where a wall of works by and about Henry James faces you as you enter—and emerged with a manuscript in hand. "This is for you," he said.

He handed me a play, the last work Jimmy completed as he suffered through his final illness, entitled "The Welcome Table." It was set in the Riviera, at a house much like his own, and among the principal characters were "Edith, an actress-singer/star: Creole, from New Orleans," "Daniel, ex-Black Panther, fledgling play-wright," with more than a passing resemblance to Cecil Brown, and "Peter Davis, Black American journalist." Peter Davis—who has come to interview a famous star, and whose prodding questions lead to the play's revelations—was, I should say, a far better and more aggressive interviewer than I was, but of course Baldwin, being Baldwin, had transmuted the occasion into a searching drama of revelation and crisis. Reading it made me think of all the questions I had left unasked. It was and is a vain regret. Jimmy loved to talk and he loved language, but his answers only left me with more questions.

Narratives of decline have the appeal of simplicity, but Baldwin's career will not fit that mold. "Unless a writer is extremely old when he dies, in which case he has probably become a neglected institution, his death must always seem untimely," Baldwin wrote in 1961, giving us fair warning. "This is because a real writer is always shifting and changing and searching." Reading his late essays, I see him embarking on a period of intellectual resurgence. I think he was finding his course, exploring the instability of all the categories that divide us. As he wrote in "Here Be Monsters," an essay published two years before his death, and with which he chose to conclude *The Price of the Ticket,* his collected nonfiction: "Each of us, helplessly and forever, contains the other—male in female, female in male, white in black, and black in white. We are a part of each other. Many of my countrymen appear to find this fact exceedingly inconvenient and even unfair, and so, very often, do I. But none of us can do anything about it." We needed to hear these words two decades ago. We need to hear them now.

Times change. An influential intellectual avant-garde in black Britain has resurrected him as a patron saint, and a new generation of readers has come to value just those qualities of ambivalence and equivocality, just that sense of the contingency of identity, that made him useless to the ideologues of liberation and anathema to so many black nationalists. Even his fiercest antagonists seem now to have welcomed him back to the fold. Like everyone else, I guess, we like our heroes dead.

# King of Cats

In the late seventies, I used to take the train from New Haven to New York on Saturdays, to spend afternoons with Albert Murray at Books & Company, on Madison Avenue. We would roam—often joined by the artist Romare Bearden—through fiction, criticism, philosophy, music. Murray always seemed to wind up fingering densely printed paperbacks by Joyce, Mann, Proust, or Faulkner; Bearden, typically, would pick up a copy of something daunting like Rilke's *Letters on Cézanne* and then insist that I read it on the train home that night.

In those days, Murray was writing Count Basie's autobiography—a project that he didn't finish until 1985. ("For years," he has remarked more than once, "when I wrote the word 'I,' it meant Basie.") But he had already published most of the books that would secure his reputation as a cultural critic—perhaps most notably, his debut collection, *The Omni-Americans* (1970), which brought together his ferocious attacks on black separatism, on protest literature, and on what he called "the social science-fiction monster." Commanding as he could be on the page, Murray was an equally impressive figure in the flesh: a lithe and dapper man with an astonishing gift of verbal fluency, by turns grandiloquent and earthy. I loved to listen to his voice—grave but insinuating, with more than a hint of a jazz singer's rasp. Murray had been a schoolmate of the novelist Ralph Ellison at the Tuskegee Institute, and the friendship of the two men over the years seemed a focal point of black literary culture in the ensuing decades. Ellison's one novel, *Invisible Man,* was among the few unequivocal masterpieces of American literature in the postwar era, satirizing with equal aplomb Garveyites, Communists, and white racists in both their Southern-agrarian and their Northern-liberal guises. Murray's works of critique and cultural exploration seemed wholly in the same spirit. Both men were militant integrationists, and they shared an almost messianic view of the importance of art. In their ardent belief that Negro culture was a constitutive part of American culture, they had defied an entrenched literary mainstream, which preferred to regard black culture as so much exotica—amusing, perhaps, but eminently dispensable. Now they were also defying a new black vanguard, which regarded authentic black culture as separate from the rest of American culture—something that was created, and could be appreciated, in splendid isolation. While many of their peers liked to speak of wrath and resistance, Murray and Ellison liked to speak of complexity and craft, and for that reason they championed the art of Romare Bearden.

In terms of both critical regard and artistic fecundity, these were good days for Bearden, a large, light-skinned man with a basketball roundness to his head. (I could never get over how much he looked like Nikita Khrushchev.) He, like Murray, was working at the height of his powers—he was completing his famous "Jazz" series of collages—and his stature and influence were greater than those which any other African-American artist had so far enjoyed. The collages combined the visual conventions of black American folk culture with the techniques of modernism—fulfilling what Murray called the "vernacular imperative" to transmute tradition into art.

After a couple of hours at the bookstore, we'd go next door to the Madison Cafe, where Romie, as Murray called him, always ordered the same item: the largest fruit salad that I had ever seen in public. He claimed that he chose the fruit salad because he was watching his weight, but I was convinced that he chose it in order to devour the colors, like an artist dipping his brush into his palette. He'd start laying the ground with the off-white of the apples and the bananas, and follow them with the pinkish orange of the grapefruit, the red of strawberries, the speckled green of kiwifruit; the blueberries and purple grapes he'd save for last. While Romie was consuming his colors, Murray would talk almost nonstop, his marvelous ternary sentences punctuated only by the occasional bite of a B.L.T. or a tuna fish on rye. Murray was then, as now, a man with definite preoccupations, and among the touchstones of his conversation were terms like "discipline," "craft," "tradition," "the aesthetic," and "the Negro idiom." And names like Thomas Mann, André Malraux, Kenneth Burke, and Lord Raglan. There was also another name—a name that never weighed more heavily than when it was unspoken—which sometimes took longer to come up.

"Heard from Ralph lately?" Bearden would almost whisper as the waitress brought the check.

"Still grieving, I guess," Murray would rasp back, shaking his head slowly. He was referring to the fire, about a decade earlier, that had destroyed Ellison's Massachusetts farmhouse and, with it, many months of revisions on his long-awaited second novel. "That fire was a terrible thing." Then Murray, who was so rarely at a loss for words, would fall silent.

Later, when Bearden and I were alone in his Canal Street loft, he'd return to the subject in hushed tones: "Ralph is mad at Al. No one seems to know why. And it's killing Al. He's not sure what he did."


The rift, or whatever it amounted to, used to vex and puzzle me. It was a great mistake to regard Murray simply as Ellison's sidekick, the way many people did, but he was without question the most fervent and articulate champion of Ellison's art. The two were, in a sense, part of a single project: few figures on the scene shared as many presuppositions and preoccupations as they did. Theirs was a sect far too small for schismatics. At the very least, the rift made things awkward for would-be postulants like me.

When *The Omni-Americans* came out, in 1970, I was in college, majoring in history but pursuing extracurricular studies in how to be black. Those were days when the Black Power movement smoldered, when militancy was the mode and rage de rigueur. Just two years before, the poets Larry Neal and Amiri Baraka had edited *Black Fire*, the book that launched the so-called Black Arts movement—in effect, the cultural wing of the Black Power movement. Maybe it was hard to hold a pen with a clenched fist, but you did what you could: the revolution wasn't about niceties of style anyway. On the occasions when Ralph Ellison, an avatar of elegance, was invited to college campuses, blacks invariably denounced him for his failure to involve himself in the civil-rights struggle, for his evident disdain of the posturings of Black Power. For me, though, the era was epitomized by a reading that the poet Nikki Giovanni gave in a university lecture hall, to a standing-room-only crowd—a sea of colorful dashikis and planetary Afros. Her words seemed incandescent with racial rage, and each poem was greeted with a Black Power salute. "Right on! Right on!" we shouted, in the deepest voices we could manage, each time Giovanni made another grand claim about the blackness of blackness. Those were days when violence (or, anyway, talk of violence) had acquired a Fanonist glamour; when the black bourgeoisie—kulaks of color, nothing more—was reviled as an obstacle on the road to revolution; when the arts were seen as merely an instrumentality for a larger cause.

Such was the milieu in which Murray published *The Omni-Americans,* and you couldn't imagine a more foolhardy act. This was a book in which the very language of the black nationalists was subjected to a strip search. Ever since Malcolm X, for instance, the epithet "house Negro" had been a staple of militant invective; yet here was Murray arguing that if only we got our history straight we'd realize that those house Negroes were practically race patriots. ("The house slave seems to have brought infinitely more tactical information from the big house to the cabins than any information about subversive plans he ever took back.") And while radicals mocked their bourgeois brethren as "black Anglo-Saxons," Murray defiantly declared, "Not only is it the so-called middle class Negro who challenges the status quo in schools, housing, voting practices, and so on, he is also the one who is most likely to challenge total social structures and value systems." Celebrated chroniclers of black America, including Claude Brown, Gordon Parks, and James Baldwin, were shown by Murray to be tainted by the ethnographic fallacy, the pretense that one writer's peculiar experiences can represent a social genus. "This whole thing about somebody revealing what it is really like to be black has long since gotten out of hand anyway," he wrote. "Does anybody actually believe that, say, Mary McCarthy reveals what it is really like to be a U.S. white woman, or even a Vassar girl?" But he reserved his heaviest artillery for the whole social-science approach to black life, whether in the hands of the psychologist Kenneth Clark (of *Brown v. Board of Education* fame) or in those of the novelist Richard Wright, who had spent too much time reading his sociologist friends. What was needed wasn't more sociological inquiry, Murray declared; what was needed was cultural creativity, nourished by the folkways and traditions of black America but transcending them. And the work of literature that best met that challenge, he said, was Ellison's *Invisible Man*.

The contrarian held his own simply by matching outrage with outrage—by writing a book that was so pissed-off, jaw-jutting, and unapologetic that it demanded to be taken seriously. Nobody had to tell this veteran about black fire: in Murray the bullies of blackness had met their most formidable opponent. And a great many blacks—who, suborned by "solidarity," had trained themselves to suppress any heretical thoughts—found Murray's book oddly thrilling: it had the transgressive frisson of samizdat under Stalinism. You'd read it greedily, though you just might want to switch dust jackets with *The Wretched of the Earth* before wandering around with it in public. "Very early on, he was saying stuff that could get him killed," the African-American novelist David Bradley says. "And he did not seem to care." The power of his example lingers. "One February, I had just delivered the usual black-history line, and I was beginning to feel that I was selling snake oil," Bradley recalls. "And right here was this man who has said this stuff. And I'm thinking, Well, *he* ain't dead yet."

As if to remove any doubts, Murray has just published two books simultaneously, both with Pantheon. One, *The Seven League Boots*, is his third novel, and completes a trilogy about a bright young fellow named Scooter, his fictional alter ego; the other, *The Blue Devils of Nada*, is a collection of critical essays, analyzing some favorite artists (Ellington, Hemingway, Bearden), and expatiating upon some favorite tenets (the "blues idiom" as an aesthetic substrate, the essentially fluid nature of American culture). Both are books that will be discussed and debated for years to come; both are vintage Murray.

The most outrageous theorist of American culture lives, as he has lived for three decades, in a modest apartment in Lenox Terrace, in Harlem. When I visit him there, everything is pretty much as I remembered it. The public rooms look like yet another Harlem branch of the New York Public Library. Legal pads and magnifying glasses perch beside his two or three favorite chairs, along with numerous ball-point pens, his weapons of choice. His shelves record a lifetime of enthusiasms; James, Tolstoy, Hemingway, Proust, and Faulkner are among the authors most heavily represented. Close at hand are volumes by favored explicants, such as Joseph Campbell, Kenneth Burke, Carl Jung, Rudolph Arnheim, Bruno Bettelheim, Constance Rourke. On his writing desk sits a more intimate canon. There's Thomas Mann's four-volume *Joseph and His Brothers*—the saga, after all, of a slave who gains the power to decide the fate of a people. There's André Malraux's *Man's Fate*, which represented for Ellison and Murray a more rarefied mode of engagé writing than anything their compeers had to offer. There's Joel Chandler Harris's *The Complete Tales of Uncle Remus*, a mother lode of African-American folklore. One wall is filled with his famously compendious collection of jazz recordings; a matte-black CD-player was a gift from his protégé Wynton Marsalis. You will not, however, see the sort of framed awards that festooned Ellison's apartment. "I have received few of those honors," he says, pulling on his arthritic right leg. "No American Academy, few honorary degrees."

A quarter of a century has passed since Murray's literary debut, and time has mellowed him not at all. His arthritis may have worsened over the past few years, and there is always an aluminum walker close by, but as he talks he sprouts wings. Murray likes to elaborate on his points and elaborate on his elaborations, until you find that you have circumnavigated the globe and raced through the whole of post-Homeric literary history—and this is what he calls "vamping till ready." In his conversation, outrages alternate with insights, and often the insights are the outrages. Every literary culture has its superego and its id; Albert Murray has the odd distinction of being both. The contradictions of human nature are, fittingly, a favorite topic of Murray's. He talks about how Thomas Jefferson was a slaveholder but how he also helped to establish a country whose founding creed was liberty. "Every time I think about it," he says, "I want to wake him up and give him ten more slaves." He's less indulgent of the conflicting impulses of Malcolm X. Dr. King's strategy of nonviolence was "one of the most magnificent things that anybody ever invented in the civil-rights movement," he maintains. "And this guy came up and started thumbing his nose at it, and, to my utter amazement, he's treated as if he were a civil-rights leader. He didn't lead anything. He was in Selma laughing at these guys. God *damn*, nigger!"

Albert Murray is a teacher by temperament, and as he explains a point he'll often say that he wants to be sure to "work it into your consciousness." The twentieth century has worked a great deal into Murray's consciousness. He was fifteen when the Scottsboro trial began, twenty-two when Marian Anderson sang at the Lincoln Memorial. He joined the Air Force when it was segregated and rejoined shortly after it had been desegregated. He was in his late thirties when *Brown v. Board of Education* was decided, when the conflict in Korea was concluded, when Rosa Parks was arrested. He was in his forties when the Civil Rights Act was passed, when S.N.C.C. was founded, when John F. Kennedy was killed. And he was in his fifties when the Black Panther Party was formed, when King was shot, when Black Power was proclaimed. Such are the lineaments of public history—the sort of grainy national drama that newsreels used to record. For him, though, the figures of history are as vivid as drinking companions, and, on the whole, no more sacrosanct.

He is equally unabashed about taking on contemporary figures of veneration, even in the presence of a venerator. Thus, about the novelist Toni Morrison, we agree to disagree. "I do think it's tainted with do-goodism," he says of her Nobel Prize, rejecting what he considers the special pleading of contemporary feminism. "I think it's redressing wrongs. You don't have to condescend to no goddam Jane Austen. Or the Brontës, or George Eliot and George Sand. These chicks are tough. You think you'll get your fastball by Jane Austen? So we don't need special pleading for anything. And the same goes for blackness." He bridles at the phenomenon of Terry McMillan, the best-selling author of *Waiting to Exhale*—or, more precisely, at the nature of the attention she has received. "I think it's a mistake to try to read some profound political significance into everything, like as soon as a Negro writes it's got to be some civil-rights thing," he says. "It's just Jackie Collins stuff."

At times, his pans somehow edge into panegyrics, the result being what might be called a backhanded insult. About Maya Angelou's much discussed Inaugural poem he says, "It's like the reaction to *Porgy and Bess*. Man, you put a bunch of brown-skinned people on-stage, with footlights and curtains, and they make *anything* work. White people have no resistance to Negro performers: they charm the pants off anything. Black people make you listen up. They're singing 'Old Man River'—'Tote that barge, lift that bale'? What the fuck is that? Everybody responded like 'This is great.' That type of fantastic charm means that black performers can redeem almost any type of pop fare."

Since discipline and craft are his bywords, however, he distrusts staged spontaneity. "He plays the same note that he perfected twenty-five years ago, and he acts like he's got to sweat to get the note out of the goddam guitar," Murray says of the contemporary blues musician B. B. King. "He's got to shake his head and frown, and it's just going to be the same goddam note he already played twenty-five years ago." Murray himself doesn't mind returning to notes he played twenty-five years ago—his nonfiction books explore the same set of issues, and can be read as chapters of a single ongoing opus. Indeed, from all accounts the fashioning of this particular cultural hero began long before the start of his writing career.

In Murray's case, heroism was a matter both of circumstance and of will. Certainly he has long been an avid student of the subject. Lord Raglan's classic *The Hero: A Study in Tradition, Myth, and Drama* (1936) is among the books most frequently cited in his writing, and it remains a part of his personal canon. Moreover, the mythic patterns that Lord Raglan parsed turn out to have had resonances for Murray beyond the strictly literary. According to Raglan's exhaustively researched generalizations, the hero is highborn, but "the circumstances of his conception are unusual," and he is "spirited away" to be "reared by foster-parents in a far country." Then, "on reaching manhood," he "returns or goes to his future kingdom," confronts and defeats the king, or a dragon, or some such, and starts being heroic in earnest. So it was, more or less, with Oedipus, Theseus, Romulus, Joseph, Moses, Siegfried, Arthur, Robin Hood, and—oh, yes—Albert Murray.

Murray was born in 1916 and grew up in Magazine Point, a hamlet not far from Mobile, Alabama. His mother was a housewife, and his father, Murray says, was a "common laborer," who sometimes helped lay railroad tracks as a cross-tie cutter and at other times harvested timber in the Turpentine woods. "As far as the Murrays were concerned, it was a fantastic thing that I finished the ninth grade," he recalls, "or that I could read the newspaper." But he had already decided that he was bound for college. Everyone in the village knew that there was something special about him. And he knew it, too.

He had known it ever since an all-night wake—he was around eleven at the time—when he had fallen asleep in the living room, his head cradled in his mother's lap. At one point, he surfaced to hear himself being discussed, but, with a child's cunning, he pretended he was still asleep.

"Tell me something," a relative was saying. "Is it true that Miss Graham is really his mama?"

"She's the one brought him into the world," Mrs. Murray replied. "But I'm his mama. She gave him to me when he was no bigger than a minute, and he was so little I had to put him on a pillow to take him home. I didn't think he was going to make it. I laid him out for God to take him two or three times. And I said, 'Lord, this child is here for something, so I'm going to feed this child and he's going to make it.' " It was a moment that Al Murray likens to finding out the truth about Santa Claus.

Murray's birth parents were, as he slowly learned, well educated and securely middle class—people who belonged to an entirely different social stratum from that of his adoptive parents. His natural father, John Young, came from a well-established family in town. His natural mother had been attending Tuskegee as a boarding student and working part time for John Young's aunt and uncle, who were in the real-estate business. When she learned that a close encounter with John Young had left her pregnant, she had to leave town—"because of the disgrace," Murray explains. As luck would have it, a cousin of hers knew a married woman who, unable to bear a child of her own, was interested in adopting one. Murray doesn't have to be prodded to make the fairy-tale connection. "It's just like the prince left among the paupers," he says cheerfully. (In *The Omni-Americans* he wrote, apropos of the 1965 Moynihan report on the breakdown of the black family structure, "How many epic heroes issue from conventional families?")

As a freshman at the Tuskegee Institute—the ancestral kingdom he was fated to enter—Murray became aware of a junior whose reading habits were alarmingly similar to his. He was a music major from Oklahoma named Ralph Waldo Ellison, and what first impressed Murray about him was his wardrobe. "Joe College, right out of *Esquire*—he had fine contrasting slacks, gray tweed jacket. He would be wearing bow ties and two-tone shoes," Murray recalls. "In those days, when you checked out a book from the library you had a little slip in the back where you would write your name, and then they would stamp the due date." Consequently, when Murray took out a book by, say, T. S. Eliot or Robinson Jeffers, he could see who had previously borrowed the book. Time and again, it was that music major with the two-tone shoes.

Ellison left Tuskegee for New York before completing his senior year: his absence was meant to be temporary, a means of saving some money, but he never went back. Murray earned his B.A. at Tuskegee in 1939, and stayed on to teach. In 1941, he married Mozelle Menefee, who was a student there. He spent the last two years of the Second World War on active duty in the Air Force. "I was just hoping I'd live long enough for Thomas Mann to finish the last volume of *Joseph and His Brothers*," he says. Two years after his discharge, he moved to New York, where, on the G.I. bill, he got a master's degree in literature from New York University. It was also in New York that the friendship between him and Ellison took off. Ellison read passages to Murray from a manuscript that would turn into *Invisible Man*. The two men explored the streets and the sounds of Harlem together; over meals and over drinks, they hashed out ideas about improvisation, the blues, and literary modernism. Even then, Murray had a reputation as a "great explainer."

The prominent black religious and literary scholar Nathan A. Scott, who was a graduate student in New York in the forties and had become a friend of Ellison's, tells about being in the Gotham Book Mart one day and noticing another black man there. "I was somewhat surprised to find this slight, dark man there, because I'd never bumped into a Negro there," Scott recounts. "And some young white chap came in, and they knew each other and immediately plunged into a spirited conversation, and at a certain point I overheard this chap say to the black man, 'Well, what are you working on these days?' To which the black chap replied, 'Oh, I am doing an essay on self-definition.' " (And Scott laughs loudly.) Later, at a dinner at Ellison's apartment, Ellison introduced Scott to his friend Albert Murray: "Immediately, I thought, By God, here is the chap who was doing that essay in self-definition! Inwardly, I laughed all over again."

If it was clear that the young man was interested in trying to write, it wasn't so clear what the results were. In the early fifties, Saul Bellow and Ralph Ellison shared a house in Dutchess County, and Bellow recalls seeing Murray from time to time down in the city. "I think he agreed with Ralph, in simply assuming that they were deeply installed in the whole American picture," Bellow says. He adds that Ellison talked about Murray's writing in those days, but that he himself never saw any of it. In 1952, Ellison published *Invisible Man*. The book was a best-seller for several months, and garnered some of the most enthusiastic critical responses anyone could remember. It was soon a classroom staple, the subject of books and dissertations. It was read and reread. Ellison, in short, had become an immortal. And Murray? With a wife and a daughter to support, he was pursuing a more conventional career—in the Air Force, which he rejoined in 1951.

As a military officer, Murray taught courses in geopolitics in the Air Force R.O.T.C. program at Tuskegee, where he was based for much of the fifties, and he oversaw the administration of large-scale technical operations both in North Africa and in the United States. While his military career has remained oddly isolated from his creative work—a matter of regret, in the opinion of some of his friends—the experience would leave him impatient with the pretensions of the by-any-means-necessary brigade. He says, in that distinctively Murrayesque tone of zestful exasperation, "Let's talk about 'the fire next time.' You know damn well they can put out the fire by Wednesday."

When Murray retired from the military, in 1962, he moved to New York, and soon his articles began to appear in periodicals *(Life, The New Leader)* and collections *(Anger, and Beyond)*. In 1964, Ellison wrote a letter about his old friend to one Jacob Cohen, who was planning to start a magazine. "Actually I find it very difficult to write about him," the letter began. "I suppose because I have known him since our days at Tuskegee, and because our contacts since that time have been so constant and our assumptions about so many matters in such close agreement that I really don't have the proper sense of perspective." Ellison went on to say of Murray, "He has the imagination which allows him to project himself into the centers of power, and he uses his imagination to deal with serious problems seriously and as though he were a responsible participant in the affairs of our nation and our time." The following year, a panel of book critics, authors, and editors found *Invisible Man* to be the most widely admired novel published since the Second World War. Meanwhile, Albert Murray, then two years out of the Air Force, was scarcely known outside the circle of his acquaintances.

However asymmetric the public stature of the pair, people who spent time with Murray and Ellison in those days were impressed by the ease and intimacy of their friendship. In the late sixties, Willie Morris, then the editor of *Harper's,* eagerly sought their company: they provided him with a refreshing contrast to what he found a suffocating literary climate. He recalls, "In every way, they were like brothers—you know, soul brothers and fellow-writers—but Ellison's star was so bright, and Al was just really getting started." Soul brothers they may have been; they were also brothers-in-arms. When Murray rose to do battle with the rising ranks of black nationalism, he knew he shared a foxhole with Ralph Ellison, and there must have been comfort in that.

It may seem ironic that the person who first urged *The Omni-Americans* on me was Larry Neal, one of the Black Arts founders. But Neal was a man of far greater subtlety than the movement he spawned, and he understood Albert Murray's larger enterprise—the one that he shared with Ellison—better than most. People who may not read Murray but like the *idea* of him reflexively label him an "integrationist"; seldom do they take in the term's full complexity. In Murray's hands, integration wasn't an act of accommodation but an act of introjection. Indeed, at the heart of Murray and Ellison's joint enterprise was perhaps the most breathtaking act of cultural chutzpah this land had witnessed since Columbus blithely claimed it all for Isabella.

In its bluntest form, their assertion was that the truest Americans were black Americans. For much of what was truly distinctive about America's "national character" was rooted in the improvisatory pre-history of the blues. The very sound of American English "is de-rived from the timbre of the African voice and the listening habits of the African ear," Ellison maintained. "If there is such a thing as a Yale accent, there is a Negro wail in it." This is the lesson that the protagonist of Ellison's novel learns while working at a paint fac-tory: the whitest white is made by adding a drop of black. For gen-erations, the word "American" had tacitly connoted "white." Murray inverted the cultural assumptions and the verbal conven-tions: in his discourse, "American," roughly speaking, means "black." So, even as the clenched-fist crowd was scrambling for cul-tural crumbs, Murray was declaring the entire harvest board of American civilization to be his birthright. In a sense, Murray was the ultimate black nationalist. And the fact that people so easily mis-took his vision for its opposite proved how radical it was.

But why stop with matters American? What did the European sa-vants of Existentialism understand about *la condition humaine* that Ma Rainey did not? In later works, most notably *Stomping the Blues* (1976), Murray took the blues to places undreamed-of by its origi-nators. It has long been a commonplace that the achievements of black music have far outstripped those of black literature—that no black writer has produced work of an aesthetic complexity compa-rable to Duke Ellington's, Count Basie's, or Charlie Parker's. This much, for Murray, was a point of departure: he sought to process the blues into a self-conscious aesthetic, to translate the deep struc-ture of the black vernacular into prose. Arguably, LeRoi Jones at-tempted something similar in his celebrated *Blues People* (1963), but there sociology gained the upper hand over art. (Ellison, writing in *The New York Review of Books,* complained that Jones's approach was enough to "give even the blues the blues.") To Murray, the blues stood in opposition to all such reductionism. "What it all rep-resents is an attitude toward the nature of human experience (and the alternatives of human adjustment) that is both elemental and comprehensive," he wrote in *Stomping the Blues,* and he continued:

It is a statement about confronting the complexities inherent in the human situation and about improvising or experimenting or riffing or otherwise playing with (or even gambling with) such possibilities as are also inherent in the obstacles, the disjunctures, and the jeopardy. It is also a statement about perseverance and about resilience and thus also about the maintenance of equilibrium despite precarious circumstances and about achieving elegance in the very process of coping with the rudiments of subsistence.

Though Murray's salvific conception of the blues may seem fantastical, it represented precisely the alternative that Larry Neal and others were searching for. In truth, you could no more capture the sublimity of music in earthbound prose than you could trap the moon's silvery reflection in a barrel of rainwater, but there was heroism, surely, in the effort. And Murray was never short on heroism.

He also had a historical sense, rare in those days, that meant that he knew when he was going down a path others had trod before him. Murray's designation for his artistic agenda was the "vernacular imperative"—namely, "to process (which is to say to stylize) the raw native materials, experiences, and the idiomatic particulars of everyday life into aesthetic (which is to say elegant) statements of universal relevance and appeal." It had to do, that is, with the assimilation of traditions, especially "nonliterary" ones; and, as a cultural policy, it came with a tradition of its own.

When I first met Murray, nearly twenty years ago, I'd wanted to talk to him about W. E. B. Du Bois—by acclamation, the greatest black intellectual in American history—and Murray had obligingly plucked from his shelves a first edition of Du Bois's *The Souls of Black Folk*. "Oh, we revered him all right," Murray said. "It's just that Du Bois was so remote, so aloof—so Olympian." Like Ellison himself, I thought. "But you know who our real hero was?" Murray asked. "James Weldon Johnson. *He* was the man to beat."

And when I thought more about it, I realized that Johnson really did make sense in the role of cultural progenitor. Johnson, who lived from 1871 to 1938, was an accomplished musician, writing a number of early Broadway hits with his brother, and a champion of rag-time; he was also a distinguished novelist (*The Autobiography of an Ex-Colored Man* is still widely taught) and a poet (every black schoolkid in my class could recite "The Creation" by heart, and so could their parents). Johnson had emigrated to New York from the provinces (Florida), as had Ellison (Oklahoma) and Murray (Alabama), but was a true man of the world: fluent in Spanish and French, Johnson served as U.S. consul in Venezuela and Nicaragua before becoming the first black executive secretary of the N.A.A.C.P. And it was Johnson who taught the first course in Negro literature at a white school, New York University. If ever there has been a true Renaissance man in black letters, Johnson was it.

More to the point, Johnson had propounded the theory—brilliantly explicated in Murray's work and exemplified in Ellison's—that great Negro art would be nourished by the loam of black vernacular culture. Here is James Weldon Johnson, writing in 1921: "What the colored poet in the United States needs to do is something like what Synge did for the Irish; he needs to find a form that will express the racial spirit by symbols from within rather than by symbols from without. . . . He needs a form that is freer and larger than dialect, but which will still hold the racial flavor; a form expressing the imagery, the idioms, the peculiar turns of thought, and the distinctive humor and pathos, too, of the Negro, but which will also be capable of voicing the deepest and highest emotions and aspirations, and allow of the widest range of subjects and the widest scope of treatment." (Compare the Malraux passage that serves as an epigraph to *The Omni-Americans:* "The individual stands in opposition to society, but he is nourished by it. And it is far less important to know what differentiates him than what nourishes him.") In a marvelously apt turn of events, Johnson's devoted secretary and amanuensis, Fanny McConnell, would, in 1946, become Ellison's wife and "best reader."

If Johnson provided the basic conception of the "vernacular imperative," he could perhaps be faulted in his execution of it. Consider, for instance, Johnson's best-known collection of poetry, *God's Trombones: Seven Negro Sermons in Verse* (1927); while his "translations" owe much to their originals, gone is the grain of the voice, the folk preacher's earthy vitality. Johnson genuinely loved the Negro idiom; he just thought that it needed a shower and a shave before showing itself downtown.

Still, Murray and Ellison knew that Johnson was right about the pitfalls: art was a matter of alchemy, not just ethnography. Their answer was to turn toward more sophisticated, nonliterary sources: jazz and, especially, the blues. "Where the hell did all those writers get the idea that folk, which is to say peasant or provincial, art (or artlessness) is adequate to the complexities of black experience in contemporary America?" Murray demands in his new essay collection, *The Blue Devils of Nada*. Moreover, there *were* successful examples of art that drew inspiration from jazz and the blues. That was where Bearden came in, and that was why his friendship with Murray had to be understood also as an artistic alliance. Bearden's mixed-media works could serve as a cultural paradigm for the kind of bricolage and hybridity that Murray favored.

In recent stanzas entitled "Omni-Albert Murray" the young African-American poet Elizabeth Alexander writes, "In my mind and in his I think a painting is a poem / A tambourine's a hip shake and train whistle a guitar." Certainly Murray proved an authoritative exponent of Bearden's works, the titles of which were frequently of his devising. The literary scholar Robert O'Meally remembers being with Bearden and Murray in Books & Company when the two were trying to decide on a name for whatever picture Bearden had brought along that day. O'Meally recalls, "It might be that Al Murray's eye was caught by the figure of a woman in one corner of the image. And he'd say, 'Who's that?' And Bearden would be looking embarrassed, because the woman in question had been an old girlfriend of his. Maybe Bearden would say, 'Oh, she's just a woman I once knew from North Carolina.' And then Murray would say, 'I've got it. Let's call it "Red-Headed Woman from North Carolina." ' Or, 'I know, call it "Red-Headed Woman from North Carolina with Rooster." ' And Bearden would go and write that on the back of his painting."

Murray stood ready to assist in other ways, too. When, in 1978,

I asked Bearden if he would conduct a seminar on Afro-American art at Yale, where I was teaching, his immediate response was "Why don't you ask Al?" But this particular appointment called for an artist, and Bearden finally did accept, though with genuine reluctance and vehement protestations of pedagogic incompetence. So reluctant was he that I was astonished by the remarkably well-organized and cogent weekly lectures he had prepared—always neatly double-spaced and fifty minutes in duration, the precise length of the academic lecturer's hour. Comprehension soon dawned. Bearden, taking matters into his own hands, had found a way to bring Murray along to New Haven: the critic had ghost-written Professor Bearden's erudite lectures.

But did Murray have debts of his own to acknowledge—in particular, to his Tuskegee schoolmate? The very similarity of their preoccupations proved a source of friction. Now it was Murray—here, there, and everywhere—spreading the glad word about the literary theorist Kenneth Burke, about Lord Raglan, about the luminous blending of craft and metaphysics represented by André Malraux and by Thomas Mann. Ellison's claim, at least to Kenneth Burke and Lord Raglan, seems clear: they were part of the swirl of ideas at Bennington College in the early fifties, when Ellison was living nearby and socializing with the faculty. One writer who had been friendly with both Murray and Ellison since the forties assures me that he has no doubt as to who was the exegete and who the originator: "This is not to say that Al was simply some sort of epigone. But *all* the fundamental ideas that are part of *The Omni-Americans* came from Ellison. Al made his own music out of those ideas, but *I* know where they came from. The course of thought that Murray began to follow in the sixties was a result of Ralph's influence, I think there is no doubt about this at all."

That has become something of a consensus view. In a recent appreciation of Murray, the jazz critic Gene Seymour writes that on such subjects as improvisation, discipline, and tradition Murray (and, by extension, disciples of his like Stanley Crouch and Wynton Marsalis) sounds "like an echo." He maintains that the recently published volume of Ellison's collected essays "makes clear [that] Ellison was the wellspring for the ideals advanced by Murray, Crouch, and Marsalis."

It's a thorny subject. At one point, Murray tells me about V. S. Naipaul's visit with him in the late eighties—a visit that was recorded in Naipaul's *A Turn in the South.* Naipaul wrote, "He was a man of enthusiasms, easy to be with, easy to listen to. His life seemed to have been a series of happy discoveries." At the same time, Naipaul identified Murray as a writer who "was, or had been, a protégé of Ralph Ellison's." Murray makes it clear that this gloss does not sit well with him. He counters by quoting something that Robert Bone, a pioneering scholar of African-American literature, told him: "I've been trying to figure out *who* is the protégé of *whom.*"

Bone, an acquaintance of both principals, suggests beginning with a different set of premises. "On Murray's part, it must have been a terribly difficult thing for him to have been overshadowed by Ralph in terms of the timing of their two careers," he says. "In a way, they started out together at Tuskegee, and then they cemented that friendship in New York, but Murray got such a later start in his career as a writer. So when he came on the scene Ralph was, of course, a celebrity." What escapes us, Bone says, is that many of the positions with which Ellison was associated were ones the two had mulled over together and corresponded about—especially "the link between Afro-American writing and Afro-American music." Reverse all your assumptions, though, and one thing remains constant: "Murray, I think, naturally must have felt a good deal of envy and resentment." Where others see Darwin and Huxley, Bone sees Watson and Crick. Of Ellison and Murray he says, "There was a time when they were both young and aspiring writers, and they shared these ideas and they worked on them together, but Ralph got into print with them first, by a kind of accident." Speaking like a true literary historian, he adds, "I think these matters will be resolved when Murray leaves his papers—he has a box full of correspondence with Ellison. I think that that correspondence is going to bring out the mutuality of these explorations and discoveries."

It's clear that beneath Ellison's unfailingly courtly demeanor, his own internal struggles may have taken their toll. The fire, in the fall of 1967, is often mentioned as a watershed moment for him, one whose symbolic freight would only increase over the years. He had been busy that summer in his Massachusetts farmhouse, making extensive revisions on his novel in progress—Murray recalls seeing a manuscript thick with interlinear emendations during a visit there. At times, Ellison had called Murray to read him some of the new material. The fire occurred on the very evening that the Ellisons had decided to return to New York. Murray says, "He packed up all his stuff and got everything together, put it all in the hallway leading out, with some of his cameras and some of his shooting equipment. Then they went out to dinner with Richard Wilbur. On the way home, when they got to a certain point, they saw this fire reflection on the skyline, and the nearer they got, the more it seemed like it was their place. And as they turned in, they saw their house going up in flames." Ellison had a copy of the manuscript in New York, but the rewriting and rethinking that had occupied him for months were lost. "So he went into shock, really. He just closed off from everybody." Murray didn't hear from him until Christmas. In the months that followed, Ellison would sometimes call Murray up and read him passages—trying to jog Murray's memory so that he would jog Ellison's. "It took him years to recover," Murray says. Meanwhile, Murray's career was following an opposite trajectory. As if making up for lost time, he spent the first half of the seventies averaging a book a year; during the same period, Ellison's block as a novelist had grown to mythic proportions. Bellow says, "Ralph was suffering very deeply from his hangup, and it was very hard to have any connection with him. He got into a very strange state, I think."

Did Ellison feel betrayed? It seems clear that he did. ("Romie used to call it 'Oklahoma paranoia,'" Murray says, musing on the froideur that settled between them.) Did Ellison have reason to? That's harder to answer. The African-American poet Michael S. Harper, an Ellison stalwart, says, "The most important word I ever heard Ralph say was the word 'honor.' I happen to know some of the difficulties they went through when Albert was in a phase of making appearances in white literary salons, and reports came back from various people." Theories of the estrangement abound. One writer acquainted with the two men says that Ellison had learned that Murray was bad-mouthing him; another suggests that Ellison simply felt crowded, that Murray was presenting himself as Ellison's confidant—"as the man to see if you want to know"—in a way that Ellison found unseemly. The chill could make things awkward for acquaintances. One of them says, "I remember on one occasion Ralph and I were lunching at the Century Club, when Al saw me in the downstairs lobby. He came up immediately and we chatted briefly, and as we were talking to each other Ralph walked away and would have nothing to do with Al. Theirs had become a difficult relationship."

Murray, for his part, is inclined to see the matter in almost anthropological terms, as falling into the behavior patterns of out-group representatives amid an in-group: "Here's a guy who figures that he's got *his* white folks over here, and he got them all hoodwinked, so he don't want anybody coming in messing things up." In anthropological terms, the native informant never relishes competition. "Hell, it was probably inevitable," Willie Morris says of the estrangement.


For all their similarities in background, education, sensibility, even dress (they shared a tailor, Charlie Davidson, himself something of a legend in sartorial circles), the two men inclined toward rather contrasting styles of public presentation. A private man who in later years grew intensely aware of being a public figure, Ellison had contrived a persona designed to defeat white expectations of black brutishness. Hence the same words come up again and again when people try to write about him—words like "patrician," "formal," "aristocratic," "mandarin," "civilized," "dignified." James Baldwin once observed, shrewdly, that Ellison was "as angry as anybody can be and still *live*." It was this banked anger that kept his back so straight in public settings, his manners so impeccable; even his spoken sentences wore spats and suspenders. Murray, who enjoyed verbal sparring as much as anybody, lacked that gift of anger, and as a conversationalist he had always taken delight in the saltier idioms of the street. (Imagine Redd Foxx with a graduate degree in literature.) The writer Reynolds Price, a friend of both Ellison and Murray, says, "Ralph had a kind of saturnine, slightly bemused quality. I thought Al always seemed the more buoyant person."

Writing is at once a solitary and a sociable act, and literary relationships are similarly compounded of opposites. So it was with Ellison and Murray, two country cousins. Many people speak of Ellison's eightieth-birthday party—to which Murray had been invited and at which he delivered a moving tribute to his old schoolmate—as a significant moment of reconciliation. "I think it was Ellison's way of reaching out to Murray," a friend of Ellison's says.

Then, too, for all his companionability, Murray's literary inclinations ran strongly toward the paternal. He takes deep satisfaction in that role, and there are many who can attest to his capacity for nurturance. James Alan McPherson, one of the fiction writers who have most often been likened to Ellison, recalls a time in the late seventies when he was in Rhode Island with a small group of his literary peers, including Ernest J. Gaines, the author of *The Autobiography of Miss Jane Pittman*. In a moment of mad enthusiasm, they hit on the idea of going to New York and letting Ellison know how much they admired him. When they phoned him, he told them, to their unbounded joy, that they should come right down. And so, after an almost mythic trek, these young black writers arrived at Riverside Drive to pay a visit to their hero.

"Mr. Ellison can't see you," they were told at the door. "He's busy working."

They were crushed. They were also adrift: with the destination of their pilgrimage closed to them, they had no place to go. "So we called Al Murray, and he picked up the slack," McPherson recounts.

"He brought us to his apartment, where he had some apples and some bourbon and some fancy French cheese. And he said, 'Have you ever met Duke Ellington's sister?' We said no, so he took us over to meet Duke Ellington's sister. And he said, 'Do you want to see the Bearden retrospective?' " He took them to the Brooklyn Museum and on to the Cordier and Ekstrom gallery, where Bearden was then showing his work. "And I'll always remember Al for that," McPherson says. (Murray tells me, "Most guys forget that I'm just two years younger than Ralph, but they feel closer to me because I'm more accessible. They kid with me all the time.") Perhaps, in the end, Ellison was the better student of Lord Raglan: he knew that patricide, or some variant of it, was a staple of heroic literature. McPherson says, quietly, "Ellison didn't want any sons."

For McPherson, what crystallized things was a ceremony that City College held in 1984 to honor Ellison. At the luncheon, one of the Ellison disciples assembled to give tributes tapped on his glass and handed Ellison a wrapped box, saying, "Ralph, here's a gift from your sons."

"Then you'd better open it yourself," Ellison replied dryly. "I'm afraid it might explode."


Albert Murray has now reached the age where his progeny have progeny, two of the most prominent in his line being, of course, Stanley Crouch and Wynton Marsalis. Both are frequent guests at Lenox Terrace, and Marsalis tells me of dinner-table conversations that roam from Homer to Galileo, from the commedia dell'arte to Faulkner and Neruda. "Murray has given me a first-class education," he says. And he speaks eloquently about the impact that *Stomping the Blues,* and Murray's very notion of jazz as an art form, had on him; he speaks about tradition, blues idioms, a poetics of inclusion. As he puts it, "I'm a Murrayite." Crouch, whose writing has brilliantly championed Murray's difficult aesthetic and emulated his pugnacious style of critique, says, "I think he's one of the foremost thinkers to appear in American letters over the last twenty-five years." (He also suggests that Murray would have been a far worthier candidate for a Nobel Prize than Toni Morrison.) "The last of the giants," McPherson calls him.

There is much to be said for having descendants. They spread the insights you have given them. They worry about why you are not better known. (Crouch has a simple explanation for Murray's relative obscurity: "It's because he spent all that time on the Basie book—there was that very long silence. I think what happened was that his career lost momentum.") They remind you, fetchingly, of your own callow youth. And they take inspiration from your fearless style of analysis and critique, and apply it to your own work—though this can be a mixed blessing.

No doubt it's the ultimate tribute to Murray's legacy of combative candor that his most fervid admirers are quite free in expressing their critical reservations—notably with regard to the new novel. *The Seven League Boots* has the distinction of being the least autobiographical of Murray's three novels: its protagonist leaves Alabama with his bass and joins up with a legendary jazz band—one not unlike Ellington's. The band is blissfully free of quarrels and petty jealousies, and Murray's alter ego, Scooter, inspires only affection in those he encounters. Indeed, this is, in no small part, a novel about friendships, about literary and intellectual conversations and correspondences, including those between Scooter and his old college roommate. On a trip across the Mississippi River Bridge, Scooter finds himself thinking about

> my old roommate again. But this time the writer he brought to mind was not Rilke but Walt Whitman, about whom he had said in response to my letter about joining the band for a while. . . . *According to my old roommate, old Walt Whitman, barnstorming troubadour par excellence that he was, could only have been completely delighted with the interplay of aesthetic and pragmatic considerations evidenced in the maps and mileage charts and always tentative itineraries.* . . . It was Ralph Waldo Emerson who spoke of "melodies that ascend and leap and pierce into the deeps of infinite time," my roommate also wrote, which, by the way, would make a very fine blurb for a Louis Armstrong solo such as the one on "Potato Head Blues."

In the next few pages, there are allusions to, among others, Melville, James Joyce, Van Wyck Brooks, Lewis Mumford, Constance Rourke, Frederick Douglass, Paul Laurence Dunbar, and Antonin Dvořák. Perhaps the critic's library overstocks his novelistic imagination. In the *Times Book Review,* the novelist and critic Charles Johnson—who must be counted among Murray's heirs, and is certainly among his most heartfelt admirers—described it as "a novel without tension." It may well be that the pleasures this novel affords are more discursive than dramatic, more essayistic than narrative. Murray tells me, "I write hoping that the most sophisticated readers of my time will think that I'm worth reading." They do, and he is.

The poet Elizabeth Alexander writes:

> *Albert Murray do they call you Al*
> *or Bert or Murray or "Tuskegee Boy"?*
> *Who are the Omni-Ones who help me feel?*
> *I'm born after so much. Nostalgia hurts.*

You could say of him what he said of Gordon Parks: "Sometimes it is as if he himself doesn't quite know what to make of what he has in fact *already* made of himself." Sometimes I don't quite, either. On the one hand, I cherish the vernacular; on the other, I've always distrusted the notion of "myth" as something deliberately added to literature, like the prize in a box of Cracker Jack. And though my first two books can be read as footnotes to *The Omni-Americans,* I, like most in the demoralized profession of literary studies, have less faith in the cultural power of criticism than he has. All the same, I find his company immensely cheering.

We live in an age of irony—an age when passionate intensity is hard to find outside a freshman dining hall, and when even the mediocre lack all conviction. But Murray was produced by another age, in which intelligence expressed itself in ardor. He has spent a career *believing* in things, like the gospel according to Ma Rainey and Jimmy Rushing and Duke Ellington. More broadly, he believes in the sublimity of art, and he has never been afraid of risking bathos to get to it. (I think the reason he took so long to write Basie's life story is that he wanted to step *inside* a great black artist, to see for himself how improvisation and formal complexity could produce high art.)

The last time I visited him at his apartment, I sat in the chair next to his writing desk as he talked me through the years of his life and his formation, and made clear much that had been unclear to me about cultural modernity. "Let me begin by saying that Romie frequently got me into trouble," Ralph Ellison told mourners at a 1988 memorial service for Bearden. "Nothing physical, mind you, but difficulties arising out of our attempts to make some practical sense of the relationship between art and living, between ideas and the complex details of consciousness and experience." In this sense, Murray, too, has always spelled trouble—for critics and artists of every description, for icon-breakers and icon-makers, for friends and foes. You learn a great many things when you sit with him in his apartment, but, summed up, they amount to a larger vision: this is Albert Murray's century; we just live in it.

# The Body Politic

It's early afternoon on Friday, November 4, 1994—the day before the Minneapolis premiere of Bill T. Jones's new work of dance theater, *Still/Here*. We are at the Northrop Auditorium, on the campus of the University of Minnesota. This is a hall with a seating capacity of about five thousand; close to a full house is expected tomorrow night. Jones is the artistic director of the Bill T. Jones/Arnie Zane Dance Company, and he is putting his dancers through their paces.

He is dressed entirely in black—a long-sleeved black cotton-knit shirt, black jeans, and black high-top shoes. Only an African amulet made of bone and amber which he wears around his neck offsets the monochrome effect. Tall, lithe, and broad-shouldered, he has been described as having the perfect dancer's body. But though Jones is the choreographer and director of *Still/Here*, he will not appear on-stage himself. Rehearsals are another matter. Coaching his dancers, he mostly stands in the middle aisle, far enough away to get the larger picture, but every few minutes he scrambles up onstage to demonstrate each movement, stance, posture that he's choreographed.

The immediate problem to be solved in this rehearsal is that the Northrop stage is vast—far larger than what the dancers are used to. They will have to make adjustments in order to fill it. "Really stretch those lines, folks!" Jones calls out, in his resonant baritone. "You have so much space around you. You can't hide anything." In defiance of classical convention, the members of his dance company come in all shapes and sizes: most noticeably, there's a distinctly portly fellow named Lawrence Goldhuber. ("When he leaves the repertory—and there's no pun intended—he will leave a big hole," Jones told me.) Jones peppers his dancers with instructions, some expressed as directives, some as questions. "Where are you going to end up, Larry?" he asks. And then "Danny, where will you be standing?" Commands alternate with cajoling and reassurance, but his authority is never in doubt. As the dancers swirl across the stage in intricate patterns, he continues to observe and to correct. "Could we space out? I have no doubt that you will be spectacular in this space." At times, he is frankly impatient. "Where *are* you folks at this moment, please? Come on, come on, get with me! Keep going—it's about spacing. Go on, go on, where do we want the material to *happen*?"

Jones believes in narrative, but narrative in a language parsed by the configuration and movement of bodies, the precisely coordinated relation that his dancers have to one another at any given moment. The storyteller is Jones; the dancers are, variously, his alphabet, his words, his syntax. "Can you guys do that phrase again? Five, six, seven, eight . . . Let's do it again, dancers." They do it again.

Tomorrow, the work will indeed be seen by about five thousand people, and it will be greeted by a standing ovation. Jones will be gratified but not surprised. When the work had its world premiere, on September 14 in Lyons, France, it was met with a standing ovation that changed into a "stomping ovation"—a rapturous audience stomping its feet in appreciation for something like fifteen minutes. Jones glows when he tells me about that audience. If you are a performer—and Jones is nothing if not a performer—there is an ecstasy to this sort of response. He is at the height of his career, and knows it. In the past year alone, he has choreographed no fewer than four new dance works, and directed Derek Walcott's play *Dream on Monkey Mountain* for the Guthrie Theatre, in Minneapolis; meanwhile, he has appeared on the cover of *Time,* been appointed resident choreographer of the Lyons Opera Ballet, in France, and received a MacArthur Foundation "genius award"—and the year isn't over yet. In short, he's become something of a poster boy for the Zeitgeist, a redoubtable achievement for someone working in the semi-sequestered, self-consciously avant-garde world of modern dance. *Still/Here*—which some esteem his masterpiece—is a two-hour multimedia work about dying and death. And Bill T. Jones has never looked more alive.

The week before, I'd met Jones one afternoon at the Astor Hotel in Milwaukee; his company was performing at the city's Pabst Theatre. The Astor was built in the early part of this century and has the tattiness that only formerly grand places can acquire; you can tell what it was in the past from the delicate dentil work around its lobby ceiling and from the threadbare elegance of its permanent residents. Two such residents, both women in their eighties, sat in the lobby like fixtures—wizened relics of a glorious past. "I'm an insomniac," Jones said to me as we passed them. "I was up at four A.M., so I walked down here to the lobby in search of a quiet corner, right past two nurses sitting where the ladies are now. They were both *on duty,* keeping watch over the near-dead." Glancing around at the faded colors of the wallpaper and the worn spots on a once magnificent carpet, Jones mused, "Some cities just don't know when to pack it in." There was no hint of disrepair or dishabille about Jones, though: I almost drooped before his erect bearing, the sinewy equipoise of his gait. He had close-cropped hair, a black suede vest buttoned over a starched white shirt, and that bone pendant which he always seems to wear. He gestured warmly toward a companion: "This is Bjorn, my partner." Bjorn Amelan, an Israeli-born Frenchman, is a quiet, tidy man in early middle age; his all-black garb and shaved head are especially arresting in this Midwestern milieu. Amelan had previously been the lover of the late Patrick Kelly, the first African-American to surmount the barricades of Paris fashion. ("I'm negotiating with Dr. Maya Angelou to write Patrick's biography," Amelan tells me excitedly before he slips off. "It will have lots of pictures.") Now he is Jones's alter ego, and, it appears, has taken on some of the other roles—manager, business partner, agent—that Arnie Zane had played for seventeen years, before his death, in 1988. (Between Zane and Amelan, Jones spent five years with Arthur Aviles, who was then and continues to be a member of the dance company.)

Jones's speech is "race neutral," his conversation strewn with easy references to Proust, Gertrude Stein, French structuralism; to film theory (and the theory of the spectatorial "gaze"); to Marcel Duchamp (and "his attempt to defeat empiricism"). Jones tells me he was "weaned on late modernism." He often speaks of himself in the third person, in the manner of athletes or presidential candidates. When he was growing up, he once thought he wanted to teach English, because he loved literature and because he was "the most vocal bullshitter in the class." His family figured him for a preacher, because he was sensitive and well spoken. He *is* remarkably eloquent: he speaks in paragraphs and can switch readily between the English of the educated classes and an earthier black vernacular. So I can believe he would have made a fine preacher, or, for that matter, English professor; but he did not go wrong in his chosen profession. Since forming his company, in 1982, Jones has received virtually every major award the dance world has to offer, including two Bessies; he has created more than forty works for his own company, as well as works for Alvin Ailey, the Boston Ballet, the Lyons Opera Ballet, the Berkshire Ballet, and the Berlin Opera Ballet. Recently, he has also branched out into other forms: he choreographed Sir Michael Tippett's opera *New Year*, which Sir Peter Hall directed for the Glyndebourne Festival Opera in 1990. About the same time, he conceived, co-directed, and choreographed Leroy Jenkins's opera *Mother of Three Sons* for the Munich Biennial, the New York City Opera, and the Houston Grand Opera.

To all his projects he brings a searching intelligence. But the world does not love him only for his mind.

A woman who once hoped for a career as a ballerina and is now a dance critic told me with wistful humor, "Every day of my life I spend *deeply* regretting the fact that he's gay." She talked about the long limbs, the trim but defined muscles, the rich mocha sheen of his skin. Certainly Jones himself has an acute sense of his physicality. He describes his face as that of "a young prizefighter, with intelligent eyes, sensitive mouth, lips not too thick, nose not too flared." He says he has "an ass that is too high, but firm like a racehorse." When he visited gay bathhouses in the late seventies and early eighties, he was, he reports, the "desired one," surrounded by competing suitors, whose attentions he would accept or reject at will. Amid the steam, the sweat, the amyl nitrite, and the sex, he seems to have realized, was another venue for performance.


William Tass Jones was born in 1952, in Bunnell, Florida, the tenth of twelve children. His father, Augustus Jones, had been a migrant worker, and in Bill's early years the family moved around the Southeast. But his father "decided to be a black Yankee," as Jones puts it, so the family moved to upstate New York—to the almost all-white village of Wayland, in the Finger Lakes region. If Jones's family roots were in Southern black culture, his accent betrays his upstate years, with pronunciations such as "elemen*tary*," and "K'yuga" for Cayuga. He recalls his father as reserved but kindly and says he can't remember his ever raising a hand to him. There's some irony in that. "My father used to cry out in his sleep," Jones tells me. "And my mother would say that's the people he killed." One person his father had killed was his mother's brother-in-law, who was apparently a drunk and a troublemaker; Gus Jones "blew him in half" with a shotgun blast—though only after giving him fair warning. (This took place when the family was living in Georgia; the sheriff chalked it up to "colored business" and let the matter drop.) By the time Bill was growing up, his father had mellowed. It was his mother, Estella,

who had the heavy hand: in her, consuming maternal love alter-
nated with near-Medean rage. With twelve kids, eight of them boys,
Estella Jones was not inclined toward the sort of indulgence
preached by Dr. Spock. "Her love was crazy, you could see it,"
Jones says. "She'd go into battle for you. By the same token, she
took a lot of liberties. She would smack your butt, smack your head,
break brooms across your back—stuff like that."

His sister Rhodessa Jones, who was born three years before him
and is now a performance artist, talks about how they kept each
other entertained when they were put to work harvesting crops together as children. Once, she remembers, Billy adapted "The Impossible Dream" to the occasion. "We stood there together in the
fields singing, 'To pick—the unpickable grape! To milk—the un-
milkable cow!' And Mama called out, 'Why are you children *taking*
so long?' "

As a boy, Jones says, he "had an aura of being a religious person."
He was sensitive, the child who couldn't watch monster flicks without suffering nightmares. Once, when he was around ten, he did
something—he can't remember what—that his father apparently
regarded as unmanly. "I never thought I'd have one of *those* in the
family," his father said acidly.

In any event, by the time he reached high school his family had
ceased to worry, because he was doing "all the things that young
boys do." He was a star athlete—a speed demon on the track team,
capturing ribbons at intermural meets. And by the time he was fourteen he had a girlfriend, too. There was a catch, though. A man who
was close to the family, whom Jones describes as "hell on wheels,"
decided to establish rules for Billy's sexual initiation. Jones speaks of
the arrangement in an almost wondering tone: "We were only allowed to sleep with each other if he was allowed to watch. And I had
to be in his bed." Jones says it happened just that once, and was not
a success. "I was traumatized," he says. Still, it's a scenario of
voyeurism that raises questions: about the man who insisted on the
arrangement, about young Billy who accommodated himself to it.
But this collision of intimacy and display—this introduction to sex
as, in the first instance, a spectator sport—seems to coincide almost

too aptly with the artist's insistence on transgressing the boundaries of public and private through the medium of performance.

It was also in high school that Jones (an admirer of Jim Morrison and Cream) joined a rock group called Wretched Souls. They used to play at the local Grange Hall, performing for kids with fringed jackets and pickup trucks. Rhodessa Jones says, "There was one song he wrote that he would sing, in a blues groove, with his shirt open. And the refrain was: 'I'm tired of you mothers fucking with me.' He was elegantly ferocious." And the audience? "They were titillated," she says.

There was no question about Jones's rebellious streak. "Growing up in an almost all-white part of the world, you sometimes had the feeling of being an alien," Rhodessa Jones says. She tells about the time that Jones, having been lambasted by a junior-high-school teacher, shouted out in class, "You want your own race riot?" And Jones's senior-year English teacher remembers him staging the "infamous Wayland Central High School sit-in of 1970"; at issue was whether girls would be allowed to wear slacks to school.

In the fall of 1970, Jones entered the State University of New York at Binghamton, where he joined the college track team. Sex led him to dance, in the form of Arnie Zane, who had graduated from the college, and who was the first man Jones slept with. When they met, in March of 1971, Jones was nineteen; Arnie was twenty-two, and was convinced that Jones's future lay not in track but in modern dance. Although Jones had already taken his first dance class, with Percival Borde, it was Zane who saw the stage as a shared vocation. Zane, of course, was white, as were all the men Jones slept with in those years: in the parlance of the subculture, Jones was a "snow queen." Not, Jones insists, because of any distaste for men who looked like him—on the contrary. When Jones was seventeen, he remembers, he went to visit an older brother in Rochester and walked in on him as he slept with his genitals exposed. Jones recounts, "I was aroused, and deeply ashamed of my arousal. I panicked and fled." So sleeping with a black man would have felt "incestuous"— like sleeping with a brother. With Arnie Zane, a short Italian-Jewish kid from Queens, there could be no such confusion.

His family represented another hurdle. Given "the brashness of the times," the early seventies, Jones was not inclined to keep secrets from his family any longer. The occasion when he brought Arnie home as his lover turned into a rather less dignified version of *Guess Who's Coming to Dinner.* He seems to have memorized every detail of the fraught moment when Estella Jones commanded him to come to her bedroom, that house's "sanctum sanctorum": the neatly made bed, the chenille bedspread, the light that filtered through drawn curtains. And his mother's words to him, as she spoke her mind: "You gotta tell me somethin'. What you doin' fuckin' some man in the ass?"

Estella then summoned Arnie to the room and turned her wrathful attention to him: "Are you a man or a woman?" A man, Arnie told her. "If you a man, then how do I know you ain't gonna take my son over there, cross that water, and leave him?" Arnie promised her that he wouldn't abandon her son, that he would protect him. And then, in Jones's account, mother and lover shook on it. Bill and Arnie's partnership, which lasted for seventeen years, until Arnie's death, proved to be a major force in contemporary dance. It was never a relationship founded on sexual fidelity, but it seemed no less powerful for that.

The first few years were nomadic—taking them from Amsterdam to San Francisco—and often hand-to-mouth. Then, in 1974, they returned to Binghamton to join with another dancer, Lois Welk, in reestablishing her American Dance Asylum, a company that had disbanded a few years earlier. To make the rent, Zane worked as a go-go dancer and Jones worked in the laundry of a geriatric hospital, where he washed countless loads of adult diapers. The larger struggle, though, was artistic. It was to find an idiom that hadn't already been claimed: to work outside the vocabulary established by the pioneers of modern dance—the Martha Grahams, the José Limóns, the Doris Humphreys, the Paul Taylors, the Merce Cunninghams. And the Alvin Aileys. "When I came into the dance world," Jones says, "everyone told me I should go to New York and let Alvin Ailey finish me. But when I met that world I realized my temperament could not have flourished there. It was very regimented. Given where they had come from and what they had to prove, there was inevitably a lot of dogma. The aesthetic—like that in the Dance Theatre of Harlem—I find very conservative. People don't want to look like fools, and dance has to work for an audience. Black folks want to come in and have a good show."

But Jones was drifting toward a markedly different aesthetic. "I wanted to make a kind of art form inspired by the cinema I had been introduced to, the non-narrative cinema of the sixties," he says. "I loved Janis Joplin, Jimi Hendrix. I had been at Woodstock." If he was out of sympathy with high modernism, he was equally unwilling to submit to the strictures of the "Black Arts" movement of the day, with its ideology of black cultural purity. "I was not a black nationalist. In the days when there were two camps, I was in the King camp. Malcolm X I didn't really know about, the rhetoric didn't have much to do with me. I had grown up since the age of twelve with white folks, people who had really shown me the greatest care outside of my family—sometimes even more than my family, because they could see things in me that I couldn't show at home. So when I came into the dance world I came in as an avant-gardist," influenced by the postmodernist manifestos of the choreographer and filmmaker Yvonne Rainer. These were the days when Jones would proudly insist that he was an artist first, a black man second. "The way I acknowledged my blackness was that I used it as a style of performance. All that stuff has to be refined."


You will find on Jones's résumé numerous dance works that he created in this period. Something that isn't on the résumé is that when Jones was around twenty-nine he became a father. He speaks of this in an almost chastened tone, punctuated with moments of defensiveness. Clearly, those were heady days: "I had reinvented myself. I was being recognized as an artist." And, just as headily, "I was flirting with girls, and guys, and doing anything." Jones was an artist-in-residence in Black Hawk County, Iowa, when he became involved with an attractive woman from inner-city Detroit, who worked as a teacher's aide. "She and I started this hot and heavy thing, every night for about a month," he says. Jones told her about Zane, but she didn't really believe it. "She told me, 'You ain't no freak.' We had relations that were *real*. That was no problem." But when the residency was over and it was time for Jones to go home, she was distraught. Later, he learned that she had given birth to his child.

"I went over to look at the child—a pretty little girl, very dark. I was trying to see myself in her. The child did not want anything to do with me. I had brought a little stuffed animal from Chicago, and the child spent the whole time beating me with it, while I sat next to her mother. The mother and I immediately fell right back into that thing. I couldn't believe it. Then she called, really upset, and she said, 'I can't handle this baby. I'm a single woman. Do you want this child?' " As it happened, Jones and Zane had been trying to adopt a baby, to no avail. "And now, suddenly, I had my *own* baby, a godsend." Jones and Zane spent a week searching their souls, and considering how they could rearrange their lives. "Then she called back and said, 'Are you crazy? I wouldn't give my child to you. I just wasn't feeling good that day. What I need is for you to send me two hundred dollars.' And she said, 'I don't want the child to know who you are. I don't want the child to know her father is a freak.' " Jones tells me this in a voice that is almost a whisper.

We are sitting together in his room, at a Radisson Hotel in Minneapolis. Jones is slumped in an armchair, one elegant leg flung over the side. His sense of injury seems real, though I can only wonder about the woman's side of the story. I ask him how it feels to be a father. He says, "My mother is on me all the time, 'When are you going to find my granddaughter?' So when you ask how does it feel to be a father, well, I feel like an embarrassment. One thing, in a family like mine, being the gay son, I've felt I'm somehow morally above my brothers. My brothers were gangsters in terms of women's lives. I was superior to that, or so I thought. So how do I feel? I feel irresponsible. Too bad there's another black child in the world without a father."

Then there is a surge of ire. Jones sits up very straight. "She didn't want me around. And she won. She has our 'issue,' as they

say. I hope my daughter finds me. That will be one angry teenager."
He softens, reflects: "I know I could find *her*, but I'm not ready."

Near the time that Jones gained and lost his daughter, his father
died. Jones tells me a story of bringing his father to the doctor's office a few years earlier, after he had suffered a stroke. "He looked
across the waiting room and there sat an old black gentleman. Probably a widower. My father said to me, 'See that old guy over there?
He could be a gay.' He said, 'You know, there are a lot of them. And
you know? They look normal, like anybody else. They get married,
too. They could be together for years and years. They really care
about each other.' Now, I'd been with Arnie since 1971, so they
knew the deal. But what my father did then was to look at me. To
give me permission to have a 'normal life.' I always thanked him for
that. It wasn't overt, but it was very sweet. And it was what I needed
to hear."


As the seventies wound to a close, Jones's professional career was
still unsettled, still in transition. Having rejected the discipline of
the modernist pioneers, Jones found himself chafing at the indiffer-
ence to audience which was cultivated by many of his vanguardist
colleagues. It was a sentiment summed up in the notorious title of
an article by the serialist composer Milton Babbitt: "Who Cares If
You Listen?" Jones recalls the time as one in which "you were supposed to be anti-performer, when the postmodern pretensions of
the day stipulated that we weren't performing but doing activities
for you, which you're allowed to watch." Jones was unabashed
about the fact that he was indeed performing, and performing for
an audience. Yet his relation to that audience was, to say the least,
ambivalent. Elizabeth Zimmer, the dance editor at the *Village Voice*
and a longtime booster of Jones's, says, "What's unusual about him
is that dancers, by and large, keep their mouths shut. But Bill talks.
And he's been talking from the beginning." Of course, what he's
had to say hasn't always been welcome. Jones now declares, "I was
saying two things—'I love you/I hate you'—but audiences heard
only the anger. People would say, 'These folks are paying to see you.

Why are you seducing them and then attacking them?' That crazi-ness came from the sense of smugness that the avant-garde has—the pretense that we are beyond those issues of class, of race."

Nor was his relationship with Zane unaffected by such tensions: "Black-white, black-Jewish—it was tough. Going to therapy was one of those survival things. He went first, and then talked me into going. I'd say to the therapist, 'Arnie's racist!' She'd say everyone is racist, but you must judge people by what they do." Jones recalls another moment of "tearful anger" in therapy. "I was complaining about being used. And my therapist said, 'You *are* being used. Why shouldn't you be used, since you refuse to use yourself?' " At the time, Jones felt that Zane had shaped his career while Jones let him-self sit back "as a pure force of nature."

Then, in the eighties, the prevailing ethos changed, and the no-tion of a black sensibility came into vogue in the downtown scene. For one thing, "multiculturalism" arrived, with much piety and posture; but in its train were some genuine innovation and origi-nality. "It became de rigueur, just as the art world went looking for black artists at this time," he says. Bill T. Jones was coming into his own. Other artists, including black artists who were clearer about their racial allegiances, regarded his ascent with a measure of cyni-cism.

"Who was I? Was I the House Negro?" Jones asks now. "Well, yes and no. Except look who I came with." It was in 1982 that Bill T. Jones/Arnie Zane & Company was founded. The slash, of course, does not do justice to the complexity of the pairing. For if black was in fashion, a white partner could be something of a critical encum-brance. Jones's brow furrows when he recalls the critical animosity toward his partner: " 'Jones is so good-looking, he moves with an-imal power, but who's that little malignant frog?' A 'malignant frog'—which is what one critic called Arnie. Or take Robert Pierce, who said that Jones and Zane are like oil and water on the stage, and that you wonder why Zane is even on the stage with him." Jones's voice is hard: "Arnie wasn't a traditional dancer. He didn't look like one, he didn't even move like one. But why do you want to exclude that from the picture? Why was the picture so much easier to understand if I was left alone? 'Well, he's just so much better a dancer.' No, that's not it! It's *easier* that way."

In a memoir, written with the assistance of Peggy Gillespie, Jones recounts going to gay bathhouses with Zane in the late seventies and early eighties. Upon arriving, each would go his own way. He describes the Byzantine courtesies of anonymous gay sex, seemingly as elaborate and as recondite to the uninitiated as the bowing practices of the Japanese. "Often you'd come across a group of men—a 'desirable' surrounded by several men vying to be chosen," he recalls. These were the years in which he "positioned" himself as a desirable. "I would advertise my body quietly, discreetly. If someone wanted me, I would choose." Sometimes he found himself pursued by people he had no interest in—presumptuous, pushy people. "On the other hand, some undesired 'suitors' seemed decent and needy. When they put their hands on me, their entreating touch merited a gentle rebuke and an apologetic smile." In the course of these visits, he found himself "rejecting and accepting up to eight men a night." He says that the dances he and Arnie were making at the time were energetic, kinetic, and that the activity in the bathhouses seemed, by comparison, "to unfold in slow motion."

AIDS, too, works in slow motion, and it entered their lives in 1985. "Arnie had been ailing for a while," Jones told me. "He had an abscess that wouldn't heal, and rashes. We had a close friend who had died in 1981 of gay-related immune deficiency—what they had been calling the 'gay cancer.' No one was sure what it was. The test came into widespread use in 1985. We got tested. The doctor—it's just like yesterday—said, 'Arnie, it's as you thought, you are H.I.V.-positive and you have an AIDS-related illness. And, Bill, you are positive, too.' " Then the couple drove from the East Village clinic back to their home, in Nyack, and let the news sink in. "I must admit, were I to dance the moment, it would be that," he says, gesturing to an imaginary person at his side. "Because for two years, it was all about him. He was the one we were taking care of. I was in good health. I was his rock. So I didn't really think about it. Of course, there was a little catch—my being positive—but I could handle it. I think that only when he died was I really able to begin to think about the ramifications for myself."

At Arnie Zane's deathbed, Bill T. Jones staged a sort of performance: something that, he says, "I orchestrated with twenty-one people in the house." There were three of Jones's sisters, who sang songs like "They Are Falling All Around Me," by Sweet Honey in the Rock. There was a rabbi who spoke about the Book of Genesis; there was a woman who sang songs in Yiddish; there was Arnie Zane, in bed, floating in and out of consciousness, hooked up to a morphine I.V. drip. At one point, Zane said, "I'm so tired, take my shoes off, I want to go now."

Jones urged Zane to hold on, telling him that the dancers would soon be arriving. In due course, the members of the dance company joined the others. Zane's parents had also been summoned. Rhodessa says that Zane's mother was initially so upset by the spectacle that she had to be persuaded not to leave, and that there were others, too, "who felt disgusted by the whole thing, who felt their emotions were being manipulated."

In some sense, what Jones orchestrated was an elaboration of an old African-American custom, and Rhodessa uses a traditional formulation when she says, "We took him over, we crossed him over." At the moment Zane died, Jones sang the spiritual "Amen." And yet there may be a distinction between ritual and theater, even if only one of degree.

Somehow, Jones seems not altogether easy with the memory. Perhaps he is less confident that a death can be *performed*, like a wedding or a bar mitzvah or a dance composition. Perhaps it is the boundary between intimacy and publicity that he is reconsidering. When I try to imagine the theater Jones created, I am not sure whether Zane was part of the performance or part of the audience. I do know that Jones, not Zane, was the choreographer. Jones sounds almost humble when he says, "I don't know what he wanted. He didn't talk about it."

. . .

Dance critics refer to Jones's current work as representing a third phase, the first phase having been the stylized American Dance Asylum performances of the seventies, and the second having been the turn the Jones/Zane partnership took from the formation of the company, in 1982, until death put their collaboration asunder in 1988. It is this third phase—producing such powerful works as *Absence* and *Last Night on Earth*—that has, in general, been the most celebrated. Though Jones bristles at those who spoke slightingly of Zane, there are critics who will tell you that while Zane made Jones into a modern dancer he also held him back. One of them says bluntly, "Had it not been for Arnie Zane, Bill would have been on Broadway—he would have been Gregory Hines. But the truth is, he's a much stronger artist than Arnie, and since Arnie's death he's really blossomed. Arnie was leading him in a direction that was superficial."

But Zane's contribution was not restricted to his artistic vision. There was also the matter of body consciousness. Jones says he did not grow up thinking he was pretty. "And you know what? Arnie helped. Because that's the way he photographed me. And the way he talked about black bodies. The Leni Riefenstahl effect: exotic beauty. And it transcended the fetish." If Jones had been, in the subcultural parlance, a snow queen, that subculture accorded his white counterparts—those, that is, who "talked about black bodies" as Zane did—the less savory designation "dinge queen."

And here we reach a rather ticklish matter. The black body has, of course, been demonized in Western culture: represented as ogreish, coarse, and highly, menacingly sexualized. But the black body has also been valorized, represented as darkly alluring—still highly, menacingly sexualized but, well, in a *good* way. And this, historically, is its ambiguous dual role in the Western imagination. The hypersexualized body of the Southern lyncher's imagination produced, as its harvest, the "strange fruit" of Billie Holiday's famous blues song: black bodies swinging from trees. But then there is the equally hypersexualized body of, say, Robert Mapplethorpe's imagination: marmoreal expanses of flesh, contours, creases, and crevices all ripely gleaming with an eroticized burnish, massive genitals in the foreground—another strange fruit, perhaps? Mapplethorpe's relation to black masculinity has frequently been denounced as "exoticizing," "fetishizing," "objectifying." And so it is. But such critiques cannot acknowledge that there may be something salutarily subversive in the way it inserts black bodies into the Western fine-art traditions of the nude—so that, as the black cultural critic Kobena Mercer slyly writes, "with the tilt of the pelvis, the black man's bum becomes a Brancusi." Jones rolls his eyes when he talks about Nureyev's rumored list of "black hustlers with the biggest dicks in the world." He asks rhetorically, "Would that be racist?" Yet if it is racist when Mapplethorpe evinces this "objectifying" gaze, why isn't it equally so when Bill T. Jones solicits it? "I've done my share of promoting racial bias," Jones says matter-of-factly. "I'm no innocent to the racial bias that comes of being born into this culture." Crucially, as Jones admits, he does not disavow the gaze of white fascination: he works within it, plays with it, *uses* it. He is accustomed to taking advantage of it—both onstage and in bed. "I've been there in situations where I've known what the deal is. Having sex with somebody and you don't really *want* to hear what he's whispering under his breath as he's allowing you to molest him, or whatever his fantasy is. It's scary—and fascinating."

But the romance of the skin has its costs. "Look, I have made a career of facing it. My eroticism, my sensuality onstage is always coupled with a wild anger and belligerence. I know that I can be food for fantasy, but at the same time I'm a person with a history—and that history is in part the history of exploitation. And I am joining it, and this costs me something, and I want you to know that it costs me something." To him there's an important difference between exploiting yourself and being exploited by another. So it's not that Jones doesn't want to be objectified; it's just that he wants to be the one to do it. When Mapplethorpe asked if he could photograph Jones, he felt uneasy about ceding that control to another. "I told him, 'I feel a little weird about being photographed by you,'" Jones recalls. "I think he had a lot of trouble dealing with black men as people, even with me. Was I flattered by it? Yeah, of course, on some level I was. But I was not stupid, either. I knew the game. I have used it in my work: the objectification of my own body, knowing when to take your shirt off, to get up close to somebody. There's a whole dynamic that I've worked with. You can fetishize yourself." In the end, Jones agreed to be Mapplethorpe's subject, but first they reached an understanding: "No dick—that was the understanding."

This is *not* an understanding that obtains in many of Jones's performances—a fact that has got him in trouble on occasion. One somewhat notorious incident took place a few summers ago, when he was performing a solo outdoors at a swank fund-raiser for his company in the Hamptons. Jones's performance became exceedingly site-specific, his interaction with the audience rather too intimate. "I kissed one woman in the audience on the mouth," he says slowly. "Sitting near her was a very handsome young man. I went over and kissed *him* on the mouth. All things were being played with, mind you. I know the effect I have when I touch someone. I was stripped down to the waist. And then I saw the children, the children of two prospective board members. The father was standing behind them. It was a blond family, very attractive. I looked at the children, and I was thinking what was there that would take it out of the realm of being posh. And that's when I did it." What he did was to drop his pants and expose himself in front of the two children. "I went over to them, and I looked at the two little innocents sitting there. And that was that: I pulled my pants back up and went on with my performance." Though Jones later apologized, he is still bemused at the sequelae of this spur-of-the-moment impulse, which ended up as an item in the press. "It was only seconds, purposely only a moment. It was like a Japanese Kabuki *mie*—the act when an intense moment happens and the protagonist stops to make a pose and crosses one eye. When that happens, the Japanese in the audience who know Kabuki shout the performer's name with excitement."

No one shouted Jones's name in Long Island. The audience was stunned and appalled. Jones recalls that the father later brought his daughter over and instructed her to ask Jones why he had done this: " 'Go ahead, *ask* him!' " I don't know what he told them; what he told me was that it was a way of "specifically making reference to the power of my body, and the taboo that it represents." It's an explanation that seems curiously inadequate to the assaultive quality of the act, even in a theater of transgression.

And nudity, in Jones's work, can be enlisted for more complex purposes—for communion rather than affront. At the end of his last major dance composition, *Last Supper at Uncle Tom's Cabin/The Promised Land* (1990), company members and forty or fifty local people, recruited for the purpose, appear naked onstage. Jones says, "It was a piece that had been about the things that separate people, and I thought, What is the most direct way I could talk about unity, and the risk that we take on all levels with our bodies? Get a sixty-five-year-old grandmother to be naked with a twenty-year-old strapping black man. Get a three-hundred-pound man to be naked—he was so fat the dick disappeared under the folds of his stomach. But they trusted me." And, he says, they believed in the project. "This piece that started off talking about slavery was, at the end, the ultimate vision of freedom. Because the nudity became a metaphor for our true commonality. Do you care at that point who's the millionaire, who's gay, who's the wife-beating heterosexual? Do you care at that moment?"

Jones's artistic attentions have more recently focused on another aspect of our shared humanity—dying. It has been almost a decade since Jones learned he was H.I.V.-positive, and though, as he's quick to say, he could be stricken tomorrow, he has never been in a hospital in his life. "That's the result of three hundred years of selective breeding. I've got a lot of good genes," he says, laughing. Completely asymptomatic, he does not take medicine, except for Zovirax—"purely precautionary against any little infection that might come up." What *has* changed as a result of the scourge is the body of his work, where themes of mourning and mortality now figure large. In 1992, Jones began conducting "Survival Workshops" in eleven cities across the country with people who were dealing or had dealt with life-threatening illnesses. These were four-hour sessions with small groups. Candidates, who ranged in age from eleven to seventy-five, were identified with the help of the Cancer Society, AIDS hospices, the local Red Cross. Jones prepared a promotional tape for them, which explained that he was after raw material for his art. "I'm not a therapist, I'm a man and an artist who is looking for information," he states flatly.

Participants in these Survival Workshops were filmed as Jones asked them a battery of highly specific questions: How did they learn their diagnosis? Where were they then—what was the room like? Who was the person who notified them? What did they do afterward? He also asked them to imagine their death. "Take us to your death," he said. "You're not going to have this chance in life. This is the one you want. You can own it—it's yours. What are the people around you saying? What are you thinking? What's the last thing you see, the last thing you say?" If the process can sound almost cruelly exploitative, the results are not. In each workshop, there is a moment when the participants form a chain and begin to literalize Jones's request to take us to their deaths. It's an image—that of a small group of triumphant souls, weary but determined, arms linked in a gloriously liminal dance with death—that's reminiscent of the one that concludes Ingmar Bergman's *The Seventh Seal.*

Certainly it has helped him transcend the ambit of his immediate personal concerns: he has moved from the specificity of AIDS— all too gravid with that metaphoric yoking of sex with death, of *Liebestod*—to the larger condition of mortality. His latest work, *Still/Here,* is less a poetics of death than a poetics of survival—or, in the current term of art, "managing mortality." It incorporates material gathered at the Survival Workshops, reassembled and set to music by the composer Kenneth Frazelle and by the rock guitarist Vernon Reid, of Living Colour. Frazelle's compositions are performed by the folksinger Odetta and by the Lark String Quartet; Reid's pieces are performed in a grittier, electronic register. The juxtaposition of the styles is oddly effective. Supporting the spectacle are video images by Gretchen Bender, costumes by Liz Prince, and lighting by Robert Wierzel.

I join an audience of about a hundred dance students at a lecture-demonstration held in the Northrop Auditorium, where Jones and members of his company explain the composition of the work. An example is the segment entitled "Tawnni's Blues." "Tawnni," Jones tells us, "was the most wonderful sprite you might ever want to meet. Even though she was literally drowning in the fluids in her lungs, she loved to talk. She'd been a gymnast, and she wanted to do all those things again. I made this trio for her." A tape is played. "My name is Tawnni Simpson," a voice says, coughing. "I think about why the hell me? Why am *I* still living, and all my friends that I've been in the hospital with are all dead? . . . I think about that constantly. But I try not to dwell on it. . . . Because you're special—that's what everybody says. . . . God has plans for you." As Tawnni speaks, Frazelle's guitar- and drum-based music keeps pace as an undercurrent, and two dancers do a sort of contemporary pas de deux.

Soon after, Jones illustrates the moment of diagnosis. "People with life-threatening illnesses have a joke—they call it the proverbial hit-by-a-truck scenario, because doctors apparently use that line frequently when informing them that they have a terminal illness. How does a choreographer begin to find a vocabulary for finding out really bad news? So we decided on the notion of being hit by something. And we tried tackling." The dancers then tackle each other, two at a time.

The portly dancer Lawrence Goldhuber talks—as he does in the performance itself—about his mother, who recently succumbed to cancer and had participated in a Survival Workshop in New York: about the devastations of chemotherapy, about her glabrous pate, about the translucency of her skin. "I told her she looked like a sperm," he says mordantly. "I've seen a lot of this kind of death lately. You know, the slow, bit-by-bit kind. So I can just go on, and pretend that it's normal, because it's become normal. Ever since I watched Arnie die, six years ago, it's been nonstop. And you know what? It's always the same."

At this point in the demonstration, a young woman seated across the aisle from me begins to sob. "That's how my father looked the last time I saw him," she says thickly.

Later, Goldhuber talks about the numbing effects of working with this material every day. "The impact it had at first was tremendous. And then I found I've become a little callous to it—not unfeeling, but it becomes part of the everyday story. It's lost the intense emotional impact for me."

"And I always say that it's art, not life," Jones puts in. "And that's a very important distinction to make, particularly when you're trying to reflect on life."

And, of course, on death. A few days after Jones and I spoke in Milwaukee, the papers carried the news that the black dancer and choreographer Pearl Primus, a legendary figure in modern dance, had died, at age seventy-four. Inevitably, we talk of her when we next meet, in Minneapolis. "She was breathtaking as a performer, with thighs like steel," Jones tells me, "but I can't say that she always drew me warmly to her bosom." Then he relates a story about how Primus, who had immersed herself in traditional African cultures, laid a curse on him. Percival Borde, Jones's teacher in college, had been her husband. In the early eighties, Jones appeared on a Future of Black Dance panel at the Brooklyn Academy of Music: "I was the young upstart, the person who said, 'I'm an artist first, a black person second'—that 'my blackness is only as important as I make it.' " But where he got in trouble was when he mentioned his favorite choreographers. "I mentioned Merce Cunningham, I mentioned Alvin Ailey—but I didn't mention Percy. He was not a choreographer of the same stripe as Merce Cunningham. And Miss Pearl! I can almost picture her coming down and turning three times and cursing me. She said, 'You will be sorry for this! Percival is turning over in his grave. You will *regret* this!' It was *cold*. I said to myself, 'Lady, you got the power, but I've got the power, too.' I showed respect for her. I'd done nothing wrong."

Certainly Jones's relations with his colleagues in the dance world are not uncomplicated. "I don't know of anybody right now who gets written about more than I," he says. "So there are a lot of levels on which they are meeting me. They're meeting this H.I.V.-

positive person. They're meeting this artist, and they might be dubious about his work. Some people avoid meeting you, some go out
of their way to meet you. I represent a lot of things, one of which is
the question 'Is *this* the Zeitgeist? Is this the artist who deserves to
be there?' " (Rhodessa says she grew up thinking of Bill as one of
her "three nappy-headed little brothers"; now, she laughs, "sometimes I feel like Shakespeare's sister.") Jones says of his peers, "They
are split about it. You have to be able to read between the lines." As
you do in the world of dance critics. Not that he is suffering any
dearth of veneration. *Newsweek*'s dance critic, Laura Shapiro, called
*Still/Here* "a work so original and profound that its place among
the landmarks of 20th-century dance seems ensured." I've heard
others describe it as a terpsichorean counterpart to Tony Kushner's
*Angels in America*. René Sirvin, writing in *Le Figaro,* said that it
landed "like a punch in the stomach" and deemed it "one of the
major events" at the festival where it had its debut.

But Bill T. Jones's ultimate stature as a choreographer remains
controversial. One critic tells me, "Jones is a charismatic performer,
but, structurally, his choreography often leaves something to be desired. His work is best when he is in it. It's also true that Bill hit his
stride when the dance boom was over—a lot of the talent was really
decimated by AIDS. That's why he and Mark Morris have the stage
to themselves. And among black artists today who work in this vein
he's far and away the strongest. Still, the reason he's getting so
many awards so soon is that people aren't gambling on his surviv-
ing: they're giving it to him now." It is clearly a commonplace, al-
beit usually an unspoken one, that the fact that Jones is both
H.I.V.-positive and black has more than a little to do with his having received so many laurels so early in his career.

Jones is not unaware of the skeptics. "My critics say that I'm a bad
artist, because I don't really know how to dance. 'Art does this, politics does this, and social work does this,' they say. I don't recognize
these boundaries." For him, art is testimony. And he values performance far more than purity. Jones *is* a formalist, plainly, but those
who like their form unadulterated find his attraction to multimedia
theater a betrayal of what they recognize as dance proper.

The critic Elizabeth Zimmer says, "You have to understand that his genre is multidisciplinary dance theater. Bill sometimes tries to stuff a twenty-pound turkey into a ten-pound bag. People want neat, pleasing elegance—single-medium artists are baffled sometimes by what he does."

Jones's relation to black culture is as complicated as his relation to the main currents of modern dance. Yet among many black artists and intellectuals, Jones commands enormous respect; he is often taken to represent a new wave of black creativity. The poet Maya Angelou says he reminds her of James Baldwin; Jessye Norman describes him as "the most soulful dancer I know." Even Arthur Mitchell—who, as a former Balanchine dancer and the founder of the Dance Theatre of Harlem, seems in so many ways Jones's opposite—calls Jones "one of the finest dance artists I've ever seen."

For his part, Jones maintains, "Artists today are criticized for being esoteric and politically correct. I'm more interested in authenticity than in originality. If originality comes, that's great. I also want to represent beauty. My paradigms of beauty have been shaped by a great deal of Eurocentric work. I want to know how pure, abstract forms work. I want to know how language can put them together." (In this vein, he talks about a "quotation" from Balanchine's neoclassical ballet *Serenade* which he inserted in a work he created for the Alvin Ailey company, and lashes out at Anna Kisselgoff, the chief dance critic for the *Times*, who, he says, wondered if he wasn't making fun of the great master. "In other words, it was 'hands off,' " he glosses.)

But it is pointless for a controversialist to bemoan controversy, and Jones is clearly still negotiating between the impersonal ideals of avant-gardism and his more populist, and personal, passions. "An artist doesn't *have* to do anything," Jones says expansively. "I know that that's an invitation to irresponsibility, but I think it's true. Artists should be the freest people in society. They don't have to pander to anyone's philosophy. But they'd better be telling me something authentic." Jones may be suspicious of race-based aesthetics, but he also maintains, "I can't even quite begin to position myself in the world matrix without taking on the issue of my humanity as a black man." Well, then, does it bother him that a black audience will probably never respond to his work as did the audiences at the premiere of *Still/Here,* in Lyons? "I make the art that I have to make and know how to make. It has to do with where I've been, with where I've been educated. It's hard to involve the black community in that." He points out that the dance companies that have a larger black audience are those with a more familiar aesthetic, like the Dance Theatre of Harlem. "I have some of those people, some adventurous persons. But my own audiences are still dominated by the white avant-garde." He remains chary of the rhetoric of black unity, and skeptical about the prospects of black-supported institutions—black patronage for black artists. "Yes, some black people will make out. People like us. But where are our David Geffens? Blacks will come and they will be ruthless. There used to be a time when everyone was my brother or sister, but I don't know if that's really the case anymore."

In his still unfinished autobiographical manuscript Jones writes, "I will never grow old. My hands will never be discolored with the spots of age. I will never have varicose veins. My balls will never become pendulous, hanging down as old men's balls do. My penis will never be shriveled. My legs will never be spindly. My belly, never big and heavy. My shoulders never stooped, rounded, like my mother's shoulders are. . . . My face will never wrinkle. . . . My teeth will never yellow." Bill T. Jones will never grow old. Recalling the passage, I later ask Jones the sort of questions he'd asked members of the Survival Workshops. For I wonder about the death of a performance artist, someone whose most intensely remembered moments are moments of spectacle: the man who watched Jones as he slept with his first girlfriend; the deathbed theater that Jones arranged for his partner of seventeen years; the sense of transport he has achieved on the stage. I try to imagine a life dedicated to the incursion of performance where performance might have seemed out of place; a craft dedicated to the exposure of his own physicality, and to the "gaze" of which he so often speaks.

"Take us to your death," he had asked members of his Survival Workshops. And so, as we sit together in his hotel room, I ask him to describe his last night on earth. I don't ask him whether he imagines his own death as having an audience, but I am curious. Must it, too, be performance?

Slowly, as if visualizing every detail, he tells me his suicide fantasy. In his scenario, he says, his affairs would be in order. The Bill T. Jones/Arnie Zane Dance Foundation would be out of debt. His will would be in place. Bjorn would be among the living, still healthy, still here. His gaze drifts off. He tells me that his death would be at home, in Nyack, but it wouldn't be like Arnie's. "A glorious fall day. I'd send notes to all my friends. Maybe no one in the office knows. The neighbors down the hill would get a note to check on me the next day. I wouldn't tell my mother or my sister: their love would be too strong."

He shuts his eyes. "And then I'd listen to music. On that day, it would be Nina Simone. It would be a long album. I'd hear the sound of the leaves outside. And I'd take pills and go to sleep." Unbidden, he answers my question. He says, very quietly, "I'd be by myself. I'd have to be by myself."

# The Powell Perplex

General Colin Powell is a man of maxims, and one of his maxims is
that you should never make a decision too early or too late. Like
many of the best maxims, this one is true by definition, and is therefore of doubtful practical use. Nonetheless, timing is one of the
General's grand subjects, and punctuality, which is timing writ
small, is something that the General sets great store by. I arrive at
his house fifteen minutes early for our appointment, even though I
stopped en route to get my shoes shined. I am vague about military
ways, but I suspect that neatness, too, counts. "First thing I no-
ticed," Powell says approvingly of my gleaming brogues when we
meet.

The Powells—Colin and Alma, his wife of thirty-three years—live
in an expensive development in McLean, Virginia. Their house,
which he bought in 1993, after his retirement, is a sprawling contemporary château, buff-colored except for white trim. In front of
a three-car garage sits a light-green '68 Volvo station wagon, the
upkeep of which is one of his chief hobbies. There is a flower bed,
and a front lawn like an advertisement for Scotts lawn-care prod-

ucts; a swimming pool is tucked discreetly out back. Barberry and yew shrubs flank the portico. The generic idea is of the French country manor reinterpreted for the upscale suburban development.

"I'm now a wealthy person," Powell says matter-of-factly. "I wasn't wealthy when I retired. I mean, I just figured out what the white guys were doing." He's speaking of investment, and reinvestment—an engine of economic growth, he'll tell you. Still, the house isn't decorated ostentatiously. It looks comfortable and lived in, if with perhaps a touch of military austerity. Alma, a poised, elegant woman with a café-au-lait complexion and blue-green eyes, ushers me through a marble-floored foyer to the center hall. Off to the left is one of the General's three home offices. This one seems to be the public office—a place more for greeting visitors than for working. Its oak floor and a red leather Queen Anne chair lend the small room an air of formality. On the walls are displayed such honors as the Medal of Freedom, the Order of Jamaica, and the Eisenhower Leadership Prize Medal. There are framed photographs of a ticker-tape parade down Fifth Avenue following Desert Storm; the assembled United States High Command; Quincy Jones standing with Nelson Mandela; Alma and the General with the Reagans at a White House Christmas party. Also framed is a statement of the creed by which the military live: "We mutually pledge to each other our lives, our fortune, and our sacred Honor." The most striking feature of this room, however, is a vertical row of framed photographs directly in the General's line of sight as he sits in his chair: from top to bottom, they are portraits of Presidents Reagan, Bush, and Clinton. This is the company he keeps even when he is alone: the three men whom he served in an executive capacity to defend the national interest.

The second time I visit, the General shows me the full-length basement, where he maintains a mini-museum of memorabilia. The basement is also where he has another of his home offices—a less public one. Here he follows his passionate avocation, black military history. If the office upstairs is the Fourth of July, this one is Black History Month. There is a large painting of the 10th United States

Cavalry—black soldiers sent in the eighteen-seventies to battle Indians and make the West safe for white settlers. (The history and commemoration of these "Buffalo soldiers," as they were known, has been a longtime concern of Powell's.) Near it is a replica of a set of Civil War epaulets from the storied 54th Massachusetts Regiment, which consisted of black soldiers who were sent into battle against desperate odds.

Mounted on another wall is a gleaming sword collection, including specimens from the Coast Guard, West Point, the Merchant Marines Academy, and the Air Force. Then your eyes fall on a photograph of Ulysses S. Grant, dated June 1, 1864; a quotation from Lincoln ("I can make a Brigadier General in five minutes, but it is not easy to replace 110 horses"); and, taking pride of place here, a tinted photograph of Franklin Delano Roosevelt, which used to hang in Powell's parents' foyer. Six Presidents keep him company as he works, along with the century-old memorabilia of blacks willing to die for a country that steadfastly refused to acknowledge their full rights as citizens. You scan the walls and you wonder: How could this man *not* be preoccupied with running for the presidency?

When I was growing up, in the late fifties and early sixties, black people would say "When a Negro is President," with all the awe and reverence of a born-again Christian saying "When Gabriel blows his trumpet and Jesus appears." A certain millenarian intonation, combined with the speaker's shining eyes, would force you to pause and marvel at the very idea. We knew we'd never live to see the day. "It'll be called the Black House then," the old joke would end. But if you are Colin Powell the prospect is no laughing matter. If you are Colin Powell, let's agree, you have heard a small voice inside your head repeating, like a mantra, one simple thought: You could be the first black man to be President. What does that do to you? Vernon Jordan—political impresario, Clinton counselor, Powell friend—says bluntly, "It's got to fuck your mind up."

Certainly the idea gives disquiet to Alma, as she makes clear on my second visit. "Soon as he would decide to run, you can bet that somebody somewhere would decide that it was his patriotic duty to shoot him," she tells me, holding a bath towel around her shoulders to cover a blue-and-white-striped bathing suit. We're in the marble foyer, waiting for the General to arrive. "But it is his decision," she adds.

There are others, too, for whom it is not a soothing prospect. "He's a phantom candidate," the Reverend Jesse Jackson snaps when I first bring up the prospect of a Powell candidacy. "We can all have positive assumptions, but we still don't know." There is a surge of ire in Jackson's voice. "We do know that very right-wing white people can trust him. They can trust him to drop bombs. We know that Reagan could trust him. Historically, there's been this search—whites always want to create the black of their choice as our leader. So for the white people this nice, clean-cut black military guy becomes something really worth selling and promoting. But have we ever seen him on a picket line? Is he for unions? Or for civil rights? Or for *anything*?" Until now, Jackson has been the soul of magnanimity—or, at least, forbearance—in his public remarks about Powell. The Reverend has been so *very* good. For the moment, his bewilderment at what he sees as Powell's free ride in the press has boiled over into outrage. He has been good long enough. "So you get some nice platitudes out of me," Jackson says, evidently marveling at the unfairness of it all. "But, I mean, *what is this?*"

Not a question, that, to be lightly disregarded. But, of course, we do know some things about Colin Powell. He was born in Harlem, on April 5, 1937, but grew up on Kelly Street in Hunts Point, in a South Bronx neighborhood known as Banana Kelly. His parents were both Jamaicans, who had immigrated to this country years before, and Powell owns to the complex bloodlines common among West Indians. He ticks off African, English, Irish, Scottish, Jewish, and probable Arawak Indian ancestry. It was appropriate, then, that he spent his childhood in a multi-ethnic neighborhood: the Powells' neighbors in Banana Kelly were Jewish, Irish, Polish, Italian, black, and Hispanic. Never a distinguished student, Powell did excel in his duties at the local Episcopal church, where he was an acolyte and a subdeacon. He tells me that in the ritual and the structure of the military he found "a little bit of the ritual and structure of the Episcopal Church."

That church, along with much else, is now gone. The Kelly Street of Powell's memory is as far from the Kelly Street of today as McLean is from the South Bronx. On the block of Kelly Street between Westchester Avenue and 163rd Street, near the Rafael Hernandez School, the eight-family, four-story tenement where Powell grew up has been replaced by a housing project. The ethnic mixture of the old days has been supplanted by a wave of Puerto Rican arrivals. Today, the building façades are festooned with artful graffiti, largely the work of someone who signs himself "Bio Nicer." The legends "Pepino's, P.R." and "Coquito de Puerto Rico" have been carefully lettered on the brick. The grocery store at the corner of Kelly and Westchester caters to an island palate, its bins filled with plantains and yams. It's a block where tattooed men with swollen bellies sit in folding lawn chairs or lean against buildings, drinking out of brown paper bags. The Powells don't live here anymore.

In 1956, soon after Colin Powell entered the City College of New York and its R.O.T.C. program, his father won ten thousand dollars playing the numbers and moved his family to the relative Arcadia of Elmira Avenue, in the Hollis section of Queens. Certainly that neighborhood can have changed little since the fifties. Drive from Kelly Street to Elmira Avenue today and the first thing that strikes you when you arrive is a feeling of calm and tidiness. Late-model Plymouths and Oldsmobiles and a Volvo or two fill the driveways. Only Queen Esther's Pentecostal Church and a billboard ad for Newports featuring a black man in a red-white-and-blue military uniform betray the fact that you are in a predominantly black neighborhood. The houses here are two-story red-brick bungalows, distinguished from one another by different patterns of ornamental masonry. The old Powell house (the General himself sold it to the current occupants just twelve years ago) has an inset of shale and granite among the red bricks. Impatiens, hosta, forsythia, hemlock—all planted by the Powells, the woman who lives there now tells me—decorate the yard. Down the street, there are kids playing tennis. Everywhere, there are squirrels chasing squirrels. And there is quiet. Booker T.

Washington, historic champion of the black working class, would have been proud.

He would also be proud of the General, whose career seems to epitomize Washington's bootstrap philosophy. And, as it happens, Powell bears an uncanny physical resemblance to the Wizard of Tuskegee. It's the same haircut, of course, but also the same sort of face—light-skinned and blunt-featured. (There are even uncanny echoes between the two men's autobiographies. Powell's boyhood account of taking a summer job mopping floors for the local Pepsi-Cola bottling plant, and doing it so skillfully that the next summer he was promoted to the "white" jobs, calls to mind the famous passage in *Up from Slavery* about the young Washington sweeping the floor at the Hampton Institute with such dedication that he was granted admission.) But whereas Booker T. Washington's eyes always appeared to be on the lookout for any potential black rival, Powell's face has a sort of yearbook openness. You can see why people trust him and feel comfortable around him. And you can see why Powell's military career was poised at an angle of ascent from the start, when, as an undergraduate in the R.O.T.C., he achieved the rank of cadet colonel. His narrative of those years is a succession of errors made and learned from—mistakes transmuted into maxims. In time, he was happy enough to skip the mistake part.

Though it's something of a journalistic commonplace to dismiss him as a "political general," Powell can point to two tours of active duty in Vietnam, where he incurred serious injuries and from which he returned a decorated veteran. His account of the war is a devastating indictment of high-level stupidity and low-level brutality; and he is impassioned when he describes the experience of returning to a nation buffeted by race. "While I had been off fighting for the freedom of foreigners, four little black girls had been killed by a bomb planted in Birmingham's 16th Street Baptist Church," he recalls in his memoir. Though he heard the voices of the black-power radicals with "uneasiness," he writes, "I came to understand that a movement requires many different voices, and the tirades of the agitators were like a fire bell ringing in the night, waking up defenders of the status quo, with the message that change had better be on the way."

For Powell, at least, change came swiftly: in Vietnam in 1968, the commander of the Americal Division made him operations officer.

After leaving Vietnam the following year, Powell enrolled in a graduate program at George Washington University. The once-indifferent student earned his Master of Business Administration with mostly A's. Soon he found himself in the White House Fellows Program, where he caught the notice of Caspar Weinberger and Frank Carlucci, the two men who so profoundly shaped his later career. In the meantime, he learned a thing or two about the White House bureaucracy, which meant picking up more maxims: "You don't know what you can get away with until you try." "Never get into fights with people who buy ink by the barrel." When Clifford Alexander was installed, in 1977, as Secretary of the Army—the only black man ever to hold the position—he tripled the number of black generals. "My method was simple," Alexander says. "I just told everyone that I would not sign the goddam [promotion] list unless it was fair." Among the beneficiaries of Secretary Alexander's aggressive new policy was Colin Powell, who achieved the rank of general at the age of forty-two.

In 1980, he cast his vote for Ronald Reagan; and three years later Reagan, in a manner of speaking, returned the favor. In 1983, with Weinberger ensconced as Secretary of Defense and Carlucci as his deputy, Powell was brought in from the field to be their valued point man and gatekeeper. From Reagan's Secretary of the Navy, John Lehman, came another maxim: "Power corrupts; but absolute power is really neat." When Carlucci was made Reagan's National Security Adviser, he insisted that Powell join him in revamping the National Security Council, which had been shaken up by the damaging revelations of the Iran-Contra scandal. Ten months later, on November 20, 1987, Powell himself was given the job of National Security Adviser. "If it hadn't been for Iran-Contra," he says, "I'd still be an obscure general somewhere. Retired, never heard of."

In the West Wing, Powell had the chance to refine his philosophy of action. "The key is not to make quick decisions, but to make timely decisions," he writes. "I have a timing formula, $P = 40$ to $70$, in which P stands for probability of success and the numbers indicate the percentage of information acquired. I don't act if I have only enough information to give me a less than forty percent chance of being right. And I don't wait until I have enough facts to be 100 percent sure of being right, because by then it is almost always too late." In 1989, the new Secretary of Defense, Dick Cheney, supported by President Bush, decided to catapult Colin Powell into the position of Chairman of the Joint Chiefs of Staff. We do not know the algorithm by which they reached the decision, but they did not regret it. The rest is not history, yet, but something closer to "current events."

People whose résumés read like Powell's are sometimes liked but not respected; sometimes respected but not liked. But if you talk to Powell's remarkably wide range of acquaintances, on and off the record, you will hear tributes that sound altogether heartfelt and unrehearsed. They say he is a "regular brother," a "mensch," "good people." He inspires loyalty even among those who aren't under his command. Vernon Jordan tells me of something that happened last year when he was hospitalized: "He came to see me every day. And he didn't just, you know, breeze in and breeze out—he did some porch-sitting with me. The look on his face of worry and concern was very real. And he did not just come when I was in the hospital, he came after I got home. He is no sunshine soldier when it comes to friendship." Warming to the subject of Powell's family-mindedness, Jordan tells me of his own mother. She had worked as a cook in the Officers' Club at Fort McPherson since the segregated days of the early nineteen-forties; so it was a matter of personal gratification when Powell took charge of U.S. Forces Command at the fort in 1989. Jordan describes a party that he threw that same year for his mother's eighty-second birthday, which Colin Powell attended. He remembers Powell telling him, "This is what it is ultimately all about—family." When Jordan adds, "And I will be there for him," it sounds like a solemn vow. Of course, Jordan makes it clear that his partisan fealty belongs to Clinton and the Democratic Party. He's talking not about political allegiances but about personal ones.

A theme that recurs when friends talk about Powell is that he is a "regular brother." Jordan explains, "You do not have to hang out on the corner to be a brother. That's number one. Number two is, you don't ask peers whether or not a guy is a regular brother. You ask the other brothers whether he is regular or not. You ask the guys at the airport, you ask the shoeshine boy. You ask the taxicab guy. And they will tell you he is a good man." Over the past few months, I *have* asked them, by the dozen, and they do tell you that. To use a word that keeps coming up, they're *proud* of him. Quincy Jones, the musician and producer, and Kurt Schmoke, the black mayor of Baltimore, told me independently about going with Colin Powell to South Africa, where he sang doo-wop and Motown tunes—accompanied by a chorus of South African youth. Not only that but when I ask him to do the Camel Walk the General gets up from his chair and does his best to perform James Brown's now classic dance. Jordan says, "The notion that he is not a regular brother is bullshit."

As the author (with Joseph E. Persico) of *My American Journey,* a book whose advance orders alone guaranteed it an impressive debut on the best-seller list, Colin Powell has been courting a wider celebrity. He makes it clear that writing the book presented a dilemma: how to achieve candor without the appearance of disloyalty. He has, by and large, brought it off. Though he describes Weinberger's "little quirks," his "Captain Queeg talisman," his "taste for pomp"—and though he seems, in the end, to be more comfortable with the policy perspectives of Weinberger's foe, George P. Shultz—the account of his great mentor is unmistakably admiring. He rates Bush highly as a commander, but he found his demeanor toward the end of his presidency so baffling as to invite a medical explanation. (Powell says, "The President calling someone a bozo? You can't do that. But the only way I could see writing it— because I'm not a medical expert—was to pose it as a rhetorical question.") And while his portrayal of President Reagan is clearly of someone who is worrisomely out of touch, it is imbued with almost filial affection. "I had trouble with the Reagan chapters," he explains, "because I have a loving relationship with him and had to be honest without being hurtful."

He also acknowledges another kind of discomfort presented by his involvement with the Reagan and Bush administrations. "When I was a young lieutenant I would have commanders come up to me and say, 'Powell, you're doing great—God damn, you're the best black lieutenant I've ever seen,'" Powell recalls. "And I'd say, 'Thank you.' Just file it away." It was good practice for his years in the White House as far as racial politics were concerned. "The problem with Reagan and Bush and Weinberger and their ilk is that they just never knew," Powell says, almost wistfully. "They were never sensitized to it. They never had to live with it. They were never close to it. And the cold political calculus is that the Republicans said, 'We can't get these people, so why spend a dime trying?' Even though Reagan and Bush are two of the closest people in my life, I've got to say that this was an area where I found them wanting. This was a difficult thing to write about in the book." He removes his photograph of Reagan from the wall and shows it to me. On it Reagan had written, in his neat, round cursive hand, "If you say so, Colin, it must be right." Powell says, "Just read it—this is from the President of the United States. And so now I'm going to turn around and say he's a racist?"

Powell tells me of an episode when Carlucci, as Reagan's National Security Adviser, sent him to see Senator Jesse Helms about a policy matter, and Helms later mentioned to Carlucci that he'd "listened to that black general you sent up here." Powell glosses, "See, now, Jesse just don't know any other way to see folks. As cordial as Jesse and I are now—and we will go out on yachts together, we'll say nice things to each other—if you think Jesse can ever see me as anything other than a black general . . ." Powell shakes his head. "Then we'd have arrived. But we ain't arrived."


The most famous black President of this century is one Douglass Dilman: he is the hero of *The Man,* a 1964 best-selling novel by Irving Wallace, which was later made into a movie starring James Earl Jones. Thrust into the Oval Office after a crisis of succession, President Dilman swiftly finds himself the target of popular animosity and Beltway intrigue. He's a man of conscience and competence, but humiliation awaits him at every turn. Half the people he invites to his first big state dinner fail to show. More nefariously, he is ensnared in a trumped-up sex scandal. His enemies seize the opportunity to begin impeachment hearings, and the Southern senator in charge of them tells him gravely, "I must decide . . . whether you acted wisely or unwisely as a President, and whether you acted as an American President or as a Negro President."

An American President or a Negro President? Though the question doesn't pose itself so starkly these days, it hasn't altogether disappeared. Powell, for one, has made his own decision on the matter. "I really don't want to be elected to be the first black American President," he tells me. "I don't want to be the poster child for the brothers, or for guilty white liberals. That would not be true to the image I have of myself."

Nor would it be true to the image that others have of him. His mentor Caspar Weinberger tells me that he doesn't see a black man when he sees Powell. "Quite a few people have talked to me recently about whether America's ready to accept a black candidate," he says. "I don't think that would be a factor at all if he should enter the presidential race. There are probably a few people left who would still be troubled by it, but I think it could be far less than one percent. The fact of the matter is that with Colin I never think of whether he's black or white or anything else."

Vernon Jordan, as a longtime veteran of the civil-rights movement, resists Weinberger's formulation. "Any time a white person says they do not see Colin Powell as black, that tells me that they cannot see," he says wearily. "What they are really saying is 'We see that he is black but we are prepared to look beyond that.' " Earl Graves, the black businessman and publisher of the magazine *Black Enterprise,* is more acerbic on the subject: "It's an affront to me when you say that, because that means that if you saw him as a black person you couldn't vote for him."

Still, there are black activists and intellectuals who wonder if the key to Powell's success may be that he is, in a phrase of the black writer Jill Nelson's, "the un-Negro." Julian Bond, the black civil-rights activist and former Georgia state legislator whose name was among those proposed for the Vice-Presidential nomination at the 1968 Democratic National Convention, develops this point: "I think first his uniform—braid, the medals—insulated him from race. Now it's in his carriage, his manner: even when he's out of uniform, even when he's in a blue serge suit, he's in uniform. You put Colin Powell and any other Mr. Black Man up there, and it becomes just that—it's Colin Powell and Mr. Black Man." Then there's the voice. "Probably because of his island heritage, he has a kind of diction that isn't black American. He's verbally not black." His podium style follows suit, Bond says. "It's just straight-ahead talking. It's almost Reaganesque—there's a kind of formal intimacy, a sense that he's speaking directly to you. There's none of that call-and-response, none of that 'Can I have just a minute more?' preacher stuff."

The racial iconography of Colin Powell goes beyond style to substance, according to the black political scientist Ronald Walters, who was Jesse Jackson's deputy campaign manager in 1984. "He doesn't speak in a racial language and therefore he's not threatening to whites," Walters says. "Right now we're having a discussion about racial mobility in American society—about things like civil rights and affirmative action. But underneath is the anger of many whites who believe that if blacks would only buckle down and play by the rules they could make it. And Powell then becomes a symbol of that—the whites' answer to the angry blacks who say racism is still here. That makes him part of this discussion, even though he hasn't engaged in it." Jesse Jackson—who eloquently indicts the supposed ideal of "color blindness" as an alibi for turning a blind eye to the social inequities of race—offers something more aphoristic. "It's not so much a problem that Weinberger says he doesn't see a black man when he sees Powell—and he *does*. It's important that Powell sees a black man when he shaves, and he does."

Ask Powell about the way he has come to be seen as a paragon of something like racial erasure, and it's clear that he has given the matter some thought. "One, I don't shove it in their face, you know?" he says. "I don't bring any stereotypes or threatening visage to their presence. Some black people do. Two, I can overcome any stereotypes or reservations they have, because I perform well. Third thing is, *I ain't that black.*" He talks about interracial social skills, skills that he fears are deficient in too many blacks. "I speak reasonably well, like a white person," he says. "I am very comfortable in a white social situation, and I don't go off in a corner. My features are clearly black, and I've never denied what I am. It fits into their general social setting, so they do not find me threatening." He pauses. "I think there's more to it than that, but I don't know what it is."

According to Bruce Llewellyn, a cousin and business partner of Powell's—and an entrepreneur whom Powell proudly describes as "one of the country's wealthiest African-Americans"—Powell's "nonthreatening" personality helps. "Have you ever heard his speeches?" Llewellyn, a formidable grizzly bear of a man, wants to know. "He gives a great speech. He gets all them white people coming up off the chairs, clapping and feeling good about themselves. He talks about America, the great land of opportunity, and how a poor West Indian kid with Jamaican parents and living in the South Bronx can work his way to be the Chairman of the Joint Chiefs of Staff."

"An all-American story," I put in.

"They all love this shit," he says, with a characteristic mixture of candor and acumen. "They all love the idea that 'Gee, we weren't prejudiced. A good man came, and we gave him his shot.' White people love to believe they're fair. One of the things that upsets the living shit out of them is when you confront them with the fact that they are really a bunch of racist, no-good motherfuckers." Llewellyn contrasts Powell's wholesome appeal with what he takes to be Jesse Jackson's forte—inspiring fear. "Jesse scares white people, because he really sounds like a fiery zealot, like he might just jump up and say 'Fuck you!' and hit you in the mouth. They really are afraid that Jesse can create violence, make people want to attack you with a baseball bat, or whatever. He missed his calling. What Jesse should be is our business shakedown artist." Llewellyn's tone is not unadmiring; he means this as a constructive suggestion. Though he is a former member of the Carter administration, he has little patience for the pieties of public discourse. This is a man who is accustomed to being in charge of his own affairs and to speaking his own mind. Later, I mention to the General something that Llewellyn had said, and he interjects, in a tone of exaggerated annoyance, "Goddam Bruce—I told him to shut up." He explains, with mock gruffness, "I put him in a closet, because he was talking to everybody."

Still, Llewellyn is far from alone in seeing the contrasts between Powell and Jackson as not only instructive but emblematic. Representative Ron Dellums told Powell that compared to Jesse Jackson, he was a "jelly maker, not a tree shaker." It's an analysis from which Powell, who speaks of Jackson with more amusement than animosity, does not exactly demur. In the words of one member of the Powell camp, "Jesse has a horrible problem. I mean, he is no longer the number one Negro in this country."

The offices of the National Rainbow Coalition, in Washington, D.C., are modestly appointed but ample in size. My appointment with Jackson is at five o'clock; not unexpectedly, Jackson is running late, by about a half hour. The office I wait in is crowded with stacks of old newspapers, a copier, and a large paper shredder that bears a sign reading "Ollie and Fawn." Over the past several weeks, I've brought up Powell with almost every black person I've spoken to. Jackson's press secretary at the Coalition, Theresa Caldwell, turns out to be effusive on the subject: "He's every-black-person-looking. In fact, without the uniform he looks like my cousin Bobby. He's the best of us in a lot of ways."

Jackson, who, at fifty-three, is five years Powell's junior, is more restrained and statesmanlike today than he was when we spoke earlier. Still, the figure recently erected by the newsweekly pundits— Powell, political panacea—has clearly been on his mind of late. "The fact is that a black is capable of being a conduit for racist positions," he tells me. "But skin color becomes a fig leaf, so if a black is elected on that premise, and you've chosen ethnicity over ethics, that's a big mistake."

Watching him light into the topic reminds you that the tradition of African-American leadership has tended to divide into contrasting couples: there's an Esau for every Jacob. The elegant ex-slave Frederick Douglass faced the militant-nationalist Henry Highland Garnet, the radical W. E. B. Du Bois faced the mainstream power broker Booker T. Washington, and the integrationist Martin Luther King, Jr., faced the separatist Malcolm X. But never before have two such rivals played out their fraternal drama in the arena of American electoral politics.

With all the obviousness of a stage set, their offices telegraph their differences. On Jackson's walls hang *his* heroes—Aristide, Mandela, and, of course, Dr. King. And then there is the matter of style, both personal and public. Powell quotes Michael Korda and Clausewitz; Jackson quotes the Bible. Powell's origins are urban; Jackson's are rural. Powell talks like a schoolmaster; Jackson talks like the Holy Ghost. Indeed, Jackson's voice is black from the first syllable, and his cadences are those of a long black preacherly tradition. Powell, as he himself says, speaks "like a white person." "When Jesse walks into a room, white people hear some sad-eyed Negro spiritual," one black politician told me. "When Powell walks in, they hear 'The Star-Spangled Banner' and 'God Bless America.' " Only their participation in the theater of presidential politics unites the two. But it divides them as well. Jackson sought to be the first black President. Powell would like to be the first President who happens to be black.

To take the measure of what Powell represents to Jackson, you have to look again at what Jackson himself represented to American politics. I remember newspaper accounts published the day after Jesse Jackson's setback in the 1988 Wisconsin primary. The gist was that, to judge by surveys, a majority of white voters went to sleep declaring that they would vote for a black man to be President but woke up realizing that they couldn't bring themselves to do it. Yet those who thought the Jackson campaign had failed missed what was really going on. Jackson's masterstroke was his use of the Democratic primaries—and his accompanying push for voter registration—as a referendum *within the African-American community* about who would inherit King's mantle. Never mind the delegate count: in 1988, Jesse Jackson was elected President of black America. His term has not lasted as long as he might have liked. Analyzing Jackson's relation to Powell, Vernon Jordan says, "It is probably the same way George Bush felt in 1992. There is no right guaranteeing a position of leadership, an opportunity to run for office or to lead an organization, that somebody holds forever." He adds delicately, "But that does not keep people from feeling that way."

There is, surely, another fundamental difference between the two men. Jesse Jackson's presidential race was, in essence, the courting of a symbol, and, as such, is representative of a movement where symbolism has long been in the ascendancy. I don't think that Jackson ever truly imagined himself in the Oval Office, except as a visitor. But few doubt that Colin Powell has. Powell—invariably tagged with the journalistic cliché "consummate insider"—has had the opportunity to witness at first hand the executive styles of Ronald Reagan, George Bush, and Bill Clinton; and if the job evaluations he has provided of his three bosses are far from dismissive, they are decidedly not overawed. He recounts their processes of decision-making in the spirit of one who means to learn from their mistakes. To Powell, whose responsibilities have ranged from planning wars to devising the first systematic reduction in the size of the military since the Second World War, the White House is an extension of a system of levers and pulleys he has helped design. No other black American has been such an integral part of the structures and processes of power.

Jackson, seated at his desk, cufflinks gleaming in the afternoon sun, offers his own analysis of how he and Powell differ. Powell represents the dominant culture, he believes, while he himself represents an oppositional culture; Powell has been "pushed along by a tailwind," as he puts it, while he has been "facing a headwind." Powell is "flowing with the culture," he says, whereas "so much of my work, so much of Dr. King's work, is countercultural." Jackson warms to his subject: "And those who go with the counterculture either die early or live on, despised. If you preach against sexism, against racism, against worker exploitation, you're going with the counterculture, and who is it you're going up against except the publishers, the bankers, the image-makers, the military, the government? Now, there is always a tendency of this society to try to position people they feel comfortable with, and what's amazing about Powell is he's created a comfort zone among the guardians of the culture. How long the right wing would express admiration if he took principled positions to their logical conclusion no one knows. But we do know that the same group that said to Jesus 'Hosanna, Hosanna' not long after that was saying 'Crucify him, crucify him.' And the same thing is already starting to happen to Powell."

"Would it surprise you to know that Powell once thought about becoming an Episcopal priest?" I ask. I'm thinking of Powell's remarks about the similarities between the two institutions.

"No," Jackson says. "Would it surprise you to know that if I hadn't won my scholarship I was going to join the Air Force?" But Jackson *has* taken the path that Powell passed by. Right now he is riffling through his Bible. Earlier, a black politician said to me, "It's very peculiar: Jackson feels that Powell has somehow *taken something* from him." Try a birth-right. It is not the story of Jacob and Esau that is today's text, however, but the story of Daniel, Mishael, and Azariah. "It's really very basic," Jackson says, and begins reading from the Book of Daniel: " 'In the third year of the reign of Jehoiakim king of Judah came Nebuchadnezzar king of Babylon unto Jerusalem, and besieged it.' And the king ordered Ashpenaz, as chief of his court officials, to bring him some of the Israelites—the invaded people, the ghetto people—from the leadership class: young men without any physical defect, handsome, showing aptitude for every kind of learning, qualified to serve in the king's palace. He was to teach them the language and culture of the Babylonians."

I'm beginning to get the picture: an elite siphoned off and coopted by the ruling culture. Jackson goes on, "The king assigned them a daily amount of food and wine from his table. They were to be trained for three years and after that they were to enter the king's service." He looks up and says, "In other words, take them away from their culture, send them to Harvard, send them to Yale, send them to the military." Then he reads again: " 'Now among these were the children of Judah, Daniel, Hananiah, Mishael, and Azariah. . . . But Daniel purposed in his heart that he would not defile himself with the portion of the king's meat.' " Jackson explains, "Daniel resolved not to defile himself—he went counterculture, and so forth. What I'm talking about is this way of taking people from their culture, getting a certain select group—get Gates, get Powell, get Cornel West, get whomever. Get—"

"Jesse," I propose.

He is having none of it. "But Jesse, like Daniel, *purposed not to defile himself.*" He gives me a stern look. "By now I could be on all kinds of boards. But I choose to transform the culture, not to conform to it." The Reverend returns to the Good Book. "So these three boys have this big religious test—would you bow to Nebuchadnezzar's golden image rather than to God?—and they passed the religious test and lived happily ever after. But the big social issue here to me is not the three boys passing the religious test and God coming and rescuing them in some miraculous way. The big issue is: What about the *rest* of them? What about those who were never chosen in the first place? What about those whose bodies were not tall and sleek like an athlete's? What about those who couldn't sing like a mockingbird? What about those who may have been short, who may have been fat, whose teeth may have been crooked, who may have been handicapped, who may have been to jail? I mean, what about the rest of them?"

To forge a career as a military man is not to be defiled, exactly; rather, it is to reject the vocabulary of defilement. And the military is more than Powell's day job. It is an integral part of his identity. His military career has created a circle of loyalists, and the odd detractor. Surprisingly, Clifford Alexander, whose term as Secretary of the Army makes him as responsible as anyone for Powell's career trajectory, seems less than pleased with the result: "Was Colin Powell exceptional? No. There were a number of black generals who were equally as good as Colin Powell. But the breaks were with

Powell. By working in the Pentagon, he was visible to the Republican leadership. And Colin, who is smart and competent, did quite well, in part because of the proximity." In Alexander's view, Powell "is now in the hands of the handlers." He tries to take the long view. Echoing Jackson, he says, "You see, this has been pulled on us many times. White America says, 'This is your new leader, and you ought to feel good about it.' " It appears that Alexander does not feel good about it.

Then, too, both Powell's record as a commander and his views on military engagement have been controversial. Two books, *The Commanders*, by Bob Woodward, and *The Generals' War*, by General Bernard E. Trainor and Michael R. Gordon, chiseled away at Powell's reputation as the helmsman of the Gulf War. The first depicted him as a reluctant warrior, who cautioned against military intervention until the die was finally cast. The second took him to task for pursuing what its authors considered a faulty endgame to the conflict—one that left Saddam Hussein's regime and military might essentially intact and able to threaten future belligerence. Both accounts have been disputed, by Powell and others. What has greater currency, however, is the unapologetic stand he has taken against intervention in the Bosnian crisis.

"The biggest mistake was recognizing all these little countries when they started to decide they were independent," Powell says, leaning back in his chair. "The Serbs had very good reason to be worried about being in a Muslim-dominated country. It wasn't just paranoia. When the fighting broke out, should the West have intervened militarily as one of the belligerents to put down all other belligerents? There was no Western leader who was willing to say, 'I have a vital interest in the outcome of this conflict.' Nobody really thinks it has a vital interest." What has become known as the Powell Doctrine cautions against military involvement where political objectives remain murky.

So Powell is wary of overseas commitments and sees nothing in Bosnia to tempt him to change course. "Bismarck once said that all the Balkans were not worth the life of one Pomeranian grenadier," Powell said when we talked first. "The man knew what he was talk-

ing about. Disraeli said something similar." The national animad-
versions of nineteenth-century statesmen aside, Powell also has serious tactical misgivings. Speaking a few weeks before the first wave
of allied air strikes began, Powell made clear his skepticism of the ultimate efficacy of such efforts. "We can bomb—but what will we ac-
complish? Tito spent forty years building this military infrastructure
so that it couldn't be bombed by the Red Air Force. This stuff is underground. Take out the artillery? This isn't like Desert Storm. You
have hills, you have trees. You have a civilian population, you have
churches, you have homes, you have schools, and they can park all
that artillery right next to any of that stuff, and you can't bomb it.
As a culture, the Air Force tends to say we can do all kinds of wonderful things. But not to a dispersed enemy in wooded, hilly terrain
which has the ability to shoot back. We bombed the hell out of Vietnam and never did stop anything on the Ho Chi Minh Trail. Bush
understood that. But we've now said, 'No, we're going to bomb,'
and what are the reasons? NATO credibility? You don't bomb people for credibility. We have repeatedly gotten in trouble thinking
that the use of military force is for the purpose of being seen as having done something. You should use military force for achieving a
specific military purpose that is linked to the achievement of a specific political purpose and goal." This conclusion is a fairly precise
statement of the Powell Doctrine—a "doctrine" being what happens to a maxim when it serves as the basis of military policy.

We're on opposite sides of the issue, and, needless to say, he has
heard my arguments many times before. But still: even beyond the
enormities in view, what about the precedent we're setting for the
next century—the implicit license our inaction confers on other attempts at "ethnic cleansing"? What kinds of signals are we sending?

"I think you ought to send a clear signal: that we're not going to
get involved in this war, and it's not going to end until people are
tired of fighting one another. If you say that every day, the Muslims
will know it and the Serbs will know it, and there will be no confusion. But for three years we've been giving these mixed signals, so
the signals are worthless, and therefore we are weakened and cheap-
ened in the eyes of the world. We have a very bad reputation around

the world now as an incontinent political entity. And it's hurt the President badly and it's hurt his statesmanship really badly. But what are the long-term consequences? I really don't think the people in places like Azerbaijan or Armenia or Liberia or Sierra Leone are calibrating their actions on the basis of what we do in Bosnia." He gives me a wry look when he says, "There are some people at that school you hang out at"—he means Harvard, where I teach—"who contribute nothing else to the national G.D.P. except to create these great schemes." Powell worries that there are certain essentials that get lost in the ozone of theory. "I believe in the bully's way of going to war," he says. "I'm on the street corner, I got my gun, I got my blade, *I'ma kick yo' ass.*' " He adds, "There was a paragraph like this in the early draft of the book, but it sounded a little too, shall we say, 'ethnic,' and a little too Bronx, so I took it out."

Annoying as he finds the Ivy League technocrats on this issue, Powell has even less time for some of my co-religionists in the press. "William Safire and Tony Lewis say this will only take a little bit of bombing and it will work. No historical precedent exists for such a position. And Safire drives me to distraction. Sometimes, because he starts down this logic trail, and every time he gets trapped he just says, 'Air power can do it.' Forget it. The technology isn't that good. Safire's outrageous: 'There's no doubt in anyone's mind that if we'd done this three years ago . . .' Bullshit, Bill. But he does that. He's getting increasingly arrogant in his old age." Still, you wonder if in allowing a maxim to become a doctrine Powell hasn't courted a paradox—that of raising pragmatism to a principle. Extremism in pursuit of moderation may be no virtue.

But Powell has a redoubtable gift for charming his opponents, even on deeply felt concerns. At a Harvard commencement a couple of years ago, I saw this gift in action. Long before the issue of gays in the military surfaced to electoral consciousness, Powell had been selected to receive an honorary degree and to give a commencement address; but the eventual salience of the debate, and Powell's well-known opposition to lifting the ban, made his appearance a matter of heated controversy on campus. The mayor of

Cambridge, Kenneth Reeves, recalls introducing himself to Powell earlier in his visit. "I said, 'General Powell, it is my great pleasure to welcome you to Cambridge. I am the mayor of Cambridge, and in Cambridge the mayor happens to be both black and a homosexual, and this homosexual is going to keep you safe all day long.' " He laughs. "The secret to Colin Powell, I found, is that he is disarmingly charming."

Just before the General was to speak before a wary crowd of twenty thousand, the graduate students' speaker delivered an impassioned and eloquent attack on his position and was loudly applauded for it. How would Powell respond? As the student was returning to her seat, Powell rose, walked over to her, and shook her hand, thanking her for her comments. A Cambridge crowd—inconceivably remote from the military ethos—cheered him, won over by the graciousness of his gesture. When we discussed the matter recently, Powell cautioned, "I never presented the case in terms of there being something wrong, morally, or any other way, with gays. I just couldn't figure out a way to handle the privacy aspect." And I can't figure out what those privacy aspects are in the first place. What's plain is that the "don't ask, don't tell" compromise receives his imprimatur in part because it *is* a compromise, and Powell is a man who believes in the golden middle.

Not surprisingly, when I ask him to contrast the military-decision-making styles of the three Presidents he advised—Reagan, Bush, and Clinton—he tells me that Bush "had the clearest sense of how to marry political objectives and military force." He tells a story about a small naval skirmish with Iranians that broke out in the Persian Gulf when he was Reagan's National Security Adviser. Reagan's approval was needed to widen the rules of engagement, and when Powell went to him with the request, he found the President sitting at his desk, signing photographs of himself. "Within a nanosecond after I got out the last phrase of my request to him, he said, 'Yes, do it, give 'em hell,' " Powell recalls. It was, he says, "vintage Reagan." Clinton, he guesses, "would have talked about it a lot more and would have been, minute by minute, into the details." As for Bush, he "was somewhere in between." Bush and his advisers would have asked a few questions about the whys and wherefores, but "we would have gotten the same quick answer," Powell says. "With Clinton, I suspect it might have taken a little bit longer."

To the chagrin of many Powell-for-President enthusiasts, Powell's own decision-making process has displayed more deliberateness than speed of late. How, for that matter, would the maxims of a lifetime in the military translate into the political arena?

Certainly Powell's relations with the black political establishment, such as it is, have sometimes been strained. He is sensitive to the hazards of criticizing black leadership ("They will jump in your face in a minute") but is undeterred by them. He views the left-listing congressional Black Caucus as a phenomenon of resegregation; it's collectively in thrall to "the redistricting of these little squirrelly black districts all over," he says. "That gives us more black congressmen, but with less power and less influence." Nor, by his reckoning, have they been eager to take responsibility for risky policies they've helped to initiate.

The Black Caucus has often sought to make American policy more sensitive to Third World concerns; racial solidarity is meant to extend beyond national boundaries. And Powell himself is not immune to the mystique of origins. He has spoken of his first visit to West Africa as a profoundly moving experience—one that reinforced his sense of an ancestral identity. "I am an African, too," he has declared. Still, his attitude toward African nations does not exactly brim with sentimentality. "We have nations in Africa that are going backward in time hundreds of years," he asserts. "They are abandoning their colonial heritage, which was sort of the passage into the twentieth century." General Abacha, the despotic ruler of Nigeria, incurs sharp disapproval—"He has the worst C.I.A. bio I've ever read, and I've read lots of them"—but then so do his subjects: "Nigeria is a nation of ninety million people. With enormous wealth. And what they could have done with that wealth over the last twenty years—they just pissed it away. They just tend not to be honest. Nigerians as a group, frankly, are marvelous scammers. I mean, it is in their national culture." So the General, to say the least, cannot be accused of knee-jerk Afrocentrism.

And yet Powell's fit with the Reagan revolution was clearly imperfect. On the one hand, he was grateful for its invigorating effect on the military, which he felt had been undervalued by Carter. On the other hand, Powell is someone for whom the adjective "right-wing" is not a positive designation; someone for whom the adjective "middle-of-the-road" is no pejorative. And though most of his political friends are Republicans, many are not. Representative Kweisi Mfume, the outspoken former leader of the congressional Black Caucus, might be expected to provide a voice of dissent, but he turns out to be an ardent booster. "General Powell is the best that we can be," he says. Would he support him? "I was at his house a week ago and I told him that whenever he decided, please count me among the persons he would call first," Representative Mfume replies. "We shook on it. That says it all."

Certainly the issue of affirmative action seems to be something of a wedge between Powell and many of his Republican friends. When he's in a formal mood, he carefully distinguishes between quotas and "equal opportunity," and discourses upon the wrongful conflation of the two. But he can also bring a certain fervor to the topic. "It's amazing how affirmative action has suddenly become issue number one. One of my Republican friends had the nerve to send me one of their newsletters a few weeks ago saying that we had to get rid of affirmative action because we couldn't keep putting these programs in place for allegations of 'vague and ancient wrongs.' I almost went crazy. I said, Vague? Vague? Denny's wouldn't serve four black Secret Service agents guarding the President of the United States. The Chicago Federal Reserve Bank just told us something that any black could have told you—that it's harder to get a loan if you're black than if you're white. And we got Pete Wilson out there saying that affirmative action is bad because there are eight-tenths of one percent more black students in the University of California school system as a result of fifteen years of affirmative action. This is the worst problem the country has? And I said, 'If there is a program that is a "get over" program, then get rid of it, sure.' But don't throw out the baby with the bathwater."

I mention the F.C.C. program granting minority set-asides of television and radio stations. He's intimately acquainted with it: it enabled him, in partnership with Bruce Llewellyn and others, to acquire a Buffalo television station ten years ago. "But it's black-owned," he says. "If you got a bunch of white guys with a brother fronting for them, get rid of it. That doesn't serve any purpose for us. What is troubling now is that we have essentially said that the principle of lowering bootstraps for people to climb up is bad." And he speaks about having been told by the Reagan adviser Stuart Spencer, who is one of the inventors of the political-consultancy business, that he was too socially conscious to mesh with the current Republican agenda.

The figure of Powell, it should be said, elicits surprising warmth among many blacks whose relation to the political establishment has often been more adversarial than not. Marian Wright Edelman, the left-liberal head of the Children's Defense Fund and herself a best-selling author, recalls, "The first time I heard him speak at the Council on Foreign Relations, he was so effective that I had to force myself to remember that we disagree on certain military policies. He certainly has a central core of integrity." Another prominent advocate, Hugh Price, who is president of the National Urban League, is sure that "if Powell is elected, he will be elected because the Americans are hungry for a person who stitches the country back together again—who brings a sense of decency, coupled with a sense of resolve and toughness." Invoking Powell's military background, the black philosopher and social critic Cornel West says, "If he could push through a Marshall Plan for the cities, that would be extraordinary. My hunch is that it would be very difficult to do, but he might be open to it. I have my own critique of the military establishment, but I think he is a man of compassion in his own way."

When I asked Roger Wilkins, the liberal commentator and an éminence grise of black politics, whether he would support Powell for President, he didn't have to pause to reflect. "Oh, yeah," he said. Even if Powell ran as a Republican? "Oh, yeah." As a third-party candidate? He grinned. "Third party? Not only would I support him, I'd work my ass off for him." And he voices a widespread grievance when he adds, "Black people are stuck in nowhere's land. Republicans don't want us. And the Democrats take us for granted."

Most of Powell's advisers take a dim view of an independent candidacy. Independent candidates for the White House do not have an inspiring record of success; the electoral college is designed in part to stabilize a two-party system. Ross Perot, several people have reminded me, spent sixty million dollars out of pocket and received not a single electoral vote. "If he had two hundred million dollars put at his disposal, he'd consider it," one friend of the General's insists. "And he may well get it." If you measure the legacy of the most successful independent candidates by sound bites rather than by electoral returns, they do have something to show for their efforts. George Wallace ("pointy-headed intellectuals"), John Anderson ("I'm a social liberal and a fiscal conservative"), and Ross Perot ("giant sucking sound") have all made contributions to the national conversation. So the General's lifelong predilection for the quotable may prove a valuable resource if at some future date he decides to hit the campaign trail.

Of course, character—solidity, strength, effectiveness—will be his main selling point. No one thinks that what will distinguish Powell is the split-the-difference approach toward policy matters which he shares with John Anderson. We know where Powell stands on many "hot button" issues, like abortion (he's pro-choice), the death penalty (he supports it), gun control (he'll support mild measures, involving registration or waiting periods), school prayer (he's opposed, but he doesn't mind a moment of silence).

Still, analysts often fail to acknowledge the extent to which elections are character-driven rather than issue-driven. Many things were portended by an electorate that switched its support from Carter to Reagan in just four years, but a massive ideological conversion was not one of them. And Powell has mastered the Rorschachian rhetoric of the well-groomed political candidate. His speeches are more evocative than substantive— short on red meat and long on uplift. Like Whitney Houston, he believes the children are our future—teach them well. "You've got to start with the families," he says of the crisis in the inner cities, "and then you've got to fix education so these little bright-eyed five-year-olds, who are innocent as the day is long and who know right from wrong, have all the education they need. And you have to do both these things simultaneously. It's like being able to support two military conflicts simultaneously." Military metaphors, the worn currency of political discourse in this country, take on a certain vitality when he deploys them. (Indeed, there are those who argue that much of the General's allure stems from a sort of transposition of realms. "I think people are hungry for a military solution to inner-city problems," the black law professor and activist Patricia Williams says reprovingly.)

"You know, I'm sort of a liberal guy, up to this point," Powell goes on, "but here's where I become a Republican: once these kids come out of school, there has got to be a capitalistic entrepreneurial system that is just burning up the place to create the jobs for these kids. And therefore you've got to get the tax burden off business. You've got to lower the capital-gains tax." Capital gains are not an abstract matter to Powell. "What have I done with my wealth? I bought my wife a nice house, I bought two new suits, leased a new car. What have I done with the rest of it? Invested it. Some of it is in bonds. Where's that bond money going? It's building things— cities. Some of it is in the equity market. What's it doing? It's financing companies. It's looking for more places to create wealth, and guess what happens when that happens. Jobs are going to be created. And so the government's got to get off people's backs. They've got to have minimum regulations, for safety and for some level of security, so we're not plundering things. But after that, get off their backs." Everything clear? Sort of a liberal, kind of a conservative. Clearly black, but, as he explains, not *too* black.


Conjecture has a way of feeding on itself: How realistic is any of this Powell-for-President stuff? Bruce Llewellyn, for one, suspects that we have got ahead of ourselves. Will his cousin run? "No. Because he can't win. The game that's being played right now has to do with selling books."

If you think that Powell's ambitions are less circumscribed than that, however, everything is a matter of the calculation of odds. The polling data are encouraging—at least, to a point.

What makes things especially tricky for the Powell pollster is the well-established distortive effect of race on polling data—many black candidates who soar in opinion surveys get sunk in the voting booth. Powell says, "Every time I see Earl Grave, he says, 'Look, man, don't let them hand you no crap. When they go in that booth, they ain't going to vote for you.' " Or as Walters explains, "When you do a public-opinion poll, what happens is that whites, particularly, lie. They don't answer the polls the way they're going to vote. So right now you have to discount some of Powell's support because of race."

Indeed, perhaps the most striking polling results aren't Powell's positives but his remarkably low negatives. It's in that respect, above all, that the familiar Eisenhower analogy gains force. And Powell himself clearly has a Republican model in Eisenhower, whose appeal he characterizes in terms that resonate with his own public profile. "Eisenhower was a person who could put together very interesting coalitions and be a natural war leader the people would respect," he says. "They saw Ike and they felt comfortable and confident. *I* like Ike." But a black Eisenhower? Well, why not? Julian Bond says of Powell, "He is a handsome, clean-cut guy, but he's not sexy. And therefore not threatening. Powell is a good-looking guy, but he's not going to steal your girl."

Alma Powell herself is widely viewed as a substantial political asset—someone who is both sophisticated and anodyne. She comes from a family that has been part of the black haute bourgeoisie for several generations. She has inherited an understated sense of cultural security and social confidence: an absolute knowledge of where she fits into society, black and white. She is also at home with power, her own and others'. Discussing what kind of First Lady she would make, Weinberger compares her with the patrician Barbara

Bush, in that "she is a lady who is perfectly comfortable with herself and therefore makes everybody else feel very much at ease." He adds that "the people who give a lot of parties and people who go to a lot of parties and people who are in various embassies around the world, they all feel the same way about her: she would also be a very fine hostess in the White House." What strikes me is that there seems to be nothing outlandish about this subject of conversation— a subject that is, historically speaking, outlandish indeed. But plausibility—supreme plausibility—is an attribute that the General and his wife have in common.

You might argue that this plausibility has never fully been put to the test—subjected to the rough-and-tumble of electoral politics. You might argue that Powell's scant unfavorable rating is simply a reflection of that. As a candidate, Powell would have to be reconciled to the sheer negativity of the modern political campaign—a particular concern for a man who, as his close friends affirm, can be short-tempered and sensitive to criticism. Something that Alma once said stays with me, too: "Even if you don't have any skeletons in your closet, someone in your family might."

"Once you get in, the knives come out, and they start poking away at you, shaving away your image," says Kurt Schmoke, whose own name was once bandied about as a possible candidate for higher office. And Vernon Jordan cites a sobering precedent: "In 1980, the press just pushed—*pushed*—Ted Kennedy into the race, and the moment he got into it they cut his dick off." Cornel West foresees another potential development on the campaign trail: "Once the ugly attacks and assaults really begin, Colin Powell will be forced, to some degree, to come out swinging. Then they'll say, 'Oh, my God, he *is* a black man. Look at him. He's full of rage. He's been that all the time.' " And many of Powell's friends would forfeit the dream of the Oval Office in order to protect the aura that he now enjoys. Quincy Jones, a man who, as an entertainment magnate, has made the manufacture of image his stock-in-trade, tells me, "I hope from the bottom of my heart that he doesn't run. Because I would not like to see that fortress attacked. And it would be an attack like you can't believe. He doesn't have to do that for us or anybody else. I would like to just see him remain an icon."

These are sentiments that Powell well understands. "You flatter me by saying, 'You're the first guy who could ever really do it,' " he tells me. "Well, isn't that, in and of itself, almost there?"

"But it's the difference between being John the Baptist and being Jesus Christ," I say. "And you have to decide how you want to be remembered." Then a thought occurs to me. "One ends up with his head on a platter, one's nailed to the cross." Put that way, there doesn't seem much to choose between. Powell roars with delighted laughter.

"Now, there's another thing that nobody recommends," Powell says. "But I have to think about it: I'm only going to be sixty-three in 1999—nine years younger than Dole is now."

Colin Powell could be the first black person to be President—and that possibility must have a magnetic pull. But he also realizes that a successful Powell run could permanently alter the political landscape—and the pull of that must be equally powerful. Nineteen ninety-nine isn't so far away. We are sitting together in his Fourth of July office, under the watchful gaze of three Presidents. Just consider, I say to Powell: if he were to secure a Republican nomination and take the black vote with him, the electoral shift would transform party politics—representing, potentially, the most significant realignment since Franklin Delano Roosevelt's second election, in 1936. "It would be a new Republican Party," I point out.

For once, his eyes seem a little misty. "It would be a new Democratic Party," he replies, not missing a beat. "They've never had to worry about a core constituency of black folks. I mean, no party has really lost its core, core constituents, before. And there's just nothing you can do to correct it. Many black congressmen have said to me, 'If you come out, I can't go nowhere. Go out and campaign against you? That'd be crazy.' They can't. They won't. A number of them have said, 'You know we'll campaign for you wherever you are.' "

Imagine, if you will, the Democrats' totemic constituents on the hustings for a Republican candidate. What if this actually came about, I ask him. What if the center held?

"It's hard to redefine or create a new center in a couple of months." The General gives me one of his owlish looks, but there is mischief in his eyes. "I could do it in four years."

# Thirteen Ways of Looking at a Black Man

❖

"Every day, in every way, we are getting meta and meta," the philosopher John Wisdom used to say, venturing a cultural counterpart to Émile Coué's famous mantra of self-improvement. So it made sense that in the aftermath of the Simpson trial the focus of attention was swiftly displaced from the verdict to the reaction to the verdict, and then to the reaction to the reaction to the verdict, and, finally, to the reaction to the reaction to the reaction to the verdict—which is to say, black indignation at white anger at black jubilation at Simpson's acquittal. It was a spiral made possible by the relay circuit of race. Only in America.

An American historian I know registers a widespread sense of bathos when he says, "Who would have imagined that the Simpson trial would be like the Kennedy assassination—that you'd remember where you were when the verdict was announced?" But everyone does, of course. The eminent sociologist William Julius Wilson was in the red-carpet lounge of a United Airlines terminal, the only black in a crowd of white travelers, and found himself as stunned and disturbed as they were. Wynton Marsalis, on tour with his band in California, recalls that "everybody was acting like they were above watching it, but then when it got to be ten o'clock—zoom, we said, 'Put the verdict on!' " Spike Lee was with Jackie Robinson's widow, Rachel, rummaging through a trunk filled with her husband's belongings, in preparation for a bio-pic he's making on the athlete. Jamaica Kincaid was sitting in her car in the parking lot of her local grocery store in Vermont, listening to the proceedings on National Public Radio, and she didn't pull out until after they were over. I was teaching a literature seminar at Harvard from twelve to two, and watched the verdict with the class on a television set in the seminar room. That's where I first saw the sort of racialized response that itself would fill television screens for the next few days: the white students looked aghast, and the black students cheered. "Maybe you should remind the students that this is a case about two people who were brutally slain, and not an occasion to celebrate," my teaching assistant, a white woman, whispered to me.

The two weeks spanning the O. J. Simpson verdict and Louis Farrakhan's Million Man March on Washington were a good time for connoisseurs of racial paranoia. As blacks exulted at Simpson's acquittal, horrified whites had a fleeting sense that this race thing was knottier than they'd ever supposed—that when all the pieties were cleared away, blacks really *were* strangers in their midst. (The unspoken sentiment: *And I thought I knew these people*.) There was the faintest tincture of the Southern slave-owner's disquiet in the aftermath of the bloody slave revolt led by Nat Turner—when the gentleman farmer was left to wonder which of his smiling, servile retainers would have slit *his* throat had the rebellion spread as was intended, like fire on parched thatch. In the day or so following the verdict, young urban professionals took note of a slight *froideur* between themselves and their nannies and babysitters—the awkwardness of an unbroached subject. Rita Dove, who recently completed a term as the United States Poet Laureate, and who believes that Simpson was guilty, found it "appalling that white people were so outraged—more appalling than the decision as to whether he was guilty or not." Of course, it's possible to overstate the tensions. Marsalis invokes the example of team sports, saying, "You want your side to win, whatever the side is going to be. And the thing is, we're still at a point in our national history where we look at each other as sides."

The matter of side-taking cuts deep. An old cartoon depicts a woman who has taken her errant daughter to see a child psychiatrist. "And when we were watching *The Wizard of Oz*," the distraught mother is explaining, "she was rooting for the wicked witch!" What many whites experienced was the bewildering sense that an entire population had been rooting for the wrong side. "This case is a classic example of what I call interstitial spaces," says Judge A. Leon Higginbotham, who recently retired from the federal Court of Appeals, and who last month received the Presidential Medal of Freedom. "The jury system is predicated on the idea that different people can view the same evidence and reach diametrically opposed conclusions." But the observation brings little solace. If we disagree about something so basic, how can we find agreement about far thornier matters? For white observers, what's even scarier than the idea that black Americans were plumping for the villain, which is a misprision of value, is the idea that black Americans didn't recognize him *as* the villain, which is a misprision of fact. How can conversation begin when we disagree about reality? To put it at its harshest, for many whites a sincere belief in Simpson's innocence looks less like the culture of protest than like the culture of psychosis.

Perhaps you didn't know that Liz Claiborne appeared on *Oprah* not long ago and said that she didn't design her clothes for black women—that their hips were too wide. Perhaps you didn't know that the soft drink Tropical Fantasy is manufactured by the Ku Klux Klan and contains a special ingredient designed to sterilize black men. (A warning flyer distributed in Harlem a few years ago claimed that these findings were vouchsafed on the television program *20/20*.) Perhaps you didn't know that the Ku Klux Klan has a similar arrangement with Church's Fried Chicken—or is it Popeye's?

Perhaps you didn't know these things, but a good many black

Americans think they do, and will discuss them with the same in-
tentness they bring to speculations about the "shadowy figure" in a
Brentwood driveway. Never mind that Liz Claiborne has never appeared on *Oprah,* that the beleaguered Brooklyn company that
makes Tropical Fantasy has gone as far as to make available an
F.D.A. assay of its ingredients, and that those fried-chicken fran-
chises pose a threat mainly to black folks' arteries. The folklorist Patricia A. Turner, who has collected dozens of such tales in an
invaluable 1993 study of rumor in African-American culture, *I
Heard It Through the Grapevine,* points out the patterns to be found
here: that these stories encode regnant anxieties, that they take root
under particular conditions and play particular social roles, that the
currency of rumor flourishes where "official" news has proved un-
trustworthy.

Certainly the Fuhrman tapes might have been scripted to confirm
the old saw that paranoids, too, have enemies. If you wonder why
blacks seem particularly susceptible to rumors and conspiracy theories, you might look at a history in which the official story was a
poor guide to anything that mattered much, and in which rumor
sometimes verged on the truth. Heard the one about the L.A. cop
who hated interracial couples, fantasized about making a bonfire of
black bodies, and boasted of planting evidence? How about the one
about the federal government's forty-year study of how untreated
syphilis affects black men? For that matter, have you ever read
through some of the F.B.I.'s COINTELPRO files? ("There is but
one way out for you," an F.B.I. scribe wrote to Martin Luther King,
Jr., in 1964, thoughtfully urging on him the advantages of suicide.
"You better take it before your filthy, abnormal, fraudulent self is
bared to the nation.")

People arrive at an understanding of themselves and the world
through narratives—narratives purveyed by schoolteachers, news-
casters, "authorities," and all the other authors of our common
sense. Counternarratives are, in turn, the means by which groups
contest that dominant reality and the fretwork of assumptions that
supports it. Sometimes delusion lies that way; sometimes not.
There's a sense in which much of black history is simply coun-

ternarrative that has been documented and legitimized, by slow, hard-won scholarship. The "shadowy figures" of American history have long been our own ancestors, both free and enslaved. In any case, fealty to counternarratives is an index to alienation, not to skin color: witness Representative Helen Chenoweth, of Idaho, and her devoted constituents. With all the appositeness of allegory, the copies of *The Protocols of the Elders of Zion* sold by black venders in New York—who are supplied with them by Lushena Books, a black-nationalist book wholesaler—were published by the white supremacist Angriff Press, in Hollywood. Paranoia knows no color or coast.

Finally, though, it's misleading to view counternarrative as another pathology of disenfranchisement. If the M.I.A. myth, say, is rooted among a largely working-class constituency, there are many myths—one of them known as Reaganism—that hold considerable appeal among the privileged classes. "So many white brothers and sisters are living in a state of denial in terms of how deep white supremacy is seated in their culture and society," the scholar and social critic Cornel West says. "Now we recognize that in a fundamental sense we really do live in different worlds." In that respect, the reaction to the Simpson verdict has been something of an education. The novelist Ishmael Reed talks of "wealthy white male commentators who live in a world where the police don't lie, don't plant evidence—and drug dealers give you unlimited credit." He adds, "Nicole, you know, also dated Mafia hit men."

"I think he's innocent, I really do," West says. "I do think it was linked to some drug subculture of violence. It looks as if both O.J. and Nicole had some connection to drug activity. And the killings themselves were classic examples of that drug culture of violence. It could have to do with money owed—it could have to do with a number of things. And I think that O.J. was quite aware of and fearful of this." On this theory, Simpson may have appeared at the crime scene as a witness. "I think that he had a sense that it was coming down, both on him and on her, and Brother Ron Goldman just happened to be there," West conjectures. "But there's a possibility also that O.J. could have been there, gone over and tried to see what was going on, saw that he couldn't help, split, and just ran away. He might have said, 'I can't stop this thing, and they are coming at me to do the same thing.' He may have actually run for his life."

To believe that Simpson is innocent is to believe that a terrible injustice has been averted, and this is precisely what many black Americans, including many prominent ones, do believe. Thus the soprano Jessye Norman is angry over what she sees as the decision of the media to prejudge Simpson rather than "educate the public as to how we could possibly look at things a bit differently." She says she wishes that the real culprit "would stand up and say, 'I did this and I am sorry I caused so much trouble.' " And while she is sensitive to the issue of spousal abuse, she is skeptical about the way it was enlisted by the prosecution: "You have to stop getting into how they were at home, because there are not a lot of relationships that could be put on television that we would think, O.K., that's a good one. I mean, just stop pretending that this is the case." Then, too, she asks, "Isn't it interesting to you that this Faye Resnick person was staying with Nicole Brown Simpson and that she happened to have left on the eighth of June? Does that tell you that maybe there's some awful coincidence here?" The widespread theory about murderous drug dealers Norman finds "perfectly plausible, knowing what drugs do," and she adds, "People are punished for being bad."

There's a sense in which all such accounts can be considered counternarratives, or fragments of them—subaltern knowledge, if you like. They dispute the tenets of official culture; they do not receive the imprimatur of editorialists or of network broadcasters; they are not seriously entertained on *MacNeil/Lehrer*. And when they do surface they are given consideration primarily for their ethnographic value. An official culture treats their claims as it does those of millenarian cultists in Texas, or Marxist deconstructionists in the academy: as things to be diagnosed, deciphered, given meaning—that is, *another* meaning. Black folk say they believe

Simpson is innocent, and then the white gatekeepers of a media culture cajolingly explain what black folk really mean when they say it, offering the explanation from the highest of motives: because the alternative is a population that, by their lights, is not merely counternormative but crazy. Black folk may mean anything at all; just not what they say they mean.

Yet you need nothing so grand as an epistemic rupture to explain why different people weigh the evidence of authority differently. In the words of the cunning Republican campaign slogan, "Who do you trust?" It's a commonplace that white folks trust the police and black folks don't. Whites recognize this in the abstract, but they're continually surprised at the *depth* of black wariness. They shouldn't be. Norman Podhoretz's soul-searching 1963 essay, "My Negro Problem, and Ours"—one of the frankest accounts we have of liberalism and race resentment—tells of a Brooklyn boyhood spent under the shadow of carefree, cruel Negro assailants, and of the author's residual unease when he passes groups of blacks in his Upper West Side neighborhood. And yet, he notes in a crucial passage, "I know now, as I did not know when I was a child, that power is on my side, that the police are working for me and not for them." That ordinary, unremarkable comfort—the feeling that "the police are working for me"—continues to elude blacks, even many successful blacks. Thelma Golden, the curator of the Whitney's "Black Male" show, points out that on the very day the verdict was announced a black man in Harlem was killed by the police under disputed circumstances. As older blacks like to repeat, "When white folks say 'justice,' they mean 'just us.' "

Blacks—in particular, black men—swap their experiences of police encounters like war stories, and there are few who don't have more than one story to tell. "These stories have a ring of cliché about them," Erroll McDonald, Pantheon's executive editor and one of the few prominent blacks in publishing, says, "but, as we all know about clichés, they're almost always true." McDonald tells of renting a Jaguar in New Orleans and being stopped by the police—

simply "to show cause why I shouldn't be deemed a problematic Negro in a possibly stolen car." Wynton Marsalis says, "Shit, the police slapped me upside the head when I was in high school. I wasn't Wynton Marsalis then. I was just another nigger standing out somewhere on the street whose head could be slapped and did get slapped." The crime novelist Walter Mosley recalls, "When I was a kid in Los Angeles, they used to stop me all the time, beat on me, follow me around, tell me that I was stealing things." Nor does William Julius Wilson—who has a son-in-law on the Chicago police force ("You couldn't find a nicer, more dedicated guy")—wonder why he was stopped near a small New England town by a policeman who wanted to know what he was doing in those parts. There's a moving violation that many African-Americans know as D.W.B.: Driving While Black.

So we all have our stories. In 1968, when I was eighteen, a man who knew me was elected mayor of my West Virginia county, in an upset victory. A few weeks into his term, he passed on something he thought I should know: the county police had made a list of people to be arrested in the event of a serious civil disturbance, and my name was on it. Years of conditioning will tell. Wynton Marsalis says, "My worst fear is to have to go before the criminal-justice system." Absurdly enough, it's mine, too.

Another barrier to interracial comprehension is talk of the "race card"—a phrase that itself infuriates many blacks. Judge Higginbotham, who pronounces himself "not uncomfortable at all" with the verdict, is uncomfortable indeed with charges that Johnnie Cochran played the race card. "This whole point is one hundred percent inaccurate," Higginbotham says. "If you knew that the most important witness had a history of racism and hostility against black people, that should have been a relevant factor of inquiry even if the jury had been all white. If the defendant had been Jewish and the police officer had a long history of expressed anti-Semitism and having planted evidence against innocent persons who were Jewish, I can't believe that anyone would have been saying that defense counsel was playing the anti-Semitism card." Angela Davis finds the very metaphor to be a problem. "Race is not a card," she says firmly. "The whole case was pervaded with issues of race."

Those who share her view were especially outraged at Robert Shapiro's famous post-trial rebuke to Cochran—for not only playing the race card but dealing it "from the bottom of the deck." Ishmael Reed, who is writing a book about the case, regards Shapiro's remarks as sheer opportunism: "He wants to keep his Beverly Hills clients—a perfectly commercial reason." In Judge Higginbotham's view, "Johnnie Cochran established that he was as effective as any lawyer in America, and though whites can tolerate black excellence in singing, dancing, and dunking, there's always been a certain level of discomfort among many whites when you have a one-on-one challenge in terms of intellectual competition. If Edward Bennett Williams, who was one of the most able lawyers in the country, had raised the same issues, half of the complaints would not exist."

By the same token, the display of black prowess in the courtroom was heartening for many black viewers. Cornel West says, "I think part of the problem is that Shapiro— and this is true of certain white brothers—has a profound fear of black-male charisma. And this is true not only in the law but across the professional world. You see, you have so many talented white brothers who deserve to be in the limelight. But one of the reasons they are not in the limelight is that they are not charismatic. And here comes a black person who's highly talented but also charismatic and therefore able to command center stage. So you get a very real visceral kind of jealousy that has to do with sexual competition as well as professional competition."

Erroll McDonald touches upon another aspect of sexual tension when he says, "The so-called race card has always been the joker. And the joker is the history of sexual racial politics in this country. People forget the singularity of this issue—people forget that less than a century ago black men were routinely lynched for merely glancing at white women or for having been *thought* to have glanced at a white woman." He adds, with mordant irony, "Now we've come to a point in our history where a black man could, potentially, have murdered a white woman and thrown in a white man to boot—and got off. So the country has become far more complex in its discussion of race." This is, as he appreciates, a less than perfectly consoling thought.

"But he's coming for me," a woman muses in Toni Morrison's 1994 novel, *Jazz*, shortly before she is murdered by a jealous ex-lover. "Maybe tomorrow he'll find me. Maybe tonight." Morrison, it happens, is less interested in the grand passions of love and requital than she is in the curious texture of communal amnesty. In the event, the woman's death goes unavenged; the man who killed her is forgiven even by her friends and relatives. Neighbors feel that the man fell victim to her wiles, that he didn't understand "how she liked to push people, men." Or, as one of them says of her, "live the life; pay the price." Even the woman—who refuses to name the culprit as she bleeds to death—seems to accede to the view that she brought it on herself.

It's an odd and disturbing theme, and one with something of a history in black popular culture. An R. & B. hit from 1960, "There's Something on Your Mind," relates the anguish of a man who is driven to kill by his lover's infidelity. The chorus alternates with spoken narrative, which informs us that his first victim is the friend with whom she was unfaithful. But then:

> Just as you make it up in your mind to forgive her, here come another one of your best friends through the door. This really makes you blow your top, and you go right ahead and shoot her. And realizing what you've done, you say: "Baby, please, speak to me. Forgive me. I'm sorry."

"We are a *forgiving* people," Anita Hill tells me, and she laughs, a little uneasily. We're talking about the support for O. J. Simpson in the black community; at least, I think we are.

A black woman told the *Times* last week, "He has been punished enough." But forgiveness is not all. There is also an element in this of outlaw culture: the tendency—which unites our lumpenproles with our postmodern ironists—to celebrate transgression for its own sake. Spike Lee, who was surprised but "wasn't happy" at the verdict ("I would have bet money that he was going to the slammer"), reached a similar conclusion: "A lot of black folks said, 'Man, O.J. is *bad*, you know. This is the first brother in the history of the world who got away with the murder of white folks, and a blond, blue-eyed woman at that.' "

But then there is the folk wisdom on the question of why Nicole Brown Simpson had to die—the theodicy of the streets. For nothing could be further from the outlaw ethic than the simple and widely shared certainty that, as Jessye Norman says, people are punished for doing wrong. And compounding the sentiment is Morrison's subject—the culturally vexed status of the so-called crime of passion, or what some took to be one, anyway. You play, you pay: it's an attitude that exists on the streets, but not only on the streets, and one that somehow attaches to Nicole, rather than to her ex-husband. Many counternarratives revolve around her putative misbehavior. The black feminist Bell Hooks notes with dismay that what many people took to be a "narrative of a crime of passion" had as its victim "a woman that many people, white and black, felt was like a whore. Precisely by being a sexually promiscuous woman, by being a woman who used drugs, by being a white woman with a black man, she had already fallen from grace in many people's eyes—there was no way to redeem her." Ishmael Reed, for one, has no interest in redeeming her. "To paint O. J. Simpson as a beast, they had to depict her as a saint," he complains. "Apparently, she had a violent temper. She slapped her Jamaican maid. I'm wondering, the feminists who are giving Simpson such a hard time—do they approve of white women slapping maids?"

Of course, the popular trial of Nicole Brown Simpson—one conducted off camera, in whispers—has further occluded anything recognizable as sexual politics. When Anita Hill heard that O. J. Simpson was going to be part of the Million Man March on Washington, she felt it was entirely in keeping with the occasion: a trial in which she believed that matters of gender had been "bracketed" was going to be succeeded by a march from which women were excluded. And while Minister Louis Farrakhan had told black men that October 16 was to serve as a "day of atonement" for their sins, the murder of Nicole Brown Simpson and Ronald Goldman was obviously not among the sins he had in mind. Bell Hooks argues, "Both O.J.'s case and the Million Man March confirm that while white men are trying to be sensitive and pretending they're the new man, black men are saying that patriarchy must be upheld at all costs, even if women must die." She sees the march as a congenial arena for Simpson in symbolic terms: "I think he'd like to strut his stuff, as the patriarch. He is the dick that stayed hard longer." ("The surprising thing is that you won't see Clarence Thomas going on that march," Anita Hill remarks of another icon of patriarchy.) Farrakhan himself prefers metaphors of military mobilization, but the exclusionary politics of the event has clearly distracted from its ostensible message of solidarity. "First of all, I wouldn't go to no war and leave half the army home," says Amiri Baraka, the radical poet and playwright who achieved international renown in the sixties as the leading spokesman for the Black Arts movement. "Logistically, that doesn't make sense." He notes that Martin Luther King's 1963 March on Washington was "much more inclusive," and sees Farrakhan's regression as "an absolute duplication of what's happening in the country," from Robert Bly on: the sacralization of masculinity.

Something like that dynamic is what many white feminists saw on display in the Simpson verdict; but it's among women that the racial divide is especially salient. The black legal scholar and activist Patricia Williams says she was "stunned by the intensely personal resentment of some of my white women friends in particular." Stunned but, on reflection, not mystified. "This is Greek drama," she declares. "Two of the most hotly contended aspects of our lives are violence among human beings who happen to be police officers and violence among human beings who happen to be husbands, spouses, lovers." Meanwhile, our attention has been fixated on the rhetorical violence between human beings who happen to disagree about the outcome of the O. J. Simpson trial.


It's a cliché to speak of the Simpson trial as a soap opera—as entertainment, as theater—but it's also true, and in ways that are worth exploring further. For one thing, the trial provides a fitting rejoinder to those who claim that we live in an utterly fragmented culture, bereft of the common narratives that bind a people together. True, Parson Weems has given way to Dan Rather, but public narrative persists. Nor has it escaped notice that the biggest televised legal contests of the last half decade have involved race matters: Anita Hill and Rodney King. So there you have it: the Simpson trial—black entertainment television at its finest. Ralph Ellison's hopeful insistence on the Negro's centrality to American culture finds, at last, a certain tawdry confirmation.

"The media generated in people a feeling of being spectators at a show," the novelist John Edgar Wideman says. "And at the end of a show you applaud. You are happy for the good guy. There is that sense of primal identification and closure." Yet it's a fallacy of "cultural literacy" to equate shared narratives with shared meanings. The fact that American TV shows are rebroadcast across the globe causes many people to wring their hands over the menace of cultural imperialism; seldom do they bother to inquire about the meanings that different people bring to and draw from these shows. When they do make inquiries, the results are often surprising. One researcher talked to Israeli Arabs who had just watched an episode of *Dallas*—an episode in which Sue Ellen takes her baby, leaves her husband, J.R., and moves in with her ex-lover and his father. The Arab viewers placed their own construction on the episode: they were all convinced that Sue Ellen had moved in with her *own* father—something that by their mores at least made sense.

A similar thing happened in America this year: the communal experience afforded by a public narrative (and what narrative more public?) was splintered by the politics of interpretation. As far as the writer Maya Angelou is concerned, the Simpson trial was an exercise in minstrelsy. "Minstrel shows caricatured every aspect of the black man's life, beginning with his sexuality," she says. "They portrayed the black man as devoid of all sensibilities and sensitivities. They minimized and diminished the possibility of familial love. And that is what the trial is about. Not just the prosecution but everybody seemed to want to show him as other than a normal human being. Nobody let us just see a man." But there is, of course, little consensus about what genre would best accommodate the material. Walter Mosley says, "The story plays to large themes, so I'm sure somebody will write about it. But I don't think it's a mystery. I think it's much more like a novel by Zola." What a writer might make of the material is one thing; what the audience has made of it is another.

"Simpson is a B-movie star and people were watching this like a B movie," Patricia Williams says. "And this is *not* the American B-movie ending." Or was it? "From my perspective as an attorney, this trial was much more like a movie than a trial," Kathleen Cleaver, who was once the Black Panthers' Minister for Communication and is now a professor of law at Emory, says. "It had the budget of a movie, it had the casting of a movie, it had the tension of a movie, and the happy ending of a movie." Spike Lee, speaking professionally, is dubious about the trial's cinematic possibilities: "I don't care who makes this movie, it is never going to equal what people have seen in their living rooms and houses for eight or nine months." Or is it grand opera? Jessye Norman considers: "Well, it certainly has all the ingredients. I mean, somebody meets somebody and somebody gets angry with somebody and somebody dies." She laughs. "It sounds like the *Ring* cycle of Wagner—it really does."

"This story has been told any number of times," Angelou says. "The first thing I thought about was Eugene O'Neill's *All God's Chillun*." Then she considers how the event might be retrieved by an African-American literary tradition. "I think a great writer would have to approach it," she tells me pensively. "James Baldwin could have done it. And Toni Morrison could do it."

What about Maya Angelou?

"I don't like that kind of stuff," she replies.

There are some for whom the question of adaptation is not entirely abstract. The performance artist and playwright Anna Deavere Smith has already worked on the 911 tape and F. Lee Bailey's cross-examination of Mark Fuhrman in the drama classes she teaches at Stanford. Now, with a dramaturge's eye, she identifies what she takes to be the climactic moment: "Just after the verdict was read I will always remember two sounds and one image. I heard Johnnie Cochran go 'Ugh,' and then I heard the weeping of Kim Goldman. And then I saw the image of O.J.'s son, with one hand going upward on one eye and one hand pointed down, shaking and sobbing. I couldn't do the words right now; if I could find a collaborator, I would do something else. I feel that a choreographer ought to do that thing. Part of the tragedy was the fact of that 'Ugh' and that crying. Because that 'Ugh' wasn't even a full sound of victory, really." In "Thirteen Ways of Looking at a Blackbird" Wallace Stevens famously said he didn't know whether he preferred "The beauty of inflections / Or the beauty of innuendoes, / The black-bird whistling / Or just after." American culture has spoken as with one voice: we like it just after.

Just after is when our choices and allegiances are made starkly apparent. Just after is when interpretation can be detached from the thing interpreted. Anita Hill, who saw her own presence at the Clarence Thomas hearings endlessly analyzed and allegorized, finds plenty of significance in the trial's reception, but says the trial itself had none. Naturally, the notion that the trial was sui generis is alien to most commentators. Yet it did not arrive in the world already costumed as a racial drama; it had to be racialized. And those critics—angry whites, indignant blacks—who like to couple this verdict with the Rodney King verdict should consider an elementary circumstance: Rodney King was an unknown and undistinguished black man who was brutalized by the police; the only thing exceptional about that episode was the presence of a video camera. But, as Bell Hooks asks, "in what other case have we ever had a wealthy black man being tried for murder?" Rodney King was a black man to his captors before he was anything else; O. J. Simpson was, first and foremost, O. J. Simpson. Kathleen Cleaver observes, "A black superhero millionaire is not someone for whom mistreatment is an issue." And Spike Lee acknowledges that the police "don't really bother black people once they are a personality." On this point, I'm reminded of something that Roland Gift, the lead singer of the pop group Fine Young Cannibals, once told a reporter: "I'm not black, I'm famous."


Simpson, too, was famous rather than black; that is, until the African-American community took its lead from the cover of *Time* and, well, blackened him. Some intellectuals are reluctant to go along with the conceit. Angela Davis, whose early-seventies career as a fugitive and a political prisoner provides one model of how to be famous *and* black, speaks of the need to question the way "O. J. Simpson serves as the generic black man," given that "he did not identify himself as black before then." More bluntly, Baraka says, "To see him get all of this God-damned support from people he has historically and steadfastly eschewed just pissed me off. He eschewed black people all his life and then, like Clarence Thomas, the minute he gets jammed up he comes talking about 'Hey, I'm black.' " And the matter of spousal abuse should remind us of another role-reversal entailed by Simpson's iconic status in a culture of celebrity: Nicole Brown Simpson would have known that her famous-not-black husband commanded a certain deference from the L.A.P.D. which she, who was white but not yet famous, did not.

"It's just amazing that we in the black community have bought into it," Anita Hill says, with some asperity, and she sees the manufacture of black-male heroes as part of the syndrome. "We continue to create a superclass of individuals who are above the rules." It bewilders her that Simpson "was being honored as someone who was being persecuted for his politics, when he had none," she says. "Not only do we forget about the abuse of his wife but we also forget about the abuse of the community, his walking away from the community." And so Simpson's connection to a smitten black America can be construed as yet another romance, another troubled relationship, another case study in mutual exploitation.

Yet to accept the racial reduction ("WHITES V. BLACKS," as last week's *Newsweek* headline had it) is to miss the fact that the black community itself is riven, and in ways invisible to most whites. I myself was convinced of Simpson's guilt, so convinced that in the middle of the night before the verdict was to be announced I found myself worrying about his prospective sojourn in prison: would he be brutalized, raped, assaulted? Yes, on sober reflection, such worries over a man's condign punishment seemed senseless, a study in misplaced compassion; but there it was. When the verdict was announced, I was stunned—but, then again, wasn't my own outrage mingled with an unaccountable sense of relief? Anna Deavere Smith says, "I am seeing more than that white people are pissed off and black people are ecstatic. I am seeing the difficulty of that; I am seeing people having difficulty talking about it." And many are weary of what Ishmael Reed calls "zebra journalism, where everything is seen in black-and-white." Davis says, "I have the feeling that the media are in part responsible for the creation of this so-called racial divide—putting all the white people on one side and all the black people on the other side."

Many blacks as well as whites saw the trial's outcome as a grim enactment of Richard Pryor's comic rejoinder "Who are you going to believe—me, or your lying eyes?" "I think if he were innocent he wouldn't have behaved that way," Jamaica Kincaid says of Simpson, taking note of his refusal to testify on his own behalf. "If you are innocent," she believes, "you might want to admit you have done every possible thing in the world—had sex with ten donkeys, twenty mules—but did not do this particular thing." William Julius Wilson says mournfully, "There's something wrong with a system where it's better to be guilty and rich and have good lawyers than to be innocent and poor and have bad ones."

The Simpson verdict was "the ultimate in affirmative action,"

Amiri Baraka says. "I *know* the son of a bitch did it." For his part, Baraka essentially agrees with Shapiro's rebuke of Cochran: "Cochran is belittling folks. What he's saying is 'Well, the niggers can't understand the question of perjury in the first place. The only thing they can understand is 'He called you a nigger.' " He alludes to *Ebony*'s fixation on "black firsts"—the magazine's spotlight coverage of the first black to do this or that—and fantasizes the appropriate *Ebony* accolade. "They can feature him on the cover as 'The first Negro to kill a white woman and get away with it,' " he offers acidly. Baraka has been writing a play called *Othello, Jr.,* so such themes have been on his mind. The play is still in progress, but he *has* just finished a short poem:

> *Free Mumia!*
> *O.J. did it*
> *And you know it.*

"Trials don't establish absolute truth; that's a theological enterprise," Patricia Williams says. So perhaps it is appropriate that a religious leader, Louis Farrakhan, convened a day of atonement; indeed, some worry that it is all too appropriate, coming at a time when the resurgent right has offered us a long list of sins for which black men must atone. But the crisis of race in America is real enough. And with respect to that crisis a mass mobilization is surely a better fit than a criminal trial. These days, the assignment of blame for black woes increasingly looks like an exercise in scholasticism; and calls for interracial union increasingly look like an exercise in inanity. ("Sorry for the Middle Passage, old chap. I don't know *what* we were thinking." "Hey, man, forget it—and here's your wallet back. No, really, I want you to have it.") The black economist Glenn Loury says, "If I could get a million black men together, I wouldn't march them to Washington, I'd march them into the ghettos."

But because the meanings of the march are so ambiguous, it would become itself a racial Rorschach—a vast ambulatory allegory waiting to happen. The actor and director Sidney Poitier says, "If we go on such a march to say to ourselves and to the rest of America that we want to be counted among America's people, we would like our family structure to be nurtured and strengthened by ourselves and by the society, that's a good point to make." Maya Angelou, who agreed to address the assembled men, views the event not as a display of male self-affirmation but as a ceremony of penitence: "It's a chance for African-American males to say to African-American females, 'I'm sorry. I am sorry for what I did, and I am sorry for what happened to both of us.' " But different observers will have different interpretations. Mass mobilizations launch a thousand narratives—especially among subscribers to what might be called the "great event" school of history. And yet Farrakhan's recurrent calls for individual accountability consort oddly with the absolution, both juridical and populist, accorded O. J. Simpson. Simpson has been seen as a symbol for many things, but he is not yet a symbol for taking responsibility for one's actions.

All the same, the task for black America is not to get its symbols in shape: symbolism is one of the few commodities we have in abundance. Meanwhile, Du Bois's century-old question "How does it feel to be a problem?" grows in trenchancy with every new bulletin about crime and poverty. And the Simpson trial spurs us to question everything except the way that the discourse of crime and punishment has enveloped, and suffocated, the analysis of race and poverty in this country. For the debate over the rights and wrongs of the Simpson verdict has meshed all too well with the manner in which we have long talked about race and social justice. The defendant may be free, but we remain captive to a binary discourse of accusation and counteraccusation, of grievance and countergrievance, of victims and victimizers. It is a discourse in which O. J. Simpson is a suitable remedy for Rodney King, and reductions in Medicaid are entertained as a suitable remedy for O. J. Simpson: a discourse in which everyone speaks of payback and nobody is paid. The result is that race politics becomes a court of the imagination wherein blacks seek to punish whites for their misdeeds and whites seek to punish blacks for theirs, and an infinite regress of score-settling ensues—yet another way in which we are daily becoming meta and meta. And so an empty vessel like O. J. Simpson becomes filled with meaning, and more meaning—more meaning than any of us can bear. No doubt it is a far easier thing to assign blame than to render justice. But if the imagery of the court continues to confine the conversation about race, it really will be a crime.

# The Charmer

❖

The drive to Louis Farrakhan's house, on South Woodlawn Avenue, took me through the heart of black Chicago—past campaign billboards for a hot city-council race, past signs for Harold the Fried Chicken King and Tony's Vienna Beef Hotdogs. Much of the area is flecked with housing projects and abandoned lots, but when you turn the corner at Woodlawn and Forty-ninth Street things abruptly look different. You can see why the late Elijah Muhammad, who led the Nation of Islam—the Black Muslims—for almost four decades, built his house in this little pocket of opulence. It's a street of large brick houses, enshrining the vision of black-bourgeois respectability, and even grandeur, that has always been at the nostalgic heart of the Nation of Islam's creed. The neighborhood, known as South Kenwood, is integrated and professional. In 1985, Farrakhan bought Elijah Muhammad's house—a yellow-brick neo-Mediterranean structure—and he has lived there ever since; the creed and the neighborhood remain intact.

It was a warm spring morning the week after Easter, 1996, and everything was peaceful, quiet, orderly, which somehow made matters all the more unsettling. I wasn't expecting the Death Star, exactly, but I wouldn't have been surprised to see a formidable security detail: the Fruit of Islam patrolling the roof and gates with automatic weapons; perhaps a few attack dogs roaming the grounds. In fact, the only security measure in evidence was a rather elegant wrought-iron fence. After I spent a minute or so fumbling around, trying to find a hinge, a baby-faced young man with close-cropped hair and gleaming black combat boots came over and flicked the gate open. Together, we walked up a short, curved driveway, past two marble lions flanking the front door, and into the house that Elijah Muhammad built.

People in the Nation of Islam refer to the house as the Palace, and it does have an undeniable, vaguely Orientalist splendor. There is a large center hall, two stories high, filled with well-tended tropical plants, some reaching up between ten and twenty feet. Sunlight floods in from a huge dome of leaded glass; at its center, Arabic characters spell out "Allahu Akbar," or "God Is Great." To the right is a large and vibrant triptych: the Nation's founder, Wallace D. Fard; his prophet, Elijah Muhammad (with a set of gold keys in his hands); and Elijah's successor as the head of the Nation, a very youthful-looking Louis Farrakhan. The walls are spanking white, the floors are tiled in white and gray marble. A C-shaped sofa is upholstered in white fabric and covered with clear vinyl—the same stuff my mother put on to protect *her* good furniture, back in Piedmont, West Virginia.

Farrakhan's wife, Khadijah, came down to check on me, and to make sure everything was tidy now that company had arrived. Khadijah Farrakhan has a soft brown face and a warm smile. I had a bad cold that day, and she offered me some advice on how to unblock my ears, which still hadn't recovered from the flight to Chicago. "Open your mouth wide, and shift your jaw from side to side," she said, helpfully demonstrating the motion. We stood facing each other, our mouths contorted like those of a pair of groupers.

That is about when America's great black Satan himself came

gliding into the room. Farrakhan was resplendent in a three-button suit of chocolate-brown silk, a brown-and-beige bow tie, and a matching pocket square. Only then did I notice that my own trousers did not match my suit jacket. Moments later, I referred to his wife as "Mrs. Muhammad," and there was a glint of amusement in his eyes. The truth is, I was having a bad case of nerves that morning. For good reason. After I criticized Farrakhan in print three years ago, a few of his more impetuous followers had shared with me their fervent hope for my death. Now that I was face to face with Farrakhan, I did feel, in fact, pretty deathly. "I'm a wounded warrior," I admitted.

Farrakhan, relaxed and gracious, made sure I was supplied with hot tea and honey. "Get the battlefield ready," he said, laughing. For the rest of a long day, we sat together at his big dining-room table, and it became clear that Farrakhan is a man of enormous intelligence, curiosity, and charm. He can also be deeply strange. It all depends on the moment and the subject. When he talks about the need for personal responsibility or of his fondness for Johnny Mathis and Frank Sinatra, he sounds as jovial and bourgeois as Bill Cosby; when he is warning of the wicked machinations of Jewish financiers, he seems as odd and obsessed as Pat Robertson.

Not long after we began talking, Farrakhan told me about an epiphany he had recently about the waning of white cultural supremacy. Farrakhan takes moments of revelation very seriously; one of his most profound occurred, he has said, while he was aboard a giant spacecraft. This particular revelation, less marvelously, took place at a Lionel Ritchie concert. There Farrakhan saw a beautiful young blond woman and her little daughter, who both clearly idolized this black performer. And when Ritchie told the mostly white crowd to raise their hands in the air almost everyone joined in. Farrakhan saw this as something not only amazing but telling.

"I see something happening in America," he said. "You go into white folks' homes, you see Michael Jackson on the wall, you see Michael Jordan on the wall, you see Hank Aaron on the wall. Their children are being influenced by black faces. And I say to myself,

'Where is this leading?' And what I see is that white supremacy is being challenged in so many subtle and overt ways, and gradually children are losing that thing about being superior."

The myths of black superiority are also going by the wayside. Someone might believe that a white cannot play the horn, he said, "then Kenny G. blows that all away." (Joe Lovano, maybe, but Kenny G.?) It used to be that white people listened to the blues but could never sing it. Now, though, "white people are experiencing that out of which the blues came," he said. "White people are suffering. Now you drive your streets and you see a white person with stringy hair sitting by the side of the road plucking his guitar, like we used to do in the South. Now *they're* into that." What people must do is "outgrow the narrowness of their own nationalistic feelings," Farrakhan declared. "When we outgrow the color thing, outgrow the race and the ethnic thing, outgrow the religious thing to see the oneness of God and the oneness of humanity, then we can begin to approach our divinity."

I scratched my head: we'd gone from Kenny G. to God in a matter of seconds; "the blue-eyed devils"—Elijah Muhammad's favorite designation for white folk—are learning the blues, and we're mightily impressed.

It turns out that there is in Farrakhan's discourse a strain that sounds awfully like liberal universalism; there is also, of course, its brutal opposite. The two tendencies, in all their forms, are constantly in tension. Pundits like to imagine that Farrakhan is a kind of radio program: the incendiary Louis Farrakhan Show. In fact, Farrakhan is more like a radio station: what you hear depends on when you tune in. His talk ranges from far-fetched conspiracy theories to Dan Quayle–like calls for family values. Farrakhan really does believe that a cabal of Jews secretly controls the world; he also suspects, I learned later in our conversation, that one of his own grandparents was a Portuguese Jew. Apologists and detractors alike feel free to decide which represents the "real" Farrakhan. The result may score debating points, but it has little to do with the man who lives at South Woodlawn and Forty-ninth Street.

Much is made of Farrakhan's capacity to strike fear into the hearts of white liberals. And it does seem that for many of them Farrakhan represents their worst nightmare: the Nat Turner figure, crying out for racial vengeance. As Adolph Reed, Jr., writes of Farrakhan, "he has become uniquely notorious because his inflammatory national- ist persona has helped to center public discussion of Afro-American politics on the only issue (except affirmative action, of course) about which most whites ever show much concern: What do blacks think of whites?"

A subject that receives far less attention is the fear that Farrakhan inspires in blacks. The truth is that blacks—across the economic and ideological spectrum—often feel astonishingly vulnerable to charges of inauthenticity, of disloyalty to the race. I know that I do, despite my vigorous efforts to deconstruct that vocabulary of re- proach. Farrakhan's sway over blacks—the answering chord his rhetoric finds—attests to the enduring strength of our own feelings of guilt, our own anxieties of having been false to our people, of having sinned against our innermost identity. He denounces the fallen in our midst, invokes the wrath of heaven against us: and his outlandish vitriol occasions both terror and a curious exhilaration.

Farrakhan is a distinctive figure with a distinctive message, but it is a message that has a context and a history. In the summer of 1930, a door-to-door salesman appeared in the Detroit ghetto selling rain- coats and silks. In those days, he was known as Wallace D. Fard; later, in the literature of the Nation of Islam, his name would be given an Arabic form—Farrad Muhammad. Some say that Fard was a white man, and others believe he was an Arab; Farrakhan has said that Fard's mother was "from the Caucasus."

Fard told his customers in the early thirties that he carried silks of the same kind that Africans were still using. He seemed to know a great deal about Africa, and soon he was holding meetings about African history at the homes of various customers. For black people at that time, this was news they could use. He had, for instance, all sorts of dietary tips: he pointed out foods that were bad for black people, explaining that the people of their native land never touched them and were always in good health. Before long, Fard moved toward religious expostulations. If the diet that your African ancestors followed was best for you, so was their religion. As time went by, the numbers of people who wanted to attend Fard's meetings grew to the point where his followers rented a hall and called it the Temple of Islam. And so, while inner-city Detroit struggled through the Great Depression, a new religion was born.

Fard taught that although the world was still dominated by "the blue-eyed devils," they were only temporary interlopers. Fard himself had been sent to awaken the consciousness of the Black Nation, the earth's "Original Man." Those who sought to join Fard could send him their current surnames—their "slave names," that is—and receive their true Islamic surnames by return mail. In time, Fard began to refer to himself as the Supreme Ruler of the Universe. And then, in June of 1934, he mysteriously vanished, never to be seen again.

After the vanishing, Fard's fiery chief minister, Elijah Muhammad, (né Poole), declared Fard to have been an incarnation of Allah, thus elevating himself to the status of Prophet, or Messenger—Muhammad's title in the Koran. Fard's birthday, February 26, became a holiday, Saviour's Day, and the organizational—and doctrinal—basis for the Nation of Islam was established.

"I must create a system, or be enslav'd by another man's," William Blake wrote in *Jerusalem*. In that spirit, Elijah Muhammad's creed offered a unique creation myth, Leviticus-like strictures on diet and behavior, and a strong component of prophecy. In the world according to Elijah Muhammad, blacks were descended from the tribe of Shabazz, which "came with the earth," when an explosion separated the earth and the moon sixty-six trillion years ago. White people, by contrast, came into existence less than seven thousand years ago, the result of the genetic experiments of a wicked scientist named Yakub. Whites were drained not only of color but of humanity: "The human beast—the serpent, the dragon, the devil, and Satan—all mean one and the same; the people or race known as the white or Caucasian race, sometimes called the European race." Black Muslim theology features no afterlife; what it offers is the promise that the reign of the blue-eyed devils is nearing its end. One could be sure of this because of a particularly splendid element of Elijah's cosmogony: the whole of history was written ahead of time, by twenty-four black scientists, under the supervision of a twenty-fifth.

Not all doctrine pertained to such lofty matters. Elijah Muhammad also published several books on "How to Eat to Live." Tobacco and alcohol were forbidden, and so were corn bread and pork. Small navy beans were permissible; lima and pinto beans were not. The Messenger instituted for members a regime of two or more temple meetings a week. Men would be expected to do some proselytizing—or "fishing for the dead," as it was known. A woman's behavior was strictly circumscribed: she was not to let herself be alone in a room with any man who wasn't her husband; her dress had to be modest.

The idiosyncrasies of the Nation of Islam should not blind one to Elijah Muhammad's organizational genius. Fard was not the only black Messiah to have achieved prominence in the thirties, or the most influential, but his was the only legacy that has thrived. Similarly, the esoteric details of Black Muslim doctrine should not obscure the real sense of absence that Elijah Muhammad addressed. Louis Farrakhan told me that the Nation of Islam might be understood as a kind of Reformation movement within the black church—a church that had grown all too accommodating to American racism. It's true that, despite the prominence of such groups as the Southern Christian Leadership Conference during the civil-rights movement, most black churches were extremely conservative when it came to race matters. Dexter Avenue Baptist Church achieved legendary status because of the leadership of Martin Luther King, Jr., and yet that same church had fired King's predecessor, Vernon Johns, for protesting racism with too much zeal. Muhammad's fierce militancy and his inversion of reigning notions of racial inferiority should be seen in relation to the failures of the black churches—especially when it came to providing a moral language in which to address the political sins of state-sponsored racial inequality.

. . .

Louis Farrakhan, for his part, remains firmly tethered to the tradition of Christian homiletics. I asked him something that my father wanted to know: How did a good Episcopalian boy like Farrakhan, born Louis Eugene Walcott, end up leaving the true church?

Farrakhan laughed, and said I should tell my father that he never really left. "I thought I did," he said, "but my love is there, my roots are the church." And that's true: references to the Koran in his speeches are perfunctory, with passages from the Old and New Testaments taking pride of place.

"We were from St. Cyprian's"—an Episcopal church in the Roxbury section of Boston, where he grew up—"and I was in the choir," he went on to tell me. He still refers to Nathan Wright, the minister when he was growing up, as "Father Wright." Roxbury retains its hold on him in other ways, too. He spent his formative years in a bustling working-class neighborhood, which was populated by immigrants from the West Indies and boasted flourishing black-owned businesses and a thriving musical scene. It has been suggested that this experience of a tight-knit, prosperous, all-black community may undergird Farrakhan's conservative social views.

Born in 1933, Gene, as he was known, was the younger of two sons of Mae Clark, who was from Barbados. Gene was named after his father, a very light-skinned man from Jamaica; he was a philanderer, whom the family seldom saw—an exceptional circumstance in what was largely a community of intact families. Nathan Wright tells me the mother was "a little old-fashioned and a disciplinarian," even "a bit too strict." Mae Clark stressed education and paid for private music lessons for both her sons. Gene played the violin.

"When I was a young boy, hardly anybody in my all-black school could not read," Farrakhan recalled. "By the time I left the eighth grade, I knew every country on this earth, every capital. I knew their lakes and rivers, I knew what those countries produced for wealth." An honor student in high school, Gene studied, among other subjects, Latin and German, calculus and medieval history. He was also a star on the track team.

A couple of decades later, an accomplished scholar, musician, and athlete like Gene Walcott would have been given the financial aid to go to one elite university or another. In fact, in his high-school year-book Walcott wrote that he wanted to attend the Juilliard School of Music. Instead, in 1950 he went off to a teachers college for blacks in Winston-Salem, North Carolina, on an athletic scholarship. It was there, in the South, that he first experienced the full impact of racism. Once, stopping over in Washington on the way down, Far-rakhan decided to take in a movie, only to be told that tickets were not sold to Negroes. "A very close friend of mine had just been killed in Korea, and I walked down the street with a twenty-dollar bill in one hand, my wallet in the other, and at that point I was very, very angry with America," he said. "I started writing a calypso song called 'Why America Is No Democracy.' "

Within a few years, Gene Walcott had dropped out of college and taken up a career as a calypso singer, styling himself the Charmer. Among those charmed, he would recount years later, were many women: "I wouldn't go to bed with them. They wanted to give me money. . . . I told them, 'You're out of your damn mind.' They said, 'I think you're a faggot.' And I said, 'I *know* what I am. *You'll* never find out.' "

At about the same time as the Charmer was making a name for himself in Boston, Malcolm X was making the rounds as a Black Muslim preacher. "A friend of mine tried to get me to go to the temple," Farrakhan told me. "He said, 'You know, Gene, the white man is the Devil.' And I looked at him and said, 'If I go home tonight and my wife is in bed with a black man, *she* has committed adultery. And if I pick up a gun and kill them, *I* have committed murder. Where's the Devil in that?' He couldn't give me an answer. So I went on about my business—I wasn't about to join the Mus-lims." Still, Farrakhan described himself as having grown disillu-sioned with the Episcopal Church: "I couldn't understand why Jesus would preach so much love and why there was so much hate demonstrated by white Christians against black Christians."

In 1955, Walcott was playing the Blue Angel nightclub in Chicago, and he ran into some old friends who had got involved with the Nation of Islam. Walcott agreed to go to hear Elijah Muhammad preach at the mosque, and when he did he liked what he heard. That night, he went back to his hotel and started copying out the standard form letter to register as a Muslim:

> Dear Saviour Allah, Our Deliverer:
> I have attended the Teachings of Islam, two or three times, as taught by one of your ministers, I believe in it. I bear witness that there is no God but Thee. And, that Muhammad is Thy Servant and Apostle. I desire to reclaim my Own. Please give me my Original name. My slave name is as follows . . .

"I wouldn't call it a conversion experience, because I wasn't thoroughly convinced," Farrakhan said. In any case, he never received a reply. Then, just a few months later, when he heard Malcolm X preach, back on the East Coast, sympathy turned into something like conviction. "I'd never heard any man talk like that," Farrakhan went on, brightening now. "*Then* I was convinced that this was where I wanted to be."

While Farrakhan was telling his story, one of his daughters—a cheerful young woman in a sari-like dress—came by with a real-estate brochure. She wanted to show her father a picture of a three-story brownstone that she and her husband were hoping to buy; Farrakhan expressed his approval. By that point, I'd already met his son Nasir, a handsome, self-possessed young man who was interested in filmmaking, and another daughter who, Farrakhan boasted, was attending law school. Farrakhan plainly was a man who was enormously proud of his children and seemed to enjoy a relaxed and affectionate relationship with them. A bit later, we were visited by a pregnant granddaughter, in her early twenties, who tapped her belly and beamed. "I'm going to be a great-grandfather again," Farrakhan said, in the tone of a happy patriarch.

Farrakhan may have grown up without a father himself, but he speaks often of his mother and her brothers. Indeed, his early interest in the Black Muslims was only a new twist on an established family tradition. Most of Farrakhan's relatives were already followers of the most widely influential black nationalist of the century—Marcus Garvey, whose Universal Negro Improvement Association achieved fame and notoriety in the early twenties. Even so, the reaction of Gene's mother to his decision to join the Muslims was less than effusive. "She was a very reserved, strong woman," Farrakhan said, "and she said, 'It's very interesting.' She didn't say nay or yea."

Before long, her son emerged as Minister Louis X, of the Boston Temple. He had been trained well by Malcolm in public speaking, and he also brought his own particular gifts to the task. He recorded a song entitled "A White Man's Heaven Is a Black Man's Hell," which was a hit in Black Muslim circles, and he swiftly established himself as one of the most promising members of the ministry. He wrote—and performed in—a play entitled *Orgena* ("A Negro" spelled backward), a satire about assimilated blacks. He also wrote *The Trial,* in which a black prosecutor (usually played by Louis) tries the White Man for his myriad sins, and at the conclusion a black jury finds the defendant guilty and sentences him to death. Audiences responded with clamorous ovations.

But the Black Muslims would soon be appearing on a far larger stage, for Elijah Muhammad was discovering that even ostensibly hostile exposure in the mass media could serve him well. In the summer of 1959, Mike Wallace and Louis Lomax produced a television documentary on the Black Muslims, a group that then numbered less than thirty thousand. The Nation seemed to arouse alarm in white audiences, but that alarm only deepened its appeal to its natural constituency. The religious scholar C. Eric Lincoln, who in 1961 published a landmark study of the Nation of Islam, points out that weeks after the documentary appeared Muhammad's following doubled in size.

Malcolm X was the public, charismatic face of the Nation of Islam in these years, while Louis, eight years his junior, proved his best student. In 1964, however, Malcolm broke with the Nation of Islam, telling newspapers that he had been disillusioned by discovering that Elijah Muhammad had fathered children with his young secretaries. (Since the facts of Muhammad's philandering had long been an open secret among the Muslim elite, Malcolm's claim to have been shocked by such revelations struck his brethren as spurious and vengeful, aimed solely at causing embarrassment.) And Louis proved himself staunchly loyal to the Nation of Islam, denouncing in thunderous tones the Judas in its midst.

In a column that appeared in December of that year in *Muhammad Speaks,* the Nation of Islam's weekly newspaper, Louis wrote some now notorious words: "The die is set, and Malcolm shall not escape. . . . Such a man as Malcolm is worthy of death." Malcolm was assassinated in Harlem on February 21, 1965. Farrakhan has been dogged by speculation that he was somehow involved in the killing. One of the men convicted of the murder said that once Malcolm had been denounced as a traitor, he simply understood it to be his duty to take him out. In recent years, Farrakhan has admitted his responsibility in helping to create the poisonous atmosphere in which the killing took place; still, he denies any more direct involvement.

Just as Fard's disappearance had propelled Elijah Muhammad into preeminence, Farrakhan was now left to fill the void left by Malcolm. By the end of the year, Farrakhan had assumed Malcolm's old position as minister of the Harlem Mosque No. 7 and as Elijah Muhammad's National Representative. Yet for some the aura of regicide would never fade. Eldridge Cleaver, who considers the assassination of Malcolm one of the crimes of the century against black people, speaks about the succession bitterly: "It was the old show-business adage: 'The show must go on.' And so, with Malcolm not being present, where was the best clone they could find? Farrakhan gravitated to the top of the heap as the slime-ball, scheming, renegade bandwagoner that he is. He was able to get that position because, unlike any of the others around him, he was able to sing Malcolm's song."

In recent years, Malcolm has been retrieved by the mainstream as a palatable culture hero, whose path to enlightenment can be contrasted with Farrakhan's blinkered vision. The civil-rights activist Julian Bond says, "Malcolm grew. Farrakhan never did." It's hard to speak conclusively about Malcolm, since he was assassinated so soon after he announced his universalist creed, but the fact remains that, his conversion to Sunni Islam aside, he never really relinquished black nationalism. Like Malcolm, Farrakhan says that we must learn to move beyond color, and transcend all the divisions of humanity; like Malcolm, he asks the black community to develop its own self-reliance in the meantime. So the supposed contrast between the two men can seem more convenient than convincing.

It's equally difficult to recapture a sense of the enmity that existed between black radicals and the civil-rights mainstream in the sixties. Malcolm and Martin Luther King (whom Malcolm used to refer to as the Reverend Dr. Chicken Wing) have in some measure been melded through martyrdom. But the Muslims' rhetoric was far from conciliatory. "I was a Muslim then," Farrakhan said to me. "I wasn't for integration—I was a separatist. I thought Dr. King wasn't going in the right direction." But he also spoke of these tensions as part of a historical pattern. "In all the years of our progress in our century, there have always been these two poles. The masses are hearing the arguments like a tennis match, and all the time there is a level of consciousness coming up." This was also true during the civil-rights era, when Malcolm X and the nationalists were squaring off against Dr. King and the integrationists.

"The argument was healthy," Farrakhan went on. "You can see it now, when you are getting old and about to die. We've tried socialism, some have tried Communism, we've tried nationalism, we've tried Americanism, we've tried integration. But in all these experiments we've become wiser, and what I see today is that there is and was good in every step that we made, and now what we need is not a thesis and an antithesis—what we need is a synthesis of the best ideas of this hundred years of struggle. And that's why in my maturity or my process of maturing I fell in love with Dr. King."

In the sixties and seventies, the Nation of Islam also began to attract followers for its level of discipline, its political savvy, and its emphasis on self-help. The eminent African-American novelist Leon Forrest served as managing editor of *Muhammad Speaks* in the early seventies, when many of its editors and writers were, like him, non-

Muslims. He recalls that Elijah Muhammad was so politically agile that he ordered the paper not to write anything bad about Richard Nixon, hoping to profit from Nixon's proposal to set up enterprise zones in the inner city. That model of economic self-reliance was altogether consonant with the preachings of the Messenger. "The base of Elijah's movement and personality was steeped in a real deep conservatism," Forrest says. "Any number of whites who knew I worked for the Nation of Islam would say, 'You know, I really admire the Muslims.' And it was because it represents all the old American values of thrift and hard work, discipline, respect for the family and the women. Keep to yourself. Build small businesses. All the old American values, really. And then Elijah put in a little radical stuff here and there. But when you think about all the in-your-face, ready-to-duke-it-out vision people have of the Muslims, how many white people did they kill?"

As Elijah Muhammad's health declined, in the early seventies, many people believed that he was grooming Farrakhan to be his successor. And yet when Muhammad lay dying, in 1975, he designated not Farrakhan but, rather, his own son, Wallace Deen Muhammad. It was a bizarre choice. Wallace—or Warith, as he then renamed himself—had sided with Malcolm X against his father in the sixties, and had even been excommunicated for several years. He had also been taking very seriously his studies of Sunni Islam, and the teachings of his father had struck him as essentially heretical. Now that he was at last at the helm of his father's movement, he renounced the doctrines of Yakub, of racial demonology, of the divinity of Fard, even of his own father's status as prophet. He also set about divesting himself of Nation properties; soon an estate thought to be worth as much as a hundred million dollars had gone the way of the original Black Muslim doctrine.

By 1977, Louis Farrakhan had had enough. He announced that he was breaking with Warith's organization in order to reestablish the Nation of Islam according to the original tenets of the Messenger. Carrying on the tradition of *Muhammad Speaks,* Farrakhan started up *The Final Call,* in which Elijah Muhammad's credo would be faithfully reproduced in every issue. Farrakhan also revived the creation myth of Yakub.

As a literary critic, I've long been impressed by Elijah Muhammad as a man who invented his own mythology. I asked Farrakhan whether he really believed the story of Yakub—or was it better understood as a metaphor?

"It is not, in our judgment, metaphorical," Farrakhan replied stolidly. "The reason it seems like an invention—and I know you meant that in the best sense—is that it was not heard before. And, rather than credit it as a revelation, intellectually we give it a name that allows us to deal with it. Personally, I believe that Yakub is not a mythical figure—he is a very real scientist."

Nevertheless, Farrakhan does seem to have quietly downgraded Elijah Muhammad's cherished demonology. Muhammad was asked, a few years before his death, whether he would really label *all* white people "blue-eyed devils." His reply was "Whether they are actually blue-eyed or not, if they are actually one of the members of that race they are devils." But now Farrakhan said, "If you saw a picture of Master Farrad Muhammad"—that is, Wallace Fard, the founder—"he looked like a white man." He went on to say that many of his own relatives, including his father and his grandfather, were fair-skinned, so how could he hate people because of the color of their skin?

While the burden of slavery and history and societal structure cannot be ignored, he argued, black men and women must accept responsibility, "more so than in any other time in our history," for their failures. "It's so easy to put it on the white man," he said. "As long as we can beat up on white people and make the world think that everything that went wrong in the world is due to them and we had nothing to do with this, then we rob ourselves of the impetus, the motivation, and the inspiration for personal change and for accepting personal responsibility. I say to black audiences today, 'There was a time when you could blame the white man and there

was a time you could say the white man is a devil, but, with the way
we're raising hell today and the way we're inflicting evil and pain on
each other, you can't say that anymore.' "


In the late seventies and early eighties, Farrakhan was busy trying to
shore up the ranks of the Nation of Islam, both economically and
ideologically, but the nation at large was barely aware of his existence. Then came 1984, Jesse Jackson's campaign for the presidency, and Farrakhan's decision to break with Elijah Muhammad's
principled abstention from politics.

Inspired by Jackson's campaign, Farrakhan registered to vote and
volunteered the Nation's Fruit of Islam to provide security for Jackson. According to Farrakhan, Jackson's bid alarmed Jews, who distrusted his attitude toward Israel, and sought to derail the campaign
by using Farrakhan's extremist rhetoric against Jackson. The wildly
menacing statements, the apocalyptic imagery of race warfare, and
all the other staples of Black Muslim oratory played well at Mosque
Maryam, in Chicago, but were less warmly received on network
television. Farrakhan complained that Jews controlled the media,
and then raised his voice even more when he was attacked as a
"black Hitler." Around the same time, Jackson got himself in trouble when a black reporter quoted him referring to New York City as
"Hymie-town." Farrakhan thereupon made things worse for Jackson by urging the black community to ostracize the reporter, and
adding that one day traitors like him would be killed. Then came
the press conference at which, in reply to a question about the
Hitler comparison, Farrakhan said that any man who is talked about
forty years after his death is a great man but that Hitler was wickedly
great. (It's clear, in context, that Farrakhan meant "great" in the
same spirit in which *Time* named Hitler Man of the Year for 1938.)

"The next day, in the *Chicago Sun-Times*, in the *New York Post*:
'JACKSON PAL HAILS HITLER,' " Farrakhan recalled. "I took umbrage
at being compared with Hitler. I haven't even been arrested for spit-
ting on the sidewalk or doing anything violent to anyone. And now

you're going to call me a Hitler, like I'm planning to do something evil to Jewish people?"

Four months later, Farrakhan made a radio broadcast during which he talked about Israelis' "using God's name to shield your dirty religion." Now he said, "Fine. I said that. They said I said 'gutter,' but it was 'dirty.' I had no reference whatsoever in my mind to Judaism. However, anybody who distilled that could say, and rightly so, that I was talking about Judaism. So the headline the next day was 'FARRAKHAN CALLS JUDAISM A GUTTER RELIGION.' "

It is true that the two things nearly everybody knows about Farrakhan—that he extolled Hitler as a great man and deplored Judaism as a "gutter religion"—are, strictly speaking, false. That point may not speak well of the accuracy of some of our leading media, but it hardly absolves him of the larger charge of anti-Semitism. And for all his talk of reconciliation, Farrakhan refuses to budge. "It doesn't make any difference what I say, how I explain myself," he said. "I have never got away from 'Judaism is a gutter religion,' 'Hitler is a great man.' " He shrugged. "I'm a *man*—I'm not afraid of white folk. And so if they got the nerve to say that about me, I got nerve enough to defend myself and to drop an accusation on them that I believe to be true. So the fight was on—me and the Jews." He spread his arms, holding up two clenched fists, like a pugilist.

If the public consternation over the Black Muslims in the late nineteen-fifties magnified Elijah Muhammad's influence, the controversy in the wake of the Jackson campaign performed a similar service for Farrakhan. David Jackson, of the *Chicago Tribune*, notes that Farrakhan's 1983 Christmas address attracted a small handful of listeners on folding chairs, whereas today he routinely commands audiences of ten thousand and more. The commentator Roger Wilkins says of Farrakhan's Jewish critics, "I'm not saying they're wrong to strike back—I'm never going to tell the guy whom somebody slams in the stomach, 'Well, here's what you must do now.' But once they struck back, he became a national figure. These attacks don't hurt him in his base; they enhance him, because he has told his people that though he is not anti-Semitic, there's this free-floating Zionist plot that is directed at him. So when the Anti-Defamation League attacks him, all he has to do is turn to his people and say 'See?' Then, of course, one of the messages is 'They are attacking me because I am supporting you and your interests.' "

Louis Farrakhan will say, up and down, that he reveres the Jewish people. Listen to him: "Personally, I don't know what this argument has served. Jewish people are the world leaders, in my opinion. They are some of the most brilliant people on this planet. The Jews are some of the greatest scientists, the greatest thinkers, the greatest writers, the greatest theologians, the greatest in music, the greatest in business. And people hate them sometimes because of envy, and because the Jews succeed in spite of the hatred of their Gentile brethren, or anybody else's hatred. I admire that, as God is my witness."

Farrakhan has a theological explanation for Jewish preeminence. His theory is that the Jews have had many prophets in their midst and so have been the greatest recipients of divine revelation, and that this elevated wisdom has translated itself into achievement of all kinds. "When you have a people who receive revelation," he says, "they can do very good things or they can become very base, evil, and use the revelation for wicked purposes."

For many years, Farrakhan has been saying that there is a small group of Jews who meet (variously) in a Park Avenue apartment or in Hollywood to plan the course of the nation. I had to ask, "Do you think that there's a cabal—that there's a central planning group within the Jewish community?"

"I do believe that," Farrakhan replied. "I believe that there are very, very wise Jews who plan good and there are very wise Jews who plan evil." He added, "I am not hateful. I am deeply respectful of the Jewish people, man. I know they are great, but I also know that there are some scoundrels among them. And those scoundrels have to be condemned by them. And if they don't condemn the scoundrels—well, that's all right. I will."

I began to focus on Farrakhan's reddish-ocher complexion and his silky, wavy hair—what we called "Jesus moss" when I was growing up. "Do you know anything about your white ancestry?" I asked him.

Farrakhan explained that his father was very light-skinned and had straight hair, and that his mother had told him his father's parentage was, in fact, white Portuguese. Then he said, "I'm going to tell you something. You really want to know what I think? I think they were members of the Jewish community." This sounds like a fantastical joke, but it is highly probable, given what we know about migration to the West Indies. Orlando Patterson, a historical sociologist at Harvard, who has made a study of merchant populations in the islands, confirms that nearly all people of Iberian descent in Jamaica and Barbados, even today, are of Sephardic Jewish ancestry.

"I believe that in my blood, and not in a bad way," Farrakhan said. "Because when I was a little boy I used to love listening to the Jewish cantors in Boston. They had a program, and every week I would listen. I was struck by the cantor, and I've always loved the way they sing or recite the Torah." Farrakhan is always happy to elaborate on his admiration for Jewish musicians. "When my mom put that violin in my hand and I fell in love with that instrument, I never was thinking Jew, Gentile, anything like that," he said. "But all my heroes were Jewish. The greatest was Jascha Heifetz, and I loved him then and I love him now. I was driving my car when it came over the news that Vladimir Horowitz, the pianist, had passed. I pulled my car over to the side of the road and I said a prayer for his soul."

He went on, "If in my lineage there are Jews, I would hope that in the end, before my life is over, I not only will have rendered a service to my own beloved community of black people but will also have rendered a service to the Jewish community." What he seemed to have in mind was not what most people would consider a service: he was evidently referring to the notorious book *The Secret Relationship Between Blacks and Jews,* published by the Nation of Islam, the implicit assumption of which is that a Jewish predilection for evil is visible throughout the centuries.

"You read *The Secret Relationship Between Blacks and Jews*," Farrakhan said.

"And critiqued it," I put in.

"And critiqued it," he said, nodding. "I didn't order anybody to research this. They wanted to defend me, so they went to research it. We are making the point that the Jewish people were involved in slavery, and seventy-five percent of the Jews owned slaves." He gave me a level look. "You have a relationship with Jews of scholarship and brilliance, whom you can admire and have a lovely friendship with," he said. "I know there are Jews like that and I could have a wonderful friendship with them. I'm hoping and I believe that in the future it will develop. Sometimes, Dr. Gates, when you are new in the neighborhood, you get in a fight and you bloody the guy's nose, and he bloodies your nose, and before you know it you end up being the best of friends. But you're not friends without mutual respect."

Farrakhan took a deep breath and continued, "But my point is I don't like our relationship with Jews. I think it's a weak relationship. I think it's a paternalistic relationship. I don't like a relationship where they are the agent or the manager and we are the talent alone. We bring a lot to the table, but we get so little from the table. The I.R.S. puts the principal in jail and the accountant gets away with the money. This is wrong. There is so much injustice here."

What is one to make of all this? Farrakhan isn't feigning admiration for Jews as a distraction from his hate-mongering. Rather, his love and his loathing flow from the same ideas. There's a sense in which Farrakhan doesn't want his followers to battle Jews, but, rather, wants them to *be* Jews. Yet when he describes Jews as "world leaders" it is a double-edged compliment. There is no sense in being gladdened when he extolls Jewish wisdom and troubled only when he warns of Jewish evil: both sentiments are sincere, and both are aspects of a single unhealthy obsession.

In speeches he has made over the past several years, Farrakhan stresses the fact that he is condemning only some Jews—the scoundrelly ones. But the question begged is one of relevance: What makes a scoundrel's ethnicity or religion of central concern to

Farrakhan or his audiences? Farrakhan protests that he didn't say all Jews, he said *some* Jews, but the protest misses the point. Partitive anti-Semitism remains anti-Semitism.

Consider, even, the figure that Farrakhan often returns to: that seventy-five percent of the Jews in the South owned slaves. He returns to it because, he says, no one has refuted it. It is a fact—the result of an 1830 survey—and not something just concocted. But facts, as Ronald Reagan once said, are stupid things. The historian Harold Brackman points out that in 1830 only a third of America's Jews lived in the South. Those Southern Jews tended to be middle-class urban dwellers, with small numbers of domestic servants; by contrast, Jewish representation among the plantation owners who held most of the slaves was minuscule. Furthermore, in 1830 black slaveowners outnumbered Jewish slaveowners by fifteen to one.

But the real question is why the results of this 1830 survey should be of such concern to a constituency that you might think had more pressing matters to contend with: mounting poverty, crime, AIDS. Farrakhan arouses the indignation of inner-city audiences when he speaks of an exploitative relationship between Jewish agents and black talent. You may cringe, but when you scan his flock you see that there's something bleakly comic about it, too. They're struggling to make ends meet. Agents? Accountants? What is Louis Farrakhan talking about? And why?

"Whenever our interests seemed diametrically opposed," Farrakhan told me, "Jews followed what they felt was in their best interest." And he cited Jewish opposition to Jackson's candidacy, and Jewish opposition to affirmative action. But since most whites opposed Jackson and most whites are hostile to affirmative action, one might think that the more interesting fact is that Jews are disproportionately represented among those whites who did support Jackson, and who favor measures like affirmative action. Blacks, Farrakhan has said, must pursue their self-interest. But hurling invective at liberal allies doesn't sound like prudent self-interest to me. Even if Farrakhan's discourse on the Jews can't be reduced purely to a matter of fear and loathing, it doesn't bespeak sweet reason, either.

. . .

The truly paranoid heart of Farrakhan's world view has been revealed in recent speeches in which he has talked about a centuries-
old conspiracy of international bankers—with names like
Rothschild and Warburg—who have captured control over the central banks in many countries, and who incite wars to increase the in-
debtedness of others and maximize their own wealth. The Federal
Reserve, the I.R.S., the F.B.I., and the Anti-Defamation League
were all founded in 1913, Farrakhan says (actually, the I.R.S. was
founded in 1862 and the F.B.I. in 1908, but never mind), and then
he poses the favorite rhetorical question of all paranoid historians:
"Is that a coincidence?"

What do you do with a religious demagogue who promulgates
the theory that Jewish financiers have manipulated world events for
centuries? Well, if you're a Republican contender for the presidency,
and the demagogue's name is Pat Robertson, you genuflect. It
turns out that Farrakhan's conspiracy theory of Jewish cabals is essentially identical to Robertson's. "Rest assured, there is a behind-
the-scenes Establishment in this nation, as in every other,"
Robertson writes in *The New World Order*, his recent best-selling
book. "It has enormous power. It has controlled the economic and
foreign policy objectives of the United States for the past seventy
years, whether the man sitting in the White House is a Democrat or
a Republican, a liberal or a conservative, a moderate or an extremist." Robertson goes on to inveigh against the tentacular Roth-
schilds and Warburgs. Michael Lind, who has analyzed Robertson's
conspiracy theories at length, suggests that not since the days of Father Coughlin has the grassroots right been as overtly anti-Semitic
as it is now.

And Farrakhan? He, too, believes all this conspiracy stuff, and
thinks he's just telling it like it is. He must realize that such talk goes
down well with inner-city audiences hungry for secret histories that
explain how things went wrong. He turns mainstream criticism to
his advantage, winning ovations by representing himself as the persecuted truth-teller. But turnabout isn't always fair play: and the

fact that Farrakhan is a black American only makes his deafness to historical context all the more dismaying. Within his own lifetime, one of every three Jews on the face of the earth died at the hands of a regime suffused by the same language about nefarious Jewish influence. Ultimately, Farrakhan's anti-Semitism has the characteristics of a psychological obsession, and once in a while he shows signs of recognizing this. "I would prefer that this whole conflict would go away, in truth," he said to me. His voice sounded husky, and a little tired. "But it's like I'm locked now in a struggle. It's like both of us got a hold on each other, and each of us is filled with electricity. I can't let them go, and they can't let me go."

Farrakhan's peculiar mixture of insight and delusion would be a matter of mainly academic interest if it weren't for his enormous populist appeal among black Americans—an appeal that was clearly demonstrated in the 1995 Million Man March. That occasion has been widely seen as an illustration both of Farrakhan's strengths and of his weaknesses. "If only somebody else had convened it," the liberal-minded are prone to say. But nobody else—not Colin Powell, not Jesse Jackson—could have.

Some of the most heartfelt tributes to the event's success are also the most grudging. There's little doubt, after all, that the Farrakhan phenomenon owes much to a vacuum of radical black leadership. (Jesse Jackson has emerged over the past decade as the leading spokesman of the American left, one could argue, rather than of black America.) "We have the worst leadership in the black community since slavery," Eldridge Cleaver maintains. "Farrakhan saw that vacuum, saw nothing motivating the people, no vision being projected to the people, and he came up with the defining event for a generation of people, this Million Man March."

Timing had a lot to do with the event's success, of course. As Roger Wilkins likes to say, Newt Gingrich was one of the main organizers of the march. "If the white middle class feels it's losing ground, the black working class and unskilled working class are being slaughtered—hit by a blitzkrieg that no one notices," Wilkins points out. "And their plight is not on anyone's agenda anymore. Farrakhan supplies an answer, and an emotional discharge."

Farrakhan's people have won some real credibility in the black community. "It's as if Malcolm was having a march on Washington," Robert Moses, the civil-rights activist and education reformer, says. And Wilkins says, "Nobody else can go into the prisons and save souls to the degree that they have. Nobody else is able to put as many neat and clean young people on the streets of the inner city as they are. You think about the fellows who are selling their papers as opposed to those fellows you see standing around the liquor stores. Their men have this enviable sense of discipline, orderliness, and human purpose." (The Nation of Islam continues to have very conservative sexual politics, and Farrakhan is vehemently anti-abortion, but he has also inveighed against domestic violence, and—in a sharp break from tradition—even named a woman to be a nation of Islam minister.) Hugh Price, the president of the National Urban League, calls the march "the largest family-values rally in the history of the United States." Indeed, another sign of its success was the number of mainstream civil-rights leaders who were present. Whatever their discomfort with Farrakhan's extremist rhetoric, they calculated that their absence might well imperil their legitimacy with the black public.

Attendance or nonattendance was a delicate decision. General Colin Powell was prominent among those blacks who decided that they could not afford to appear. When I asked Farrakhan if he would consider supporting a future Powell presidential bid, he said, "I don't want to support anybody because he's black—I think I have outgrown the need to support somebody because of the color of his skin. What is in the best interest of our people is really in the best interest of the country. So if General Powell had an agenda that is good for the totality of our people—the American people first—and in that package is something that can lift our people, he's got our support."

Farrakhan's level of support among black Americans is vigorously debated. If you gauge his followers by the number who regularly attend mosques affiliated with the Nation of Islam and eschew lima beans and corn bread, they are not very numerous. Estimates range from twenty thousand to ten times that. On the other hand, if you go by the number of people who consider him a legitimate voice of black protest, the ranks are much larger. (In a recent poll, more than half the blacks surveyed reported a favorable impression of him.) The march was inspired by the Muslims but not populated by them. Farrakhan knows that the men who came to the march were not his religious followers. They tended to be middle class and college-educated and Christian. Farrakhan is convinced that those men came "to a march called by a man who is considered radical, extremist, anti-Semitic, anti-white" because of a yearning "to connect with the masses."

Not everyone, to be sure, was quite so deeply impressed. "This was an opportunity for the black middle class to feel this symbolic connection, but what were the solutions that were proposed, except atonement?" Angela Davis asks. Julian Bond says bluntly, "You know, that Negro didn't even vote until 1984. He's the leader in the sense that he can gather people to him, but they don't go anyplace when they leave him." And Jesse Jackson, who addressed the marchers, now views the march as fatally flawed by its failure to reach out to Capitol Hill. "The 1963 March on Washington was connected to public policy—public accommodations," he says, and notes that the result was the signing into law of the Civil Rights Act the following year. By contrast, he argues, the Million Man March had "essentially a religious theme—atonement—disconnected from public policy," so it brought no political dividends in its aftermath. "On the very next day—the very next day, *the very next day*—there was the welfare bill," he said, referring to the House and Senate conferences to work out a final draft of a bill excusing the federal government from a degree of responsibility toward the poor. "The next day was the vote on the unfair sentence guidelines. The next day was the Medicare bill," another hostile measure. "The big debates in Congress took place between that Wednesday and Thursday. And so those who were taking away our rights and attacking us did not see any connection between the gathering and public policy." The lesson he draws is straightforward: "The march was essentially disconnected from our political leadership. Any mass action must be connected to the public-policy leaders."

Some critics express a sense that the mass mobilization may itself be a relic of a bygone era. It was an arena where Farrakhan was able to stake a claim for mass black leadership, in part because of the near-sacralization of the 1963 precursor; but its continued political viability has not been demonstrated. Indeed, the growing fragmentation of black leadership—the irrelevance of the old-fashioned notion of a "head nigger in charge"—is one sign that an elite now exists in black America that does enjoy an unmediated relation to power. Privately, many black leaders say that Farrakhan's moment has passed. Such remarks inevitably carry an air of wishful thinking. White liberal allies sometimes worry that pressure is required to keep black leaders from being "soft on Farrakhan": in reality, no love is lost among those who would compete for the hearts and souls of black America. At the helm of the mainstream black-advocacy groups are men and women who may say conciliatory things about the Nation of Islam, but their jaws are tense and their smiles are tight. They reassure themselves that Farrakhan is bound to remain a marginal phenomenon because of his extremism. Yet the organic leaders of the disenfranchised are seldom moderate in tone; and since, from all indications, the underclass is continuing to expand, Farrakhan's natural power base will only increase.

In the months following the march, Farrakhan dropped out of public view, and he spoke of having suffered from depression, in part because he was still being misrepresented by the press. This response highlights Farrakhan's paradoxical relation to the wider public—that of a pariah who wants to be embraced. "Both Malcolm and Farrakhan had a very tough ideology but at the same time wanted a degree of public acceptance in the white community," Ron Walters, a political scientist and an adviser to Jackson, says. "To me, that's a tremendous contradiction. I don't know whether it's a personality thing or just what happens to you when you reach a certain level of prominence—that you do want a sort of universal acceptance."

Such acceptance has been elusive so far. A few weeks before the

Million Man March, Farrakhan gave an interview to make it clear that when he referred to Jewish "bloodsuckers" he didn't mean Jews in particular—he meant all nonblack shopkeepers in the inner city, some of them Jewish but these days more often Koreans or Arabs. He must have found it galling when many newspapers wrested his remarks out of context, leaving the impression that he had merely repeated the original accusation: Farrakhan calls Jews bloodsuckers. Farrakhan's image also suffered when, early last year, the *Chicago Tribune* published an investigative series, by David Jackson and William Gaines, revealing financial disarray among Nation-owned businesses. Farrakhan's calls for economic self-sufficiency, it appeared, were not matched by his organization's performance.

Farrakhan hurt himself yet again, with his so-called World Friendship Tour, in January and February. He claims that his decision to make this trip to Third World capitals was a matter of divine inspiration, but it isn't hard to imagine human motivations as well. Public figures who feel that they have been badly used by the local papers often find that solace awaits them in admiring throngs overseas: call it the Jerry Lewis syndrome. Besides, how better to shore up your position as the leader of black America than by being received as such by foreign potentates?

The domestic fallout, however, has lingered. Even many of those who supported Farrakhan were chagrined to find him holding friendly meetings with some of the world's worst dictators: Nigeria's Sani Abacha, Libya's Muammar Qaddafi, Zaire's Mobutu, and Sudan's Omar al-Bashir. Ron Walters observes, "He gave all those people who wanted an opportunity not to have to deal with him the golden reason. The tremendous political capital of the march had been dissipated." Black nationalists were among those who were the most horrified. Molefi Kete Asante, the Afrocentric scholar, says, "What Farrakhan did, in my judgment, was to take the legitimacy of the march and put it in his back pocket, and march around to these terrible governments, as if somehow he were the leader of a million black people. That upset me."

It is a sore subject with Farrakhan. Sure, he met with dictators, he

said to me, but when you are dealing with atonement, sin, and reconciliation you don't travel to the blameless. "It's all right for Jesse
to sit down with George Wallace in Alabama and for them to pray
together—and there's applause," he went on. "But I can't go sit
down with my brother who is a sinner? Nixon died a hero, but I
cannot forgive a black man?" There was a surge of anger in his voice.
"That's the damnable thing that I hate about this whole damned
thing," he said. "If I go to a black man to retrieve him, all of a sudden I'm cavorting with a damned dictator, but Jesus could sit down
with the sinners and you give him honor and credit. And Reagan
can sit down with Gorbachev, and he gets honor and credit. He sits
with the evil empire, but I can't sit with my own brother. To hell
with you for that. That's why I am not a politician."

"Has the tour compromised the achievement of the march?" I
asked him.

He sounded subdued when he said, "If I lost momentum, I believe it's only temporary."


Farrakhan lays much stress on the imagery of dialogue and concili-
ation these days. Certainly the Farrakhan I met was a model of ci-
vility and courtesy. I was reminded of Eric Lincoln's account of the
last couple of visits he had paid to Farrakhan at his home: "Louie
insisted on getting down on his hands and knees on the floor to take
my shoes off. You know, I'm overweight and it's a difficult task to
get shoes and socks off. And so Louis said, 'I will do that.' And I
said, 'No, no.' And Louis said, 'No, I want to do it.' He took my
shoes off and rubbed my feet to get the blood circulating."

If the Farrakhan phenomenon remains disquieting, the man himself seems oddly, jarringly vulnerable. I met someone who was
eager, even hungry, for conversation; someone of great intelligence
who seemed intellectually lonely. In fiery speeches before packed
auditoriums, Farrakhan speaks of plots against his life, and does so
in alarmingly messianic tones. ("I don't care nothing about my
life," he told his audience on Saviour's Day in 1995, his voice breaking. "It's *your* life that I want to save!") To me he spoke of his mor-

tality in a quieter mode. He spoke movingly of watching the funeral of Yitzhak Rabin—about the tragedy of a wise and tempered elder statesman assassinated by a callow extremist. He spoke about having a growing appreciation for compromise, about coming to see the value in the positions of his ideological antagonists within the civil-rights tradition. And he told me about a fight of his own, against prostate cancer, over the past several years.

"At first, it was frightening to me—how could I have cancer? I've eaten well, I've tried to live clean. Then I fasted and I prayed and I went into the desert, and after a month I went and had an M.R.I. and one of those rectal ultrasounds, and all they could find was a little scar." He paused, and added quietly, "But then it came back." He looks in splendid health: he is sixty-three, and his skin remains soft and almost unlined. He recently made a health-and-exercise video, which shows him going through an arduous regimen of weight-training. And he *is* remarkably fit. He has undergone seed-implantation radiation-therapy for his cancer, and remains optimistic about the results. "I've never had to take a pain pill, and I hope and pray that God will bless me ultimately to overcome it. At least, all accounts up to date, the P.S.A."—the blood-screening test for prostate cancer—"has been normal. And so I'm going on with my life, but warning all of us that this is such a hell of a killer of our people. And when you reach your early forties, many of us won't like somebody poking around in our rectum, but we have to encourage our young men and our middle-aged brothers, and the population as a whole, to do that for themselves, because all we have is our health."

We all know that the world isn't divided between saints and sinners. And yet the private Farrakhan's very humanness—those traits of kindness, concern, humor—makes his paranoia all the more disconcerting. He rails against the way the mainstream has demonized him, and yet he refuses to renounce the anti-Semitic conspiracy theories that have made him anathema: to him, it would be like denying the law of gravity. And so he is trapped, immobilized by his contradictory desires. His ongoing calls for dialogue are seemingly heartfelt; he genuinely wants a seat at the table, craves the legitima-

tion of power. Yet he will not engage in the compromises and con-
cessions that true dialogue requires. He cannot afford to. This is a
man whose political identity is constituted by antagonism to the
self-image of America. To moderate his stance of unyielding opposition would be to destroy the edifice he has spent his life constructing. Moreover, Farrakhan knows that there are people around
him whose militancy puts his to shame. Some of them are former
lieutenants of his in the Nation of Islam, such as Khalid Muhammad, whom Farrakhan suspended after judging him to have been
*too* intemperate in his public pronouncements. Others have established an independent base of support, such as Silas Muhammad,
another Elijah loyalist who split with the organization, and whose
sect is now based in Atlanta. For leaders whose appeal is based on
intransigence, outrage, and wrath, there is always the danger of
being outflanked by those even more intransigent, more outrageous, more wrathful. This, in part, is why Farrakhan could not
truly atone even at his own day of atonement.

In the end, however, it isn't Farrakhan but Farrakhan's following
that demands explanation. We might start by admitting the moral
authority that black nationalism commands even among those
blacks who ostensibly disapprove of it. In the village where I grew
up, there was a Holiness Church, where people spoke in tongues
and fell down in religious ecstasy. It was not my church; my family
and I shunned the Pentecostal fervor. And yet, on some level, we
believed it to be the real thing, realer than our own, more temper-
ate Episcopal services. It was the place to go if you really needed
something—if you got desperately sick, say—because the Holy
Ghost lived there. (There are Reform Jews who admit to a similar
attitude toward their Hasidic brethren.) In this same vein, the assimilated black American, who lives in Scarsdale and drives a Lexus,
responds to Farrakhan and Farrakhanism as a presence at once
threatening and exhilarating, dismaying and cathartic. Though
blackness isn't exactly a religion, it has become invested with a

quasi-religious structure. Black nationalism is a tradition extending at least back to Martin R. Delany, in the nineteenth century. Cross it with the black messianic tradition—which spawned the legendary likes of Father Divine, Daddy Grace, and Prophet Jones—and you have the Nation of Islam.

Hard as it is to take stock of the organization's membership, it's harder to take stock of Farrakhan's place in the mind of black America. For his dominion is, in a sense, a dominion of metaphor, which is to say that it is at once factitious and factual. The political theorist Benedict Anderson has defined nations as "imagined communities," and the black nation is even more imaginary than most. We know that thirty-six million sepia Americans do not a collective make, but in our minds we sometimes insist upon it.

The Million Man March had all the hallmarks of a watershed event, yet a march is not a movement. I asked Farrakhan at one point what the country would look like if, by magic, he could turn his hopes into reality. The answer he gave me was long and meandering, but it centered on things like "revamping the educational system" to make it less Eurocentric—proposals of the sort debated by the New York State Board of Regents, rather than something that was radically transformative in any obvious way.

That was, in a sense, the most dismaying response I'd heard all day. Farrakhan is a man of visions. Just weeks before the march, he told congregants in a Washington, D.C., church about the "Mother Wheel"—a heavily armed spaceship the size of a city, which will rain destruction upon white America but save those who embrace the Nation of Islam. ("Ezekiel saw the wheel, way up in the middle of the air," in the words of the old spiritual.) What gave me pause was the realization that such visions coexist in Farrakhan's mind with a real poverty of—well, vision, which is to say a broader conception of the human future.

Farrakhan is a man of unhealthy fixations, but the reciprocal fixation on Farrakhan that you find in the so-called mainstream is a sign of our own impoverished political culture. Thirteen decades have passed since Emancipation, and half of our black men between twenty-four and thirty-five are without full-time employment. One black man graduates from college for every hundred who go to jail. Almost half of black children live in poverty. People say that Farrakhan is now the leading voice of black rage in America. One day, America will realize it got off easy.

# Belafonte's Balancing Act

❖

For one week in February of 1968, something strange happened to the *Tonight Show* with Johnny Carson: it became the *Tonight Show* with Harry Belafonte. I was a high-school student, growing up in Piedmont, West Virginia, a partly segregated hamlet in the Allegheny Mountains, and television was the only thing that connected any of us there with the larger world. Night after night, my father and I stayed up late to watch a black man host the highest-rated show in its time slot—history in the making.

This was the year my father and I bonded over the Vietnam War—or, anyway, over our ongoing arguments on the subject, the point being that it gave us something to talk about. By now, I knew I had the moral high ground, a fact I determined by a rough head count of the celebrities who had weighed in on my side. So it was in that spirit—vindication on my part, mistrust on his—that my father and I sat together on our rust-red brocatelle sofa in front of the television set. Who had ever seen so many famous black folks (Sidney Poitier, Bill Cosby, Lena Horne, Wilt Chamberlain, for starters) on the *Tonight Show?*

On the second evening, Martin Luther King, Jr., emerged from behind the curtain. "What do you have in store for us *this* summer?" Belafonte asked him, flashing a provocative smile: white folks were still reeling from the riots that had come with the previous year's long hot summer. The studio audience laughed nervously.

King, looking tired and a little heavy, announced that he was shifting his emphasis from strictly racial issues. "The time has come to bring to bear the power of the nonviolent direct-action movement on the basic economic conditions that we face all over the country," he said, in his rich, rolling baritone. He pointed out that poverty among blacks, Mexican-Americans, Puerto Ricans, American Indians, and Appalachian whites had reached "Depression levels."

"Then someone is lying to the American people," Belafonte declared, in a voice that was half silk, half outrage.

Back in Piedmont, I rose from my seat. "Go ahead, brother!" I shouted: Johnny Carson was never like this.

King went on to argue that the war in Vietnam was at odds with the war on poverty. "A major myth, the guns-and-butter philosophy," King said. All the money spent on that senseless war meant that "you don't get butter—in fact, you don't even get oleo!"

"Right on, Dr. King!" I yelled at the TV set. And my father snapped, "I *told* you he was a Communist."

"Do you fear for your life?" Belafonte asked King, abruptly striking a sombre note. King explained that he'd reconciled himself to the danger he faced. "Suffering is redemptive," he said. "If something happens to me, maybe something good will come of it." Enormous applause burst forth from the studio audience, and my eyes misted over.

Harry Belafonte: Was he not Negro manhood at its finest? Was he not the perfect hybrid of popular culture and political conscience? It was the air of principle, of moral certitude, of engagement—not to mention those teeth, those cheekbones. You simply didn't hear this kind of thing in those days, not on network TV. That week, I knew I had been witness to a great event, though in time it became less clear whether it was the start of something or the end. Two months after his appearance on the show, King was assassinated; Robert F. Kennedy, who had appeared later that week with Belafonte, was shot in June.


It's close to three decades later, and Harry Belafonte is giving me a tour of his Manhattan apartment, on West End Avenue. He's closing in on seventy, and his face isn't uncreased, but his mocha skin still has a glow and his movements have a rangy, almost feline grace. Two physical anomalies lend his presence a peculiar intensity. First, he's ever so slightly walleyed, and somehow the result is to make his gaze seem especially intimate. Second, his speaking voice is a husky whisper, which has the inadvertent effect of giving everything he says a tone of confiding urgency, though in fact it's just the aftermath of a long career. ("My chronic laryngitis," he said back in the fifties, "is the organic symptom of subconscious feelings of guilt about my success.") He's still the great talker he always was, though. Get him started on international politics and he'll perorate like Che Guevara or, anyway, Jesse Jackson. If he hadn't been Mr. Entertainment, he would have been huge on the hustings.

Belafonte bought the apartment building, one of the grandest on the street, in the late fifties; he sold off the apartments as co-ops a couple of years later but kept a floor for himself. Martin Luther King, Jr., who was a guest here often, described it as "palatial," and after visiting all twenty-one rooms I can see why. Belafonte and Julie, his wife of forty years, have made the place into a sort of museum. There are paintings by Marc Chagall and Diego Rivera; there must be half a dozen works by the African-American social realist Charles White. The décor has the settled air of mid-century leftism: canvases by artists who had congenial views on the relation between art and social action.

Photographs of Paul Robeson are prominent here, and for good reason. If Belafonte had a hero in life, it was Robeson, the legendary singer, actor, intellectual, social activist, and left-wing martyr. The shadow of Robeson haunted a generation of black artists and performers, and Belafonte, who loved him and witnessed his destruction during the Red Scare, was part of that generation. Belafonte's pronouncements on the state of the world retain an old-time Robesonian fervor. He says things like "Monopoly capitalism is bigger than government—it buys and sells governments." Despite the hushed gravel of his conversation, his singing voice is actually quite well preserved: even now, his "Daaay-o!" comes out full-throated enough for any banana loader to hear. A good thing, too, because— what with the legacy of colonial exploitation and the depredations of the United Fruit Company—he still worries about those dockworkers.

Politics, it sometimes seems, is what Belafonte did instead of the more wholesome, more *normal* preoccupations of the American superstar—namely, drugs, debauchery, and dissipation. On some level, surely, we want our idols to engage in the sins of the flesh— on our behalf, as it were—and, being obliging souls, they usually do. By contrast, the celebrity who makes heavy weather of his political convictions strikes us (when they are not our convictions) as recklessly indulgent: what's violated is the intricate, unwritten covenant between celebrities and their fans. We elevate them to godlike stature, but heaven forbid they should think they're better than us. If you follow.

Harry Belafonte was radical before it was chic and remained so long after it wasn't. He made decisions, in consequence, that hurt his career. Many of these decisions strike me as misguided, contradictory, shortsighted, and bullheaded—but impossible not to admire. If Belafonte is, as publicists say, "back," it helps to know what, in Belafonte's case, "back" really means.

For a couple of years in the late fifties, Belafonte was arguably the most desirable man in the Western world. He was the first black matinée idol in the history of the film industry. He was the first artist (of any color) in the history of the recording industry to have a platinum album. As a live performer, he was unrivaled both in the size of the crowds he attracted and in the size of his contracts. Such success could be explained by his being a brilliant actor with an amazing voice, except that he wasn't a brilliant actor and didn't have an amazing voice. It was nothing so undemocratic as supernal talent that made Belafonte a demigod.

Over the past year, I've heard dozens of explanations of what did make him one, and why he survived. The critic Stanley Crouch says, "I never underestimate the skin-tone factor. The thing is, he wasn't *black* black." Johnny Carson tells me, "I think people perceive him as a nice person, and if people seem to like you, that's half the game in the entertainment business." And, Carson delicately explains, the comfort factor figures all the larger when you bring in the race factor: "That's why today, for example, a lot of white Americans find great comfort with a Colin Powell and find *dis*comfort with a Jesse Jackson. Jesse Jackson, who has the strident cadence of a preacher, gets people excited. Colin Powell is not perceived as a threat. Perception is a lot in this business." The explanation I like the best, though, comes from the great folk singer Odetta. Speaking as if to a slow child, she says, "Did you get a look at the man?"


Belafonte points out that he was born the same year, 1927, that Marcus Garvey was deported to Jamaica from the United States. But while Garvey wasn't without his influence in the Belafonte family, neither was he the household god he had been for many other West Indians in New York. Though Belafonte's mother was from Jamaica and his father from Martinique, both his mother's mother and his father's father (a gentleman named Bellanfanti, from Marseilles) were white. Belafonte was born in New York and spent most of his early years there; but in 1935, when riots and looting erupted in Harlem, his mother, a domestic worker, decided to take her family back to Jamaica. Belafonte spent the next five years in the Blue Mountains, in St. Anne's, and in Kingston.

Sidney Poitier, who is Belafonte's best friend and nearly exact contemporary, says that the childhood years they spent in the West Indies gave them a psychological advantage: colonialism aside, growing up in a black-majority country meant that most of the doctors, nurses, lawyers, and policemen you encountered were black. "I firmly believe," Poitier says, "that we both had the opportunity to arrive at the formation of a sense of ourselves without having it fucked with by racism as it existed in the United States."

In 1940, Belafonte returned to Harlem, and ended up in a largely Italian neighborhood. On the streets, kids squared off as the Hawks versus the Scorpions. Most of Belafonte's relatives in America, he recalls, were in rackets like the numbers business. Nor did school provide any respite: burdened by dyslexia, he dropped out after ninth grade. He finally escaped from the neighborhood, at seventeen, by joining the Navy. He scrubbed the decks of ships in port— the sort of menial work that most Negroes were assigned. It wasn't a career, but it was an education. For it was in the Navy that he was radicalized.

"I ran into a group of young men who, as it turned out, were the intellectuals in our crowd—Pullman-car porters, college graduates," Belafonte says. He mostly sat and listened until one of them handed him *Color and Democracy,* by W. E. B. Du Bois. Belafonte struggled with the words, spending hours poring over a single paragraph. He recalls, "I discovered that at the end of some sentences there was a number, and if you looked at the foot of the page the reference was to what it was all about—what source Du Bois gleaned this information from. So when I was on leave, going into Chicago, I went to a library with a long list of books. The librarian said, 'That's too many, young man. You're going to have to cut it down.' I said, 'I can make it very easy. Just give me everything you got by Ibid.' She said, 'There's no such writer.' I called her a racist. I said, 'Are you trying to keep me in darkness?' And I walked out of there angry."

In the Navy, stationed near Newport News, Virginia, in 1944, he met Margurite Byrd, a campus beauty at the nearby Hampton Institute. They were an odd couple from the start. Margurite was a sorority sister and a class officer, from a middle-class family in Washington, D.C. She had grown up in the insular comfort of the black bourgeois world, segregated but secure; her perspective on racial politics couldn't have contrasted more strongly. She later recalled, "Our courtship was one long argument over racial issues."

And Belafonte really was, by all accounts, an angry young man out of a juvie-menace flick. For instance, he was given to defacing subway posters that annoyed him—like one for a skin lotion that promised to preserve the soft white beauty of your hands. "What about *Negro* hands?" the young Belafonte scrawled in pencil. Margurite has said, "He reminded me of a big kid who was about to get into trouble if somebody didn't watch and help him. I had to keep him from becoming a delinquent." They were married in June, 1948, and their first child, Adrienne, was born the following year.

Shortly after leaving the Navy, Belafonte saw a play at the American Negro Theatre, in Harlem, and decided that he had glimpsed his destiny. He joined the A.N.T., initially working backstage, and there he and another aspiring actor, Sidney Poitier, began their nearly fifty-year friendship. From the beginning, it was a complicated relationship—compounded of affection, admiration, and rivalry. "Harry was then very competitive and I was then very competitive," Poitier says. "Harry Belafonte is today very competitive and Sidney Poitier is today very competitive. And then there was the fact that we were eligible for pretty much the same kind of parts."

Belafonte made his stage debut as the juvenile lead in an A.N.T. production of *Juno and the Paycock;* parts in other plays followed. Paul Robeson was in the audience at one of those performances, and told him afterward, "Job well done, young man." Belafonte felt anointed. Poitier says, "I remember times when he and I would meet Robeson in a bar on Fifth Avenue just off a Hundred and Twenty-fifth Street, and sit there and talk. He was very fond of Harry. And Harry loved him."

These were tough times for Belafonte and Poitier both; and they were better at concocting schemes to get rich quick than at making ends meet. Poitier still remembers a plan to bottle and sell an extract of conch, a shellfish that, in the Caribbean, anyway, was reputed to be an aphrodisiac. At another point, the two decided that their fortune lay in standup comedy, and they spent weeks practicing routines that they'd perform as the comic duo Belafonte & Poitier, until they figured out that their routine was about as effective as their aphrodisiac.

In 1948, Belafonte was performing in an A.N.T. production of a play called *Days of Our Youth,* with Poitier serving as his understudy.

Belafonte had a job as a janitor's assistant, bagging garbage, but he paid someone else to cover for him during his evening performances. "This particular night, the person who was covering for me couldn't do it, and I had to go take care of the garbage," he recalls. "That was the night Sidney Poitier went on for me. That was also the night some people from downtown were coming up to look at casting an all-black show of *Lysistrata*. So Sidney got the job, which led to his being cast opposite Richard Widmark in the film *No Way Out*—and on from there." As a result, Belafonte has long joked that Poitier's career is "based on garbage." His daughter Shari Belafonte-Harper sees it as a joke with dimensions: "They've been best friends forever, but—and I'm being a junior psychologist here—Daddy has never forgiven Sidney for stealing his career."

Belafonte's break came when a friend coaxed him into appearing on amateur night at the Royal Roost jazz tavern, and he ended up landing a full-time gig. He'd done some singing in a musical once, but singing had never been a consuming passion. Still, a job was a job. He started as a jazz singer but soon switched to a pop repertoire—songs like "Lean on Me," "Pennies from Heaven," and one of his own composition, entitled "Recognition." In clubs, he was billed as the Gob with a Throb, and for his act he sat on a stool wearing a dinner jacket and a St. Christopher medal. Jack Rollins, who was soon to be his manager, describes his routine in those days as a "vanilla imitation of Billy Eckstine." "That's probably a fair description," Belafonte admits.

In 1950, Belafonte, with two friends, opened a hamburger joint in the Village, called the Sage; it lasted all of eight months, but it did provide him with rehearsal space to work after hours on his new act—as a folksinger. Certainly folk music was in the air: the jukebox at the Sage played Burl Ives, Josh White, and the Weavers. And this was a musical genre that somehow resonated with his political sensibilities. "People see Harry as the Adonis—sensual and sexy, and all that," Poitier points out. "But when the same remarkable presence was singing ballads they did not electrify the world. He wanted what he believed in to be a part of his work. That's what took him to folksinging. The whole history of black people was in the texture of folksinging." To the usual folk repertoire Belafonte added a particular emphasis on West Indian folk songs.

The larger cultural milieu was changing in auspicious ways, too. Imprinted on Belafonte's memory to this day is a photograph he saw in the April 24, 1950, issue of *Life,* which showed Billy Eckstine being embraced by a white woman. "Nat King Cole, who was one of the greatest singers in pop culture, didn't quite make it across the line, because of his physical cut, his fully Afrocentric being," Belafonte says matter-of-factly. "Billy Eckstine—light-skinned, gloriously good-looking, suave—just had people swooning all over the place. And when that photo hit, in this national publication, it was as if a barrier had been broken."

In 1951, another light-skinned, gloriously good-looking, suave crooner presented his new act as a folksinger at Max Gordon's already legendary Village Vanguard. His folk songs—"John Henry," "A Man Ain't Nothing but a Man," "Mark Twain," "Hold 'Em Joe"—were interspersed with songs that had something of an island lilt, like "Venezuela Matilda" and "Coconut Woman." As his following grew—and it rapidly did—he moved uptown to the posher Blue Angel, another Max Gordon venue, where he met with even greater success. Before long, he found himself booked at the upper echelon of night clubs and hotels across the country, and under contract as a recording artist at RCA. If being a singer had never been one of Belafonte's dreams, the world clearly had its own plans for him.

These were years that mixed exhilaration with humiliation: the bigger he got, the harder it was for him to ignore the petty indignities of Jim Crow. The exhilarating part was, for instance, being booked to play the swanky Thunderbird Hotel, in Las Vegas. The humiliating part was then being forced to sleep in a Negro boarding house on the outskirts of town, and denied use of any of the hotel's facilities.

In 1953, enjoying his first real taste of affluence, Belafonte moved from Washington Heights into a white neighborhood in

Elmhurst, Queens. "Right when we moved in," Margurite recalls, "you suddenly saw a number of 'For Sale' signs appearing." One day soon afterward, Adrienne, who was then four, announced, "Mother, we've got to move! There are Niggeroes moving into the neighborhood." It seemed that one of her playmates had confusedly let her in on the neighborhood anxiety. "Why don't we wait to see what these Niggeroes are like?" Margurite replied.

That same year, John Murray Anderson signed Belafonte for *Almanac,* his annual talent show on Broadway, and Belafonte, the only black member of the cast, wound up winning a best-performance Tony. This, in turn, earned him an appearance on the annual "musical evening" of the *Ed Sullivan Show*—which led to many more appearances. Indeed, Belafonte went on to become perhaps the most frequently heard singer on the show.

Belafonte was receiving his greatest popular exposure so far, but he was also—and not for the last time, either—experiencing the bitterness of being shunned by his own people. "A lot of people on the left turned against me, because they thought there was no way I could get on the Sullivan show if I hadn't talked to the Committee, or whatnot. I had to live for a long time with the pain of rejection from people who were in the same camp." As I have learned, there are a number of people around who still harbor such suspicions. (Even Paul Robeson, Jr., the son of Belafonte's great hero, says, "I just have to leave it as an open question.") Poitier, though, says, "Harry escaped Robeson's fate partly because Robeson paid the dues. They crucified him—and the black community knew it, the white liberal community knew it. It stained an awful lot of hands."

What really changed Belafonte's life was the 1954 film *Carmen Jones*—adapted from Mike Todd's all-black version of Bizet's opera—in which Belafonte played the dashing young Army officer whose romance with Carmen Jones (Dorothy Dandridge) proves fatal. Not all the critics were impressed, but for many black viewers, in particular, the performances were electrifying, and remain so. "It was incredibly evocative and very sexy, and it was two of the physically most beautiful human beings on the planet," the theatre director George Wolfe says.

During this time, Belafonte's marriage to Margurite was disintegrating. Margurite, who had done graduate work at the Sorbonne and the University of Heidelberg and was soon to earn a Ph.D. in psychology, found herself temperamentally at odds with the milieu in which Belafonte traveled. "I just found the show-biz world to be shallow, and false," she recalls. "And, more and more, that was his whole life." (Their daughter Adrienne observes, "Mom had the drive and focus of many black contemporaries. She came from a family that was striving to be in the upper echelon of black society, which then moves you into the middle echelon of white society. For Dad, it was about changing all of society.")

Then, during the filming of *Carmen Jones,* Belafonte met a dancer named Julie Robinson, and things soon grew serious. Robinson, who had been dating Marlon Brando, had the distinction of being the only white dancer in the Katherine Dunham Company. Though she was of Russian-Jewish ancestry, she knew a lot more about African and African-American folk culture than Belafonte did: she had attended the Little Red School House, in the Village, and was involved with the N.A.A.C.P. In short, she was a thoroughly modern bohemian. Margurite, soon after giving birth to Shari, in 1954, discovered a cache of love letters that Julie Robinson had written to her husband. The Belafontes separated soon thereafter. (More acrimonious was Belafonte's breakup with his manager, Jack Rollins, around the same time. Rollins went on to become a high-profile agent and producer, but he remains bitter. "You look at this guy, and some people might say he's a credit to his race," Rollins says now. "The guy's a bum!")

In the winter of 1957, following the shooting of his next film, *Island in the Sun,* Belafonte managed to conceal two legal events: his divorce from Margurite and his subsequent marriage to Julie Robinson. Alas, news of his revised marital status leaked out shortly before the new film was released. *Island in the Sun* itself provoked controversy, with its story of an interracial love affair between characters played by Belafonte and his co-star, Joan Fontaine. (In fact, a bill was introduced in the South Carolina legislature proposing to fine any theater that showed the film.) But many blacks felt equally troubled by the developments in Belafonte's personal life. In the spring of 1957, the *Amsterdam News* ran the headline "BELAFONTE WEDS WHITE DANCER," and the paper cited in its story a saying from the twenties: "Give a Negro man fame and fortune, and he's got to have a white woman, a Packard car, and a bulldog." Readers were further informed that "Belafonte's popularity with his own race is hanging in the balance at the moment." That wasn't the wild hyperbole it may seem. In the late fifties, Eartha Kitt said, "I am not sure that Harry has completely healed the breach." She went on, "This is something that no Negro performer can afford. It has to play havoc with him inside."

What made the issue of particular moment was the fact that by 1957 Harry Belafonte had emerged as perhaps the country's most popular performer. The album *Harry Belafonte—Calypso*, released at the end of 1956, ended up selling more than a million and a half copies, more than any single-artist album ever had before, and it remained on the charts for a year and a half. Elvis and Sinatra were big in 1957, yet Belafonte—the King of Calypso, as he was touted—outsold both of them. (With fetching modesty, Belafonte told one reporter, "I don't want to be known as the guy who put the nail in the coffin of rock and roll.")

Belafonte had plenty of help, to be sure. "Listen to his voice without looking at him, and it is clear that his sound is not a sexy one, as the sound of Sinatra, of Nat Cole, and even of Billy Daniels, are sexy," the music executive Arnold Shaw wrote in 1960. "What Harry sounds like and what he looks like are not the same thing." So what he looked like was crucial, and his managers worked hard on sexing up his image: putting him in tight, form-fitting mohair pants, and colorful silk shirts that opened nearly to his navel. The King of Calypso also had a lot of help from his court—including the Juilliard-educated musician and songwriter Irving Burgie—or Lord Burgess, as he called himself, calypso style—who helped write or arrange most of the songs on the *Calypso* album.

The Belafonte craze swept the country. Claims adjusters in Tucson, driving to work in their white Hudsons, chorused along with their radios, "Daylight come and me wan' go home," at least when they weren't worrying about having "left a little girl in Kingston-town." Pete Seeger explains, " 'Day-O'—it's something that just makes you feel like taking a lungful of air and singing. A lot of people who never thought of themselves as singers could sing it."

In fact, to purists the problem with Belafonte was that he was too much of a singer, and not a calypsonian at all. As Daisann McLane, a calypso scholar—and singer—points out, *echt*-calypso is less about crooning than about percussion: "You don't necessarily have to be on key, but you do have to be on time." The King of Calypso title caused outrage for other reasons, too. Calypso—which had enjoyed brief spells of popularity in this country in the thirties (largely due to Rudy Vallee's radio show) and again in the forties—is a distinctively Trinidadian tradition; its French and Yoruba influences reflect the peculiar history of the island's settlement. In Trinidad, where calypsonians had long since formed something like a trade guild, a king of calypso was determined during an annual carnival known as the Calypso War: the calypsonian who most inventively insults his competitors wins the title. So Trinidadian calypso, which was traditionally extemporized, and which zestfully blended political protest and personal invective, was thus a far different creature from what usually passed under that name in the United States. As for what Belafonte brought in the guise of calypso, McLane says, "I would call it calypso with a conk."

Belafonte is unapologetic. "There were great calypsonians who could never see the light of day in this country, because they were so distanced from this culture. Now I came along and I modified the dialect, I put it into a rhythm that was more closely identified with the American scene. If, instead, I came in and sang this stuff with a thick Jamaican accent, it would have been like listening to Italian opera."

He recalls a press conference where a Trinidadian journalist berated him for styling himself King of Calypso when he had never been to Trinidad and had no contact with its traditions. Belafonte replied that he had no control over how his record label promoted him, and conceded that he wasn't really a calypso singer. "And then I said, 'I'll tell you, though, that I find that most of the culture coming out of Trinidad among calypso singers is not in the best interests of the people of the Caribbean community. I think that it's racist, because you sing to our own denunciation on color. You sing about our sexual power, and our gift of drinking, and rape, and all the things we do to which I have, and want, no particular claim. What I have sought to do with my art is take my understanding of the region and put it before people in a positive way. And doing these songs gives people another impression than the mythology they have that we're all lazy, living out of a banana tree, fucking each other to death.' "

But then Belafonte was never going to get any benedictions from the keepers of the *Volksgeist*. The mighty Odetta says, "There were lots of times when the folky-poos, as I call them, loved some particular singer, until his records became popular, and then all of a sudden they decided he wasn't a folksinger anymore. It depended on what they thought the bank account was. Isn't that pitiful?" By that yardstick, too, Belafonte was handily disqualified.


Belafonte had known the worship of strangers since his mid-twenties; but it was in 1957 that he experienced for the first time what Leo Braudy calls the "frenzy of renown." Each week brought more articles in newspapers and magazines, biographical sketches in *Life* and *Time* and the *Saturday Evening Post*. And this declaration from *Look:* "Singer-actor Harry Belafonte, one of the most acclaimed entertainers in America today, has also become the first Negro matinee idol in our entertainment history." That he succeeded where so many others failed was, in the eyes of some, no real mystery. Belafonte's friend and collaborator Bill Attaway observed, in the late fifties, "At the present stage of the struggle for human freedom, the need is for a bridge Negro—one who serves to connect white and Negro. Harry fills that need remarkably. Although he is brown-skinned and unmistakably Negro, he is acceptable in terms of white standards of beauty. Brown up Tab Hunter and you could hardly tell him from Harry Belafonte."

The status of bridge Negro did not sit very well with Belafonte, who wanted to be adored as much as the next man, but whose political sensibilities were in rebellion against the terms of that adoration. Nevertheless, he concedes, "I think the whole thing came in a package that was quite comfortable—attractive, articulate. With all my passion, I've never driven people to extremes. And what they loved so much was 'Banana Boat' and 'Jamaica Farewell,' and all that stuff." Indeed, you get the sense that in the late fifties Belafonte's political commitments were regarded, in Hollywood, as a fairly benign idiosyncrasy, rather on the order of Dean Martin's boozing.

Belafonte recalls that at about that time Otto Preminger wanted to cast him in a film version of *Porgy and Bess*. He found the script racially offensive—a romance between a druggie and a whore, wasn't it? "A host of people in the black community said no. The one who broke the chain was Sidney, who agreed to do it." In the event, the movie didn't do much business when it came out, in 1960, and it was roundly criticized in the black press. But a pattern was established. Belafonte's disenchantment with Hollywood grew. Over the next decade, his friend Poitier made seventeen major motion pictures; Belafonte made exactly none.

For one thing, the scripts he was offered appalled him. He mentions a couple of movies that he turned down. "One was a film called *To Sir with Love*."

"You turned that down?" I'm aghast.

"Oh, shit, yeah. And also *Lilies of the Field*."

This, of course, was the 1963 film that established Poitier as a significant presence in postwar cinema: noble, selfless, saintly. When I saw it, at thirteen, I was moved to tears. It was the perfect civil-rights vehicle for its moment. Its message to white America was practically telegraphed: We are a friendly and kind-hearted people; we are good citizens.

Belafonte had another take on it. "When I read *Lilies of the Field*,

I was furious. You've got these nuns fleeing Communism, and out of nowhere is this black person who throws himself whole-heartedly into their service, saying nothing, and doing nothing except being commanded by these Nazi nuns? He didn't kiss anybody, he didn't touch anybody, he had no culture, he had no history, he had no family, he had nothing. I just said, 'No, I don't want to play pictures like that.' What happened was that Sidney stepped in—and got the Academy Award."

Which was just typical, according to Belafonte. "In the early days, Sidney participated in left affairs, but once he became anointed he gave it up," he says, without bitterness. "Sidney was always more pliable, more accommodating. He handpicked each one of those pictures to continue to exercise that beauty and make sure that he never, ever disturbed the white psyche in anything he did. Not once. Not in public utterance or in private utterance." In the meantime, Belafonte says, "I put script after script before people who just rejected them out of hand, and I just said there's no point in trying to change this monster. They would not listen to my gods." In the end, Belafonte decided that "Hollywood was symptomatic, and the problem was the nation: I figured unless you change the national vocabulary, the national climate, the national attitude, you're not going to be able to change Hollywood."

Belafonte's involvement with the civil-rights movement in the sixties was no parlor project, and his friendship with King was no celebrity air kiss, either. Belafonte first met King in 1956, during the Montgomery bus boycotts. Though the black clergy's betrayals of Du Bois and Robeson had left him skeptical of the breed, King won him over by his humility and his earnestness. "I need your help," King told him. "I have no idea where this movement is going." An alliance was forged that lasted until King's death. King was a frequent guest of Belafonte's in New York, and Belafonte was one of the few who could serve as trusted conduits between King and the Southern Christian Leadership Conference, on the one hand, and the Washington establishment, on the other. He put up the seed money to support the newly founded Student Nonviolent Coordinating Committee. He financed a group that included Fannie Lou Hamer, Julian Bond, Bob Moses, Jim Foreman, and John Lewis to tour Africa and establish international liaisons there. It was Belafonte who bailed King out of the Birmingham jail, and who raised money to bail out a number of jailed student activists. Belafonte can be oddly reticent at times, and, though he's obviously proud of the role he played in the civil rights era, he speaks of these matters with some hesitancy. King's widow, Coretta Scott King, is more forthcoming. She recalls a day in the early sixties when Belafonte told King, laughing, "Martin, one of these days some of these crackers are going to kill you, and I'm going to end up having to take care of your family." Both things came to pass, Belafonte having insured King's life heavily for his family's sake. Mrs. King describes him as a member of King's small "strategy committee," a trusted adviser as well as one of the few effective fund-raisers in the movement; and in moments of crisis Belafonte's friendship with Robert Kennedy, then Attorney General, proved invaluable.

Meanwhile, Belafonte held on to his day job, continuing to tour and make television appearances. But TV had its vexations for him, too. In 1960, for example, he received an Emmy for a television special he did for the *Revlon Hour,* called "Tonight with Belafonte." Since the show was also a hit with viewers, Revlon decided that it was on to a good thing. According to Belafonte, an agreement was reached in which he would be given a million dollars to produce and serve as host of five shows. The second show, featuring black and white luminaries from jazz, folk, and pop, earned raves. Then he was brought up short by reality.

"Now I get called by Charlie Revson to have a meeting," he told me. "Would I come alone? I can't wait—I'm figuring he wants to give me half the company, or something. So we're having lunch in his private dining room, and he's saying, 'As a Jew in Jersey City, I understand oppression'—da, da, da, da—'but we have to talk about the show. Good ratings. Good reviews. Very nice. But we're getting some response that says you should do it all-black. If you could just take all the white people out . . .' I couldn't believe it. And I said,

'Mr. Revson, let me tell you something. If you'd asked me to put on a flowery shirt and sing more calypso tunes, and dance more, because that's what white people would like, I would consider it. But what you've asked me to do—there's no way to square it. I cannot become resegregated.' He said, 'O.K.' Four o'clock that afternoon, I had a check for eight hundred thousand dollars. Charlie Revson said, 'Goodbye. You're off the air.' "

Belafonte's first impulse, he says, was to raise a stink, but on talking it over with friends he reconsidered. Revson was just one of a number of advertisers who were looking to sponsor the occasional black entertainer. "If I blew the whistle and it became very political, they were going to run scared on black folk. People said, 'Just walk soft on this one, Harry. Don't say anything. It'll make it difficult for others.' So I didn't say anything." Seven years later, he was co-host of a TV special with Petula Clark, and at one point their hands touched. This time, when objections were raised by one of the marketing vice-presidents Belafonte did not walk softly. "I was thinking, After all the marches and protests—not this again." Belafonte told some journalist friends and was not displeased by the small ruckus that ensued.

But, if the political climate was changing in ways that were congenial to him, racial aesthetics were changing in ways that were less clearly advantageous. In 1967, Sidney Poitier was Hollywood's largest-grossing matinée star (*In the Heat of the Night, To Sir with Love,* and *Guess Who's Coming to Dinner* all having been released that year), and this happenstance was not lost on his friend. "From a Hollywood perspective, ironically, Sidney cut the mustard more than I did in terms of appearance," Belafonte says. "They were looking for somebody who was truly African in his heritage line. He certainly reflected that more than I." So Belafonte had been caught in what amounted to a temporal double bind: in earlier years, the material was too tame to suit his sense of amour propre; in later years, the Tab Hunter-with-a-tan look wasn't providing the racial frisson that filmmakers, and audiences, were seeking.

. . .

As we sit in what Belafonte refers to as the Red Room of his West End Avenue apartment, he tells me about a recent countrywide tour. Hunched slightly forward on a nine-foot damask sofa, he sounds depleted. "I'm going to tell you, man," he says. "I never saw so many white people in my life."

Neither had I. Belafonte's road show today consists of the standards he has sung for forty years, which he performs in a colorful silk shirt before a cardboard set of palm trees. When I caught up with him in Minneapolis, I saw a sold-out auditorium—the audience, from the looks of it, consisting of the same people who had bought his albums back in the fifties. But they loved him still. Onstage, he radiated energy and charisma, and you could see what it was that made him keep at it: the ovation was tremendous. It's also true that I was practically the only black person in the house. But then what was I expecting? Banjee boys in gold-fronts and skullies? Besides, it *was* Minneapolis.

Belafonte now says, sadly, "Let me tell you something. I don't know of any artist at my level who has ever been as much on the line for black liberation as I have and has as few black people in attendance at anything that he does as I do."

"That must hurt," I venture.

"Oh, I've layered it over so heavily it's stopped hurting now," he says, and for a moment I almost believe him. Then he shrugs. "Even before, because of my social and political position, most black people distanced themselves from me," he says. "Because I'm a tough package. In California, I walked into a place and somebody said, 'Here comes Mr. Conscience,' and all the cocaine left the room— you know? On the other hand, there's always been that noise and roar, and that approval I think in many ways saved me. Because, whether it was out of envy or jealousy or just plain fear, there was always that—I've always been out of the loop. I didn't grow up in the church, I didn't grow up in Mississippi, I didn't come out of the blues valleys of the Mississippi Delta. But most black Americans don't support anybody." And he cites such international performing artists as Miriam Makeba and Milton Nascimento. "There's a handful of people in the end who respect you and know you, but that's it. No black American artist has ever got the support of black America." I suppose he is overstating the case, but I know what he means. Belafonte goes on, "So there was some comfort in the fact that I was in a crowd."

Later, Sidney Poitier reflects on the vagaries of crossover success. "Let me tell you something," he says heavily. "We both suffer from that a lot. That kind of success is a bitch."

Longevity is one advantage that the career of the activist has over that of the entertainer, and in the last couple of decades Belafonte has devoted most of his energies to charitable organizations, among them UNICEF; indeed, it was Belafonte who conceived the idea of "We Are the World," the 1985 concert and recording that raised a hundred million dollars for famine relief in Ethiopia. Of course, for his own children, and now grandchildren, the competition for his attention could be something of a strain. Adrienne—who, like all her siblings, speaks of him with doting candor—says, "The family calls him 'As Soon As.' You know—'I'll come see you as soon as I get back from South Africa, Europe, the West Coast, etc. I'll call you as soon as I get off the phone with Bishop Tutu, Sidney, the President . . .' " Still, I'm impressed with the way he's kept things together. Julie and Margurite have become good friends, and the children of Belafonte's second marriage, David and Gina, are genuinely close to those of his first.

Belafonte has also been a force to be reckoned with behind the camera: he spent much of the eighties as a producer, trying to package a television miniseries that would narrate the history of apartheid in South Africa. It would have been a perfect project for him, uniting his interest in narrative filmmaking with his interests in global politics and social justice. Instead, it ended one friendship and strained another. First, he got in a dispute with Bill Cosby over who had the rights to the Nelson Mandela story. Evidently, Winnie Mandela had signed over exclusive rights to each of them in turn, though Belafonte viewed his rights as prior and preemptive. "So I called Bill, and he said, 'My wife has the rights, and you have to deal with her.' And his wife and I had never got on particularly well. After several frustrating attempts to work this out, I said to him, 'Look, it's a legal matter, and I have the rights. We have to work this out, and if we don't we'll have to turn it over to our lawyers.' And Cosby said, 'Well, call your best shot.' So I did. Shortly after that, his people backed down."

What particularly galled Belafonte was that *The Cosby Show* was a top-rated television show in apartheid South Africa, despite the cultural boycott of that country. Compounding the insult was the fact that Cosby had subsequently been asked to join the board of TransAfrica, an organization that Belafonte had helped found and had long supported. "I went to a board meeting one day, and they said, 'Bill Cosby's coming on board.' And I said, 'Wait a minute. Where's your integrity?' Here was a major violator of the boycott. Well, they smelled money, they smelled power. I said, 'Fine. I resign.' And Bill and I have had no exchanges since then. We see each other in public places and we give each other the nod. But the line is drawn."

Finally, after Belafonte secured backing and lined up a director and a cast, Sidney Poitier, who had long been slated to play Mandela, backed out, explaining that he had script problems, and had been offered another Mandela project, which he preferred. "So that killed it," Belafonte says. "I reported it to the network, and they said, 'Well, the game's over.' "

"Of course he had to have been disappointed," Poitier says flatly. "But Harry knows and accepts that there have not been and never will be any artistic favors done between us. It can't happen."

Belafonte says of Poitier's film, "I can't wait to see it—to see what he crucified us to get."

This sort of skirmishing is far from straightforward, largely because Poitier and Belafonte really are like brothers, with all the conflict and ambivalence that usually exists between brothers. When Belafonte explains why he won't live in Hollywood, for example, he cites the conflict between his ideals and the dominant ethos of the place, and adds, "That couldn't have been described more clearly than in my relationship with Sidney. Sidney just picked and chose when he wanted me to come to dinner. He still does it now. Even if I'm a guest in his house, there are some things he just will not invite me to—situations where he feels it will just make it uncomfortable for the people he's going to be with." Then he half relents: "It's O.K. I let him live in his comfort zone."

Shari Belafonte elaborates: "You see where Sidney's career has gone in terms of film, which is what Dad always wanted to do. And then you see where Dad's career has gone. It's one thing to have enormous success. It's another thing to be enormously successful in something you *want* to be enormously successful in." For her, the reason isn't far to seek. "I don't think Dad was a very good actor," she says bluntly. She thinks he had moments in the two Poitier-directed farces he did in the early seventies, *Buck and the Preacher* and *Uptown Saturday Night,* but "they were all caricature and he was hiding behind them—'acting,' as opposed to just being," she says. "And I think that now—he's soon to be seventy—he is getting to be comfortable in his own skin. And also Gina worked hard and it shows. I think he is getting better now."

Certainly Belafonte's performance in *Kansas City*—as a garrulous gangster known as Seldom Seen—has been heralded as a real turnaround in an acting career that has had few high points since the fifties; and he gives a lot of the credit to the coaching he received from Gina Belafonte, his and Julie's younger child. "Mainly, he wrote the lines," Altman says. "When I sent him the script, after we'd talked about him playing Seldom Seen, there were no lines in it. And he said, 'What kind of part is this?' I said, 'The one thing about you, Harry, I know, is the thing you're best at is talking.' " The two have since become close; indeed, Bob and Kathryn Altman are now frequent dinner guests of the Belafontes—part of a group of friends that includes Eli Wallach and Anne Jackson and (since they moved their primary residence to Manhattan, two years ago) Sidney and Joanna Poitier.

When Altman first proposed that Belafonte should play the role of a cold-blooded villain, though, he winced. "I said, 'That's a lot of pressure. I can play a leading-man type. Give me a horse and a gun—I can get away with that. But this is serious business.' A few drinks later, Altman says to me, 'I need to ask you something. Who started that rumor that you're an actor?' " The point was taken. Besides, if Belafonte were truly protective of his image he wouldn't have become involved in Altman's latest project, *Amos 'n' Andy.*

The other week, I got an excited phone call from Belafonte, who was on tour in Monte Carlo. "I talked to Altman. The project is a go!" he said. Then he laughed. "People are going to say, '*Amos 'n' Andy*? What the fuck is Harry Belafonte doin' with that?' "

*Amos 'n' Andy*—an all-black show about an inveterate schemer and his perpetual dupe—was once among the most popular shows in the country, first on radio, then on television. In the early fifties, however, the program was canceled, following protests from civil-rights organizations, which found its depiction of black people demeaning. "I think that was the right thing to do at the time," says Belafonte, who joined in that protest. But Altman persuaded him that the time had come to take another look at the show and its history.

Actually, what fascinated Altman most was the story behind *Amos 'n' Andy*—the story of its originators, two black comedians, named Aubrey Lyles and Flournoy Miller, who themselves had to don blackface, minstrel style, to entertain audiences both black and white. There's no script yet, but the idea is to interweave an *Amos 'n' Andy* narrative with the earlier story of the historical creation of *Amos 'n' Andy*—a story, in part, of exploitation, as white producers took the show away from its creators in the process of bringing it before a mass audience.

"When he told me about wanting to do *Amos 'n' Andy,* he said it was because he saw in it not only a hell of a piece of drama but a metaphor of human existence, especially as American culture is defined by him," Belafonte explains. "Everybody lives an *Amos 'n' Andy* existence, and not just the racial connotation that we have suffered: it is the façade that we put on every day in order to advance our ambitions. We're all living out these little plays every day in order to advance our interests."

Belafonte's association (presumably as a producer) will be no vaccine against controversy; the complexity of Altman's sensibility will have to suffice. But Belafonte says, "If we can successfully crack the back of telling that story, I think we'll have launched into the most troublesome subject in American culture, and that is the issue of race."

These days, of course, Americans are disposed to react to talk of racism the way you might to a discussion of one of those now banned artificial sweeteners: Cyclamates, cyclamates—didn't we already *do* something about that? And as for Harry Belafonte's perorations about social injustice, didn't that kind of talk go out with—well, with Harry Belafonte? But that's the thing: he's still here.

A cultural punishment is exacted from those lucky few to whom it has been given to embody the Zeitgeist: in the fullness of time, they become ridiculous. The former idol now headlining in second-string venues, cheesily reprising the smash hits of yesteryear, is uniquely a figure of bathos: the has-been can seem absurd in a way that the never-was doesn't. Unlike Engelbert Humperdinck, say, Belafonte has largely escaped that fate: his road show may verge on camp, but it doesn't cross over. In the funniest scene in Tim Burton's 1988 movie *Beetlejuice,* a malevolent ghost compels the members of a straitlaced dinner party to perform "The Banana Boat Song." Against their will, they find themselves dancing to a Caribbean beat and belting out "Day-O!" But the impression you're left with isn't how silly the song was but how bewitchingly catchy it still is: even without any supernatural agency, you find yourself wanting to join in the chorus.

Belafonte's daughter Adrienne told me, "One of my father's songs has a line about 'A secret soldier with pieces inside broke,' and that's how I see him. He wants to fix the world, and he's sad because he sees it slipping away. I believe he feels alone." A secret soldier with pieces inside broke: I watch Harry Belafonte relax in the elegant comfort of the Red Room, amid oversized club chairs with eighteenth-century needlepoint pillows, a wide fireplace flanked with wrought-iron church candlesticks, and carved religious figures from Bahia and the Philippines on the mantelpiece. A restive energy emanates from him all the same: he seems both perfectly at home and somehow caged.

We're speaking about a recent cancer scare he had, the prostate surgery from which he's still mending, and the way he dealt with the usual questions raised by such reminders of mortality. "There wasn't all that much I would have done differently, when I look back on it," he muses. He's still acutely conscious of being an autodidact, and he says he wishes he'd read more, learned more. I think he wishes he were loved more, too. I was struck by something a friend of his remarked decades ago, when Belafonte was a young man on top of the world: "Friends had to love him. Business associates had to love him. Relatives had to love him. And so on down the line—to children, animals, insects, and perhaps even bacteria." I was equally struck by the realization that Belafonte is one of the few mortals around to have come close to that blessed state. He stares straight ahead when he recalls the exhilaration of being shoulder to shoulder with Dr. King, and the "onrush of love" he felt from civil-rights marchers when he'd get up to speak. "Ask most black Americans," he says, "and they'll say, 'Oh, he's a standup guy. Oh, yeah, you can always count on Harry.' " He breaks off, sags a little, and sounds almost resigned when he adds, "But then don't ask them very much past that."

# The Passing of
# Anatole Broyard

❖

In 1982, an investment banker named Richard Grand-Jean took a summer's lease on an eighteenth-century farmhouse in Fairfield, Connecticut; its owner, Anatole Broyard, spent his summers in Martha's Vineyard. The house was handsomely furnished with period antiques, and the surrounding acreage included a swimming pool and a pond. But the property had another attraction, too. Grand-Jean, a managing director of Salomon Brothers, was an avid reader, and he took satisfaction in renting from so illustrious a figure. Anatole Broyard had by then been a daily book reviewer for the *Times* for more than a decade, and that meant that he was one of literary America's foremost gatekeepers. Grand-Jean might turn to the business pages of the *Times* first, out of professional obligation, but he turned to the book page next, out of a sense of self. In his Walter Mittyish moments, he sometimes imagined what it might be like to be someone who read and wrote about books for a living—someone to whom millions of readers looked for guidance.

Broyard's columns were suffused with both worldliness and high culture. Wry, mandarin, even self-amused at times, he wrote like a man about town, but one who just happened to have all of Western literature at his fingertips. Always, he radiated an air of soigné self-confidence: he could be amiable in his opinions or waspish, but he never betrayed a flicker of doubt about what he thought. This was a man who knew that his judgment would never falter and his sentences never fail him.

Grand-Jean knew little about Broyard's earlier career, but as he rummaged through Broyard's bookshelves he came across old copies of intellectual journals like *Partisan Review* and *Commentary*, to which Broyard had contributed a few pieces in the late forties and early fifties. One day, Grand-Jean found himself leafing through a magazine that contained an early article by Broyard. What caught his eye, though, was the contributor's note for the article—or, rather, its absence. It had been neatly cut out, as if with a razor.

A few years later, Grand-Jean happened on another copy of that magazine, and decided to look up the Broyard article again. This time, the note on the contributor was intact. It offered a few humdrum details—that Broyard was born in New Orleans, attended Brooklyn College and the New School for Social Research, and taught at New York University's Division of General Education. It also offered a less humdrum one: the situation of the American Negro, the note asserted, was a subject that the author "knows at first hand." It was an elliptical formulation, to be sure, but for Anatole Broyard it may not have been elliptical enough.

Broyard was born black and became white, and his story is compounded of equal parts pragmatism and principle. He knew that the world was filled with such snippets and scraps of paper, all conspiring to reduce him to an identity that other people had invented and he had no say in. Broyard responded with X-Acto knives and evasions, with distance and denials and half-denials and cunning half-truths. Over the years, he became a virtuoso of ambiguity and equivocation. Some of his acquaintances knew the truth; many more had heard rumors about "distant" black ancestry (wasn't there a grandfather who was black? a great-grandfather?). But most were entirely unaware, and that was as he preferred it. He kept the truth even from his own children. Society had decreed race to be a matter of natural law, but he wanted race to be an elective affinity, and it was never going to be a fair fight. A penalty was exacted. He shed a past and an identity to become a writer—a writer who wrote endlessly about the act of shedding a past and an identity.

Anatole Paul Broyard was born on July 16, 1920, in New Orleans to Paul Broyard and Edna Miller. His father was a carpenter and worked as a builder, along with his brothers; neither parent had graduated from elementary school. Anatole spent his early years in a modest house on St. Ann Street, in a colored neighborhood in the French Quarter. Documents in the Louisiana state archives show all Anatole's ancestors, on both sides, to have been Negroes, at least since the late eighteenth century. The rumor about a distant black ancestor was, in a sense, the reverse of the truth: he may have had one distant white ancestor. Of course, the conventions of color stratification within black America—nowhere more pronounced than in New Orleans—meant that light-skinned blacks often inter-married with other light-skinned blacks, and this was the case with Paul and his "high yellow" wife, Edna. Anatole was the second of three children; he and his sister Lorraine, two years older, were light-skinned, while Shirley, two years younger, was not so light-skinned. (The inheritance of melanin is an uneven business.) In any event, the family was identified as Negro, and identified itself as Negro. It was not the most interesting thing about them. But in America it was not a negligible social fact. The year before Anatole's birth, for example, close to a hundred blacks were lynched in the South and anti-black race riots claimed the lives of hundreds more.

While Anatole was still a child, the family moved to the Bedford-Stuyvesant area of Brooklyn, thus joining the great migration that took hundreds of thousands of Southern blacks to Northern cities during the twenties. In the French Quarter, Paul Broyard had been a legendary dancer, beau, and *galant*; in the French Quarter, the Broyards—Paul was one of ten siblings—were known for their craftsmanship. Brooklyn was a less welcoming environment. "He should never have left New Orleans, but my mother nagged him into it," Broyard recalled years later. Though Paul Broyard arrived there a master carpenter, he soon discovered that the carpenters' union was not favorably inclined toward colored applicants. A stranger in a strange city, Paul decided to pass as white in order to join the union and get work. It was strictly a professional decision, which affected his work and nothing else.

For Paul, being colored was a banal fact of life, which might be disguised when convenient; it was not a creed or something to take pride in. Paul did take pride in his craft, and he liked to boast of rescuing projects from know-nothing architects. He filled his home with furniture he had made himself—flawlessly professional, if a little too sturdily built to be stylish. He also took pride in his long legs and his dance-hall agility (an agility Anatole would share). It was a challenge to be a Brooklyn *galant*, but he did his best.

"Family life was very congenial, it was nice and warm and cozy, but we just didn't have any sort of cultural or intellectual nourishment at home," Shirley, who was the only member of the family to graduate from college, recalls. "My parents had no idea even what *The New York Times* was, let alone being able to imagine that Anatole might write for it." She says, "Anatole was different from the beginning." There was a sense, early on, that Anatole Broyard—or Buddy, as he was called then—was not entirely comfortable being a Broyard.

Shirley has a photograph, taken when Anatole was around four or five, of a family visit back to New Orleans. In it you can see Edna and her two daughters, and you can make out Anatole, down the street, facing in the opposite direction. The configuration was, Shirley says, pretty representative.

After graduating from Boys High School, in the late thirties, he enrolled in Brooklyn College. Already, he had a passion for modern culture—for European cinema and European literature. The idea that meaning could operate on several levels seemed to appeal to him. Shirley recalls exasperating conversations along those lines: "He'd ask me about a Kafka story I'd read or a French film I'd seen and say, 'Well, you see that on more than one level, don't you?' I felt like saying 'Oh, get off it.' Brothers don't say that to their sisters."

Just after the war began, he got married, to a black Puerto Rican woman, Aida, and they soon had a daughter. (He named her Gala, after Salvador Dali's wife.) Shirley recalls, "He got married and had a child on purpose—the purpose being to stay out of the Army. Then Anatole goes in the Army anyway, in spite of this child." And his wife and child moved in with the Broyard family.

Though his military records were apparently destroyed in a fire, some people who knew him at this time say that he entered the segregated Army as a white man. If so, he must have relished the irony that after attending officers' training school he was made the captain of an all-black stevedore battalion. Even then, his thoughts were not far from the new life he envisioned for himself. He said that he joined the Army with a copy of Wallace Stevens in his back pocket; now he was sending money home to his wife and asking her to save it so that he could open a bookstore in the Village when he got back. "She had other ideas," Shirley notes. "She wanted him to get a nice job, nine to five."

Between Aida and the allure of a literary life there was not much competition. Soon after his discharge from the Army, at war's end, he found an apartment in the Village, and he took advantage of the G.I. bill to attend evening classes at the New School for Social Research, on Twelfth Street. His new life had no room for Aida and Gala. (Aida, with the child, later moved to California and remarried.) He left other things behind, too. The black scholar and dramatist W. F. Lucas, who knew Buddy Broyard from Bed-Stuy, says, "He was black when he got into the subway in Brooklyn, but as soon as he got out at West Fourth Street he became white."

He told his sister Lorraine that he had resolved to pass so that he could be a writer, rather than a Negro writer. His darker-skinned younger sister, Shirley, represented a possible snag, of course, but then he and Shirley had never been particularly close, and anyway she was busy with her own life and her own friends. (Shirley graduated Phi Beta Kappa from Hunter College, and went on to marry Franklin Williams, who helped organize the Peace Corps and served as ambassador to Ghana.) They had drifted apart: it was just a matter of drifting farther apart. Besides, wasn't that why everybody came to New York—to run away from the confines of family, from places where people thought they knew who and what you were? Whose family *wasn't* in some way unsuitable? In a *Times* column in 1979 Broyard wrote, "My mother and father were too folksy for me, too colorful. . . . Eventually, I ran away to Greenwich Village, where no one had been born of a mother and father, where the people I met had sprung from their own brows, or from the pages of a bad novel. . . . Orphans of the avant-garde, we outdistanced our history and our humanity." Like so much of what he wrote in this vein, it meant more than it said; like the modernist culture he loved, it had levels.

In the Village, where Broyard started a bookstore on Cornelia Street, the salient thing about him wasn't that he was black but that he was beautiful, charming, and erudite. In those days, the Village was crowded with ambitious and talented young writers and artists, and Broyard—known for calling men "Sport" and girls "Slim"— was never more at home. He could hang out at the San Remo bar with Dwight Macdonald and Delmore Schwartz, and with a younger set who yearned to be the next Macdonalds and the next Schwartzes. Vincent Livelli, a friend of Broyard's since Brooklyn College days, recalls, "Everybody was so brilliant around us—we kept dueling with each other. But he was the guy that set the pace in the Village." His conversation sparkled—everybody said so. The sentences came out perfectly formed, festooned with the most apposite literary allusions. His high-beam charm could inspire worship but also resentment. Livelli says, "Anatole had a sort of dancing attitude toward life—he'd dance away from you. He had people understand that he was brilliant and therefore you couldn't hold him if you weren't worthy of his attention."

The novelist and editor Gordon Lish says, "Photographs don't suggest in any wise the enormous power he had in person. No part of him was ever for a moment at rest." He adds, "I adored him as a

man. I mean, he was really in a league with Neal Cassady as a kind
of presence." But there was, he says, a fundamental difference between Broyard and Kerouac's inspiration and muse: "Unlike Cassady, who was out of control, Anatole was *exorbitantly* in control.
He was fastidious about managing things."

Except, perhaps, the sorts of things you're supposed to manage.
His bookstore provided him with entrée to Village intellectuals—
and them with entrée to Anatole—yet it was not run as a business,
exactly. Its offerings were few but choice: Céline, Kafka, other hard-
to-find translations. The critic Richard Gilman, who was one of its
patrons, recalls that Broyard had a hard time parting with the in-
ventory: "He had these books on the shelf, and someone would
want to buy one, and he would snatch it back."

Around 1948, Broyard started to attract notice not merely for his
charm, his looks, and his conversation but for his published writings. The early pieces, as often as not, were about a subject to which
he had privileged access: blacks and black culture. *Commentary*, in
his third appearance in its pages, dubbed him an "anatomist of the
Negro personality in a white world." But was he merely an anthropologist or was he a native informant? It wasn't an ambiguity that
he was in any hurry to resolve. Still, if all criticism is a form of autobiography (as Oscar Wilde would have it), one might look to
these pieces for clues to his preoccupations at the time. In a 1950
*Commentary* article entitled "Portrait of the Inauthentic Negro,"
he wrote that the Negro's embarrassment over blackness should be
banished by the realization that "thousands of Negroes with 'typical' features are accepted as whites merely because of light complexion." He continued:

> The inauthentic Negro is not only estranged from whites—he is
> also estranged from his own group and from himself. Since his com-
> panions are a mirror in which he sees himself as ugly, he must reject
> them; and since his own self is mainly a tension between an accusa-
> tion and a denial, he can hardly find it, much less live in it. . . . He is
> adrift without a role in a world predicated on roles.

A year later, in "Keep Cool, Man: The Negro Rejection of Jazz," he wrote, just as despairingly, that the Negro's

> contact with white society has opened new vistas, new ideals in his imagination, and these he defends by repression, freezing up against the desire to be white, to have normal social intercourse with whites, to behave like them. . . . But in coolness he evades the issue . . . he becomes a pacifist in the struggle between social groups—not a conscientious objector, but a draft-dodger.

These are words that could be read as self-indictment, if anybody chose to do so. Certainly they reveal a ticklish sense of the perplexities he found himself in, and a degree of self-interrogation (as opposed to self-examination) he seldom displayed again.

In 1950, in a bar near Sheridan Square, Broyard met Anne Bernays, a Barnard junior and the daughter of Edward L. Bernays, who is considered the father of public relations. "There was this guy who was the handsomest man I have ever seen in my life, and I fell madly in love with him," Bernays, who is best known for such novels as *Growing Up Rich* and *Professor Romeo*, recalls. "He was physically irresistible, and he had this dominating personality, and I guess I needed to be dominated. His hair was so short that you couldn't tell whether it was curly or straight. He had high cheekbones and very smooth skin." She knew that he was black, through a mutual friend, the poet and Blake scholar Milton Klonsky. (Years later, in a sort of epiphany, she recognized Anatole's loping walk as an African-American cultural style: "It was almost as if this were inside him dying to get out and express itself, but he felt he couldn't do it.")

After graduation, she got a job as an editor at the literary semiannual *Discovery*. She persuaded Broyard to submit his work, and in 1954 the magazine ran a short story entitled "What the Cystoscope Said"—an extraordinary account of his father's terminal illness:

> I didn't recognize him at first, he was so bad. His mouth was open and his breathing was hungry. They had removed his false teeth, and

his cheeks were so thin that his mouth looked like a keyhole. I leaned over his bed and brought my face before his eyes. "Hello darlin'," he whispered, and he smiled. His voice, faint as it was, was full of love, and it bristled the hairs on the nape of my neck and raised goose flesh on my forearms. I couldn't speak, so I kissed him. His cheek smelled like wax.

Overnight, Broyard's renown was raised to a higher level. "Broyard knocked people flat with 'What the Cystoscope Said,' " Lish recalls. One of those people was Burt Britton, a bookseller who later co-founded Books & Co. In the fifties, he says, he read the works of young American writers religiously: "Now, if writing were a horse race, which God knows it's not, I would have gone out and put my two bucks down on Broyard." In *Advertisements for Myself*, Norman Mailer wrote that he'd buy a novel by Broyard the day it appeared. Indeed, Bernays recalls, on the basis of that story the Atlantic Monthly Press offered Broyard a twenty-thousand-dollar advance—then a staggeringly large sum for a literary work by an unknown—for a novel of which "Cystoscope" would be a chapter. "The whole literary world was waiting with bated breath for this great novelist who was about to arrive," Michael Vincent Miller, a friend of Broyard's since the late fifties, recalls. "Some feelings of expectation lasted for years."

Rumor surrounded Broyard like a gentle murmur, and sometimes it became a din. Being an orphan of the avant-garde was hard work. Among the black literati, certainly, his ancestry was a topic of speculation, and when a picture of Broyard accompanied a 1958 *Time* review of a Beat anthology it was closely scrutinized. Arna Bontemps wrote to Langston Hughes, "His picture . . . makes him look Negroid. If so, he is the only spade among the Beat Generation." Charlie Parker spied Broyard in Washington Square Park one day and told a companion, "He's one of us, but he doesn't want to admit he's one of us." Richard Gilman recalls an awkwardness that ensued when he stumbled across Anatole with his dark-skinned wife and child: "I just happened to come upon them in a restaurant that was not near our usual stomping grounds. He introduced me, and it was fine, but my sense was that he would rather not have had anyone he knew meet them." He adds, "I remember thinking at the time that he had the look of an octoroon or a quadroon, one of those—which he strenuously denied. He got into very great disputes with people."

One of those disputes was with Chandler Brossard, who had been a close friend: Broyard was the best man at Brossard's wedding. There was a falling out, and Brossard produced an unflattering portrait of Broyard as the hustler and opportunist Henry Porter in his 1952 novel, *Who Walk in Darkness*. Brossard knew just where Broyard was most vulnerable, and he pushed hard. His novel originally began, "People said Henry Porter had Negro blood," as does the version published in France. Apparently fearing legal action, however, Brossard's American publisher, New Directions, sent it to Broyard in galley form before it was published.

Anne Bernays was with Broyard when the galleys arrived. Broyard explained to her, "They asked me to read it because they are afraid I am going to sue." But why would he sue, she wanted to know. "Because it says I'm a Negro," he replied grimly. "Then," Bernays recalls, "I said, 'What are you going to do?' He said, 'I am going to make them change it.' And he did."

The novel went on to be celebrated as a groundbreaking chronicle of Village hipsters; it also—as a result of the legal redactions—reads rather oddly in places. Henry Porter, the Broyard character, is rumored to be not a Negro but merely an illegitimate":

> I suspect [the rumor] was supposed to explain the difference between the way he behaved and the way the rest of us behaved. Porter did not show that he knew people were talking about him this way. I must give him credit for maintaining a front of indifference that was really remarkable.
>
> Someone both Porter and I knew quite well once told me the next time he saw Porter he was going to ask him if he was or was not an illegitimate. He said it was the only way to clear the air. Maybe so.

But I said I would not think of doing it. . . . I felt that if Porter ever wanted the stories about himself cleared up, publicly, he would one day do so. I was willing to wait.

And that, after all, is the nature of such secrets: they are not what cannot be known but what cannot be acknowledged.

Another trip wire seems to have landed Broyard in one of the masterpieces of twentieth-century American fiction, William Gaddis's *The Recognitions*. Livelli explains, "Now, around 1947 or '48, William Gaddis and Anatole were in love with the same gal, Sheri Martinelli. They were rivals, almost at each other's throats. And Willie was such a sweetheart that he had a mild approach to everything, and Anatole was sort of a stabber: he injected words like poison into conversations." When *The Recognitions* came out, in 1955, "Anatole caught on to it right away, and he was kind of angry over it." The Broyard character is named Max, and Gaddis wrote that he "always looked the same, always the same age, his hair always the same short length," seemingly "a parody on the moment, as his clothes caricatured a past at eastern colleges where he had never been." Worse is his "unconscionable smile," which intimates "that the wearer knew all of the dismal secrets of some evil jungle whence he had just come."

Broyard's own account of these years—published in 1993 as *Kafka Was the Rage*—is fueled by the intertwined themes of writing and women. Gaddis says, "His eyes were these great pools—soft, gentle pools. It was girls, girls, girls: a kind of intoxication of its own. I always thought, frankly, that that's where his career went, his creative energies."

Anne Bernays maintains, "If you leave the sex part out, you're only telling half the story. With women, he was just like an alcoholic with booze." She stopped seeing him in 1952, at her therapist's urging. "It was like going cold turkey off a drug," she says, remembering how crushing the experience was, and she adds, "I think most women have an Anatole in their lives."

Indeed, not a few of them had Anatole. "He was a pussy gangster, really," Lucas, a former professor of comparative literature, says

with Bed-Stuy bluntness. Gilman recalls being in Bergdorf Good-
man and coming across Broyard putting the moves on a salesgirl. "I
hid behind a pillar—otherwise he'd know that I'd seen him—and
watched him go through every stage of seduction: 'What do you
think? Can I put this against you? Oh, it looks great against your
skin. You have the most wonderful skin.' And then he quoted
Baudelaire."

Quoting Baudelaire turns out to be key. Broyard's great friend
Ernest van den Haag recalls trolling the Village with Broyard in
those days: "We obviously quite often compared our modus
operandi, and what I observed about Anatole is that when he liked
a girl he could speak to her brilliantly about all kinds of things which
the girl didn't in the least understand, because Anatole was really
vastly erudite. The girl had no idea what he was talking about, but
she loved it, because she was under the impression, rightly so, that
she was listening to something very interesting and important. His
was a solipsistic discourse, in some ways." Indeed, the narrator of
"What the Cystoscope Said" tells of seducing his ailing father's
young and ingenuous nurse in a similar manner:

> "Listen," I said, borrowing a tone of urgency from another source,
> "I want to give you a book. A book that was written for you, a book
> that belongs to you as much as your diary, that's dedicated to you
> like your nurse's certificate." . . . My apartment was four blocks away,
> so I bridged the distance with talk, raving about *Journey to the End
> of the Night*, the book she needed like she needed a hole in her head.

Broyard recognized that seduction was a matter not only of talking but of listening, too, and he knew how to pay attention with an
engulfing level of concentration. The writer Ellen Schwamm, who
met Broyard in the late fifties, says, "You show me a man who talks,
and I'll show you a thousand women who hurl themselves at his
feet. I don't mean just talk, I mean dialogues. He *listened*, and he
was willing to speak of things that most men are not interested in:
literature and its effect on life." But she also saw another side to
Broyard's relentless need to seduce. She invokes a formulation

made by her husband, the late Harold Brodkey: "Harold used to say that a lot of men steal from women. They steal bits of their souls, bits of their personalities, to construct an emotional life, which many men don't have. And I think that Anatole needed something of that sort."

It's an image of self-assemblage which is very much in keeping with Broyard's own accounts of himself. Starting in 1946, and continuing at intervals for the rest of his life, he underwent analysis. Yet the word "analysis" is misleading: what he wanted was to be refashioned—or, as he told his first analyst, to be *transfigured*. "When I came out with the word, I was like someone who sneezes into a handkerchief and finds it full of blood," he wrote in the 1993 memoir. "I wanted to discuss my life with him not as a patient talking to an analyst but as if we were two literary critics discussing a novel. . . . I had a literature rather than a personality, a set of fictions about myself." He lived a lie because he didn't want to live a larger lie: and Anatole Broyard, Negro writer, was that larger lie.

Alexandra Nelson, known as Sandy, met Broyard in January of 1961. Broyard was forty, teaching the odd course at the New School and supporting himself by freelancing: promotional copy for publishers, liner notes for Columbia jazz records, blurbs for the Book-of-the-Month Club. Sandy was twenty-three and a dancer, and Broyard had always loved dancers. Of Norwegian descent, she was strikingly beautiful, and strikingly intelligent. Michael Miller recalls, "She represented a certain kind of blonde, a certain kind of sophisticated carriage and a way of moving through the world with a sense of the good things. They both had marvelous taste."

It was as if a sorcerer had made a list of everything Broyard loved and had given it life. At long last, the conqueror was conquered: in less than a year, Broyard and Sandy were married. Sandy remembers his aura in those days: "Anatole was very hip. It wasn't a pose—it was in his sinew, in his bones. And, when he was talking to you, you just felt that you were receiving all this radiance from him." (Van den Haag says, "I do think it's not without significance that Anatole married a blonde, and about as white as you can get. He may have feared a little bit that the children might turn out black. He must have been pleased that they didn't.")

While they were still dating, two of Broyard's friends told Sandy that he was black, in what seemed to be a clumsy attempt to scare her off. "I think they really weren't happy to lose him, to see him get into a serious relationship," she says. "They were losing a playmate, in a way." Whatever the cultural sanctions, she was unfazed. But she says that when she asked Broyard about it he proved evasive: "He claimed that he wasn't black, but he talked about 'island influences,' or said that he had a grandmother who used to live in a tree on some island in the Caribbean. Anatole was like that—he was very slippery." Sandy didn't force the issue, and the succeeding years only fortified his sense of reserve. "Anatole was very strong," she says. "And he said about certain things, 'Just keep out. This is the deal if you get mixed up with me.' " The life that Broyard chose to live meant that the children did not meet their Aunt Shirley until after his death—nor, except for a couple of brief visits in the sixties, was there any contact even with Broyard's light-skinned mother and older sister. It was a matter of respecting the ground rules. "I would try to poke in those areas, but the message was very direct and strong," Sandy explains. "Oh, when I got angry at him, you know, one always pushes the tender points. But over time you grow up about these things and realize you do what you can do and there are certain things you can't."

In 1963, just before their first child, Todd, was born, Anatole shocked his friends by another big move—to Connecticut. Not only was he moving to Connecticut but he was going to be commuting to work: for the first time in his life, he would be a company man. "I think one of his claims to fame was that he hadn't had an office job—somehow, he'd escaped that," Sandy says. "There had been no real need for him to grow up." But after Todd was born—a daughter, Bliss, followed in 1966—Anatole spent seven years working full-time as a copywriter at the Manhattan advertising agency Wunderman Ricotta & Kline.

Over the next quarter century, the family lived in a series of eighteenth-century houses, sometimes bought on impulse, in places like Fairfield, Redding, Greens Farms, and Southport. Here, in a land of leaf-blowers and lawnmowers, Bed-Stuy must have seemed almost comically remote. Many of Broyard's intimates from the late forties knew about his family; the intimates he acquired in the sixties did not, or else had heard only rumors. Each year, the number of people who knew Buddy from Bed-Stuy dwindled; each year, the rumors grew more nebulous; each year, he left his past further behind. Miller says, "Anatole was a master at what Erving Goffman calls 'impression management.' " The writer Evelyn Toynton says, "I remember once going to a party with Sandy and him in Connecticut. There were these rather dull people there, stockbrokers and the usual sorts of people, and Anatole just knocked himself out to charm every single person in the room. I said to him, 'Anatole, can't you ever *not* be charming?' " Miller observes, "He was a wonderful host. He could take people from different walks of life—the president of Stanley Tools or a vice-president of Merrill Lynch, say, and some bohemian type from the Village—and keep the whole scene flowing beautifully. He had perfect pitch for the social encounter, like Jay Gatsby."

It was as if, wedded to an ideal of American self-fashioning, he sought to put himself to the ultimate test. It was one thing to be accepted in the Village, amid the Beats and hipsters and émigrés, but to gain acceptance in Cheever territory was an achievement of a higher order. "Anatole, when he left the Village and went to Connecticut, was able not only to pass but even to be a kind of influential presence in that world of rich white Wasps," Miller says. "Maybe that was a shallower part of the passing—to be accepted by Connecticut gentry."

Broyard's feat raised eyebrows among some of his literary admirers: something borrowed, something new. Daphne Merkin, another longtime friend, detected "a 'country-squire' tendency—a complicated tendency to want to establish a sort of safety through bourgeoisness. It was like a Galsworthy quality."

Even in Arcadia, however, there could be no relaxation of vigilance: in his most intimate relationships, there were guardrails. Broyard once wrote that Michael Miller was one of the people he liked best in the world, and Miller is candid about Broyard's profound influence on him. Today, Miller is a psychotherapist, based in Cambridge, and the author, most recently, of *Intimate Terrorism*. From the time they met until his death, Broyard read to him the first draft of almost every piece he wrote. Yet a thirty-year friendship of unusual intimacy was circumscribed by a subject that they never discussed. "First of all, I didn't *know*," Miller says. "I just had intuitions and had heard intimations. It was some years before I'd even put together some intuition and little rumblings—nothing ever emerged clearly. There was a certain tacit understanding between us to accept certain pathways as our best selves, and not challenge that too much." It was perhaps, he says a little sadly, a limitation on the relationship.

In the late sixties, Broyard wrote several front-page reviews for the *Times Book Review*. "They were brilliant, absolutely sensational," the novelist Charles Simmons, who was then an assistant editor there, says. In 1971, the *Times* was casting about for a new daily reviewer, and Simmons was among those who suggested Anatole Broyard. It wasn't a tough sell. Arthur Gelb, at the time the paper's cultural editor, recalls, "Anatole was among the first critics I brought to the paper. He was very funny, and he also had that special knack for penetrating hypocrisy. I don't think he was capable of uttering a boring sentence."

You could say that his arrival was a sign of the times. Imagine: Anatole Broyard, downtown flaneur and apostle of sex and high modernism, ensconced in what was, literarily speaking, the ultimate establishment perch. "There had been an awful lot of very tame, very conventional people at the *Times,* and Broyard came in as a sort of ambassador from the Village and Village sophistication," Alfred Kazin recalls. Broyard had a highly developed appreciation of the paper's institutional power, and he even managed to use it to avenge wrongs done him in his Village days. Just before he started his job at the daily, he published a review in the *Times Book Review* of a new novel by one Chandler Brossard. The review began, "Here's a book so transcendently bad it makes us fear not only for the condition of the novel in this country, but for the country itself."

Broyard's reviews were published in alternation with those of Christopher Lehmann-Haupt, who has now been a daily reviewer at the *Times* for more than a quarter century, and who readily admits that Broyard's appointment did not gladden his heart. They hadn't got along particularly well when Lehmann-Haupt was an editor at the *Times Book Review,* nor did Lehmann-Haupt entirely approve of Broyard's status as a fabled libertine. So when A. M. Rosenthal, the paper's managing editor, was considering hiring him, Lehmann-Haupt expressed reservations. He recalls, "Rosenthal was saying, 'Give me five reasons why not.' And I thoughtlessly blurted out, 'Well, first of all, he is the biggest ass man in town.' And Rosenthal rose up from his desk and said, 'If that were a disqualification for working for *The New York Times*'—and he waved—'this place would be empty!' "

Broyard got off to an impressive start. Lehmann-Haupt says, "He had a wonderful way of setting a tone, and a wonderful way of talking himself through a review. He had good, tough instincts when it came to fiction. He had taste." And the jovial Herbert Mitgang, who served a stint as a daily reviewer himself, says, "I always thought he was the most literary of the reviewers. There would be something like a little essay in his daily reviews."

Occasionally, his acerbic opinions got him in trouble. There was, for example, the storm that attended an uncharitable review of a novel by Christy Brown, an Irish writer who was born with severe cerebral palsy. The review concluded:

> It is unfortunate that the author of "A Shadow on Summer" is an almost total spastic—he is said to have typed his highly regarded first novel, "Down All the Days," with his left foot—but I don't see how the badness of his second novel can be blamed on that. Any man who can learn to type with his left foot can learn to write better than he has here.

Then, there was the controversial review of James Baldwin's piously sentimental novel of black suffering, *If Beale Street Could Talk*. Broyard wrote:

> If I have to read one more description of the garbage piled up in the streets of Harlem, I may just throw protocol to the winds and ask whose garbage is it? I would like to remind Mr. Baldwin that the City Health Code stipulates that garbage must be put out in proper containers, not indiscrimately "piled."

No one could accuse Broyard of proselytizing for progressive causes. Jason Epstein, for one, was quick to detect a neoconservative air in his reviews, and Broyard's old friend Ernest van den Haag, a longtime contributing editor at *National Review*, volunteers that he was available to set Broyard straight on the issues when the need arose. Broyard could be mischievous, and he could be tendentious. It did not escape notice that he was consistently hostile to feminist writers. "Perhaps it's naïve of me to expect people to write reasonable books about emotionally charged subjects," one such review began, irritably. "But when you have to read and review two or three books each week, you do get tired of 'understanding' so much personal bias. You reach a point where it no longer matters that the author's mistakes are well meant. You don't care that he or she is on the side of the angels; you just want them to tell the truth."

Nor did relations between the two daily reviewers ever become altogether cordial. Lehmann-Haupt tells of a time in 1974 when Broyard said that he was sick and couldn't deliver a review. Lehmann-Haupt had to write an extra review in less than a day, so that he could get to the Ali-Frazier fight the next night, where he had ringside seats. Later, when they discussed the match, Broyard seemed suspiciously knowledgeable about its particulars; he claimed that a friend of his had been invited by a television executive to watch it on closed-circuit TV. "I waited about six months, because one of the charming things about Anatole was that he never remembered his lies," Lehmann-Haupt says, laughing. "And I said,

'Did you see that fight?' And he said, 'Oh, yeah—I was there as a guest of this television executive.' *That's* why he couldn't write the review!"


Broyard had been teaching off and on at the New School since the late fifties, and now his reputation as a writing teacher began to soar. Certainly his fluent prose style, with its combination of grace and clarity, was a considerable recommendation. He was charismatic and magisterial, and, because he was sometimes brutal about students' work, they found it all the more gratifying when he was complimentary. Among his students were Paul Breslow, Robert Olen Butler, Daphne Merkin, and Hilma Wolitzer. Ellen Schwamm, who took a workshop with him in the early seventies, says, "He had a gourmet's taste for literature and for language, and he was really able to convey that: it was a very sensual experience."

These were years of heady success and, at the same time, of a rising sense of failure. An arbiter of American writing, Broyard was racked by his inability to write his own magnum opus. In the fifties, the Atlantic Monthly Press had contracted for an autobiographical novel—the novel that was supposed to secure Broyard's fame, his place in contemporary literature—but, all these years later, he had made no progress. It wasn't for lack of trying. Lehmann-Haupt recalls his taking a lengthy vacation in order to get the book written. "I remember talking to him—he was up in Vermont, where somebody had lent him a house—and he was in agony. He banished himself from the Vineyard, was clearly suffering, and he just couldn't do it." John Updike, who knew Broyard slightly from the Vineyard, was reminded of the anticipation surrounding Ellison's second novel: "The most famous non-book around was the one that Broyard was not writing." (The two non-book writers were in fact quite friendly: Broyard admired Ellison not only as a writer but as a dancer—a high tribute from such an adept as Broyard.)

Surrounded by analysts and psychotherapists—Sandy Broyard had become a therapist herself by this time—Broyard had no shortage of explanations for his inability to write his book. "He did have a total writer's block," van den Haag says, "and he was analyzed by various persons, but it didn't fully overcome the writer's block. I couldn't prevent him from going back to 'The Cystoscope' and trying to improve it. He made it, of course, not better but worse." Broyard's fluency as an essayist and a reviewer wasn't quite compensation. Charles Simmons says, "He had produced all this charming criticism, but the one thing that mattered to him was the one thing he hadn't managed to do."

As the seventies wore on, Miller discussed the matter of blockage with his best friend in relatively abstract terms: he suggested that there might be something in Broyard's relationship to his family background that was holding him back. In the eighties, he referred Broyard to his own chief mentor in gestalt therapy, Isador From, and From became perhaps Broyard's most important therapist in his later years. "In gestalt therapy, we talk a lot about 'unfinished business': anything that's incomplete, unfinished, haunts the whole personality and tends, at some level, to create inhibition or blockage," Miller says. "You're stuck there at a certain point. It's like living with a partly full bladder all your life."

Some people speculated that the reason Broyard couldn't write his novel was that he was living it—that race loomed larger in his life because it was unacknowledged, that he couldn't put it behind him because he had put it beneath him. If he had been a different sort of writer, it might not have mattered so much. But Merkin points out, "Anatole's subject, even in fiction, was essentially himself. I think that ultimately he would have had to deal with more than he wanted to deal with."

Broyard may have been the picture of serene self-mastery, but there was one subject that could reliably fluster him. Gordon Lish recalls an occasion in the mid-seventies when Burt Britton (who was married to a black woman) alluded to Anatole's racial ancestry. Lish says, "Anatole became inflamed, and he left the room. He snapped, like a dog snapping—he *barked* at Britton. It was an ugly moment." To people who knew nothing about the matter, Broyard's sensitivities were at times simply perplexing. The critic Judith Dunford used to go to lunch with Broyard in the eighties. One day, Broyard mentioned his sister Shirley, and Dunford, idly making conversation, asked him what she looked like. Suddenly, she saw an extremely worried expression on his face. Very carefully, he replied, "Darker than me."

There was, finally, no sanctuary. "When the children were older, I began, every eighteen months or so, to bring up the issue of how they needed to know at some point," Sandy Broyard says. "And then he would totally shut down and go into a rage. He'd say that at some point he would tell them, but he would not tell them now." He was the Scheherazade of racial imposture, seeking and securing one deferral after another. It must have made things not easier but harder. In the modern era, children are supposed to come out to their parents: it works better that way around. For children, we know, can judge their parents harshly—above all, for what they understand as failures of candor. His children would see the world in terms of authenticity; he saw the world in terms of self-creation. Would they think that he had made a Faustian bargain? Would they speculate about what else he had not told them—about the limits of self-invention? Broyard's resistance is not hard to fathom. He must have wondered when the past would learn its place, and stay past.

Anatole Broyard had confessed enough in his time to know that confession did nothing for the soul. He preferred to communicate his truths on higher frequencies. As if in exorcism, Broyard's personal essays deal regularly with the necessary, guilt-ridden endeavor of escaping family history: and yet the feelings involved are well-nigh universal. The thematic elements of passing—fragmentation, alienation, liminality, self-fashioning—echo the great themes of modernism. As a result, he could prepare the way for exposure without ever risking it. Miller observes, "If you look at the writing closely enough, and listen to the intonations, there's something there that is like no writer from the completely white world. Freud talked about the repetition compulsion. With Anatole, it's interesting that he was constantly hiding it and in some ways constantly revealing it."

Sandy speaks of these matters in calmly analytic tones; perhaps because she is a therapist, her love is tempered by an almost profes-

sional dispassion. She says, "I think his own personal history continued to be painful to him," and she adds, "In passing, you cause
your family great anguish, but I also think, conversely, do we look
at the anguish it causes the person who is passing? Or the anguish
that it was born out of?"

It may be tempting to describe Broyard's self-positioning as arising
from a tortured allegiance to some liberal-humanist creed. In fact,
the liberal pieties of the day were not much to his taste. "It wasn't
about an ideal of racelessness but something much more complex
and interesting," Miller says. "He was actually quite anti-black,"
Evelyn Toynton says. She tells of a time when she was walking with
him on a street in New York and a drunken black man came up to
him and asked for a dollar. Broyard seethed. Afterward, he remarked to her, "I look around New York, and I think to myself, If
there were no blacks in New York, would it really be any loss?"

No doubt this is a calculation that whites, even white liberals,
sometimes find themselves idly working out: How many black
muggers is one Thelonious Monk worth? How many Willie Hor-
tons does Gwendolyn Brooks redeem? In 1970, Ellison published
his classic essay "What America Would Be Like Without Blacks," in
*Time*; and one reason it is a classic essay is that it addresses a question that lingers in the American political unconscious. Commanding as Ellison's arguments are, there remains a whit of defensiveness
in the very exercise. It's a burdensome thing to refute a fantasy.

And a burdensome thing to be privy to it. Ellen Schwamm recalls
that one of the houses Broyard had in Connecticut had a black
jockey on the lawn, and that "he used to tell me that Jimmy Baldwin had said to him, 'I can't come and see you with this crap on
your lawn.' " (Sandy remembers the lawn jockey—an antique—as
having come with the house; she also recalls that it was stolen one
day.) Charles Simmons says that the writer Herbert Gold, before introducing him to Broyard, warned him that Broyard was prone to
make comments about "spades," and Broyard did make a few such
comments. "He personally, on a deeper level, was not enamored of

blacks," van den Haag says. "He avoided blacks. There is no question he did." Sandy is gingerly in alluding to this subject. "He was very short-tempered with the behavior of black people, the sort of behavior that was shown in the news. He had paid the price to be at liberty to say things that, if you didn't know he was black, you would misunderstand. I think it made him ironical."

Every once in a while, however, Broyard's irony would slacken, and he would speak of the thing with an unaccustomed and halting forthrightness. Toynton says that after they'd known each other for several years he told her there was a "C" (actually, "col," for "colored") on his birth certificate. "And then another time he told me that his sister was black and that she was married to a black man." The circumlocutions are striking: not that *he* was black but that his birth certificate was; not that *he* was black but that his family was. Perhaps this was a matter less of evasiveness than of precision.

"Some shrink had said to him that the reason he didn't like brown-haired women or dark women was that he was afraid of his own shit," Toynton continues. "And I said, 'Anatole, it's as plain as plain can be that it has to do with being black.' And he just stopped and said, 'You don't know what it was like. It was horrible.' He told me once that he didn't like to see his sisters, because they reminded him of his unhappy childhood." (Shirley's account suggests that this unhappy childhood may have had more to do with the child than with the hood.)

Ellen Schwamm remembers one occasion when Broyard visited her and Harold Brodkey at their apartment, and read them part of the memoir he was working on. She says that the passages seemed stilted and distant, and that Brodkey said to him, "You're not telling the truth, and if you try to write lies or evade the truth this is what you get. What's the real story?" She says, "Anatole took a deep breath and said, 'The real story is that I'm not who I seem. I'm a black.' I said, 'Well, Anatole, it's no great shock, because this rumor has been around for years and years and years, and everyone assumes there's a small percentage of you that's black, if that's what you're trying to say.' And he said, 'No, that's not what I'm trying to say. My father could pass, but in fact my mother's black, too. We're black as far back as I know.' We never said a word of it to anybody, because he asked us not to."

Schwamm also says that she begged him to write about his history: it seemed to her excellent material for a book. But he explained that he didn't want notoriety based on his race—on his revealing himself to be black—rather than on his talent. As Toynton puts it, Broyard felt that he had to make a choice between being an aesthete and being a Negro. "He felt that once he said, 'I'm a Negro writer,' he would have to write about black issues, and Anatole was such an aesthete."

All the same, Schwamm was impressed by a paradox: the man wanted to be appreciated not for being black but for being a writer, even though his pretending not to be black was stopping him from writing. It was one of the very few ironies that Broyard, the master ironist, was ill equipped to appreciate.

Besides, there was always his day job to attend to. Broyard might suffer through a midnight of the soul in Vermont; but he was also a working journalist, and when it came to filing his copy he nearly always met his deadlines. In the late seventies, he also began publishing brief personal essays in the *Times*. They are among the finest work he did—easeful, witty, perfectly poised between surface and depth. In them he perfected the feat of being self-revelatory without revealing anything. He wrote about his current life, in Connecticut: "People in New York City have psychotherapists, and people in the suburbs have handymen. While anxiety in the city is existential, in the country it is structural." And he wrote about his earlier life, in the city: "There was a kind of jazz in my father's movements, a rhythm compounded of economy and flourishes, functional and decorative. He had a blues song in his blood, a wistful jauntiness he brought with him from New Orleans." (Wistful, and even worrisome: "I half-expected him to break into the Camel Walk, the Shimmy Shewobble, the Black Bottom or the Mess

Around.") In a 1979 essay he wrote about how much he dreaded family excursions:

> To me, they were like a suicide pact. Didn't my parents know that the world was just waiting for a chance to come between us?
>
> Inside, we were a family, but outside we were immigrants, bizarre in our differences. I thought that people stared at us, and my face grew hot. At any moment, I expected my father and mother to expose their tribal rites, their eccentric anthropology, to the gape of strangers.
>
> Anyone who saw me with my family knew too much about me.

These were the themes he returned to in many of his personal essays, seemingly marking out the threshold he would not cross. And if some of his colleagues at the *Times* knew too much about him, or had heard the rumors, they wouldn't have dreamed of saying anything. Abe Rosenthal (who did know about him) says that the subject never arose. "What was there to talk about? I didn't really consider it my business. I didn't think it was proper or polite, nor did I want him to think I was prejudiced, or anything."

But most people knew nothing about it. C. Gerald Fraser, a reporter and an editor at the *Times* from 1967 until 1991, was friendly with Broyard's brother-in-law Ambassador Franklin Williams. Fraser, who is black, recalls that one day Williams asked him how many black journalists there were at the *Times*. "I listed them," he says, "and he said, 'You forgot one.' I went over the list again, and I said, 'What do you mean?' He said, 'Shirley's brother, Anatole Broyard.' I was dumbstruck, because I'd never heard it mentioned at the *Times* that he was black, or that the paper had a black critic."

In any event, Broyard's colleagues did not have to know what he was to have reservations about *who* he was. He cultivated his image as a trickster—someone who would bend the rules, finesse the system—and that image only intensified his detractors' ire. "A good book review is an act of seduction, and when he did it there was nobody better," John Leonard says, but he feels that Broyard's best was not always offered. "I considered him to be one of the laziest book reviewers to come down the pike." Soon a running joke was that Broyard would review only novels shorter than two hundred pages. In the introduction to *Aroused by Books,* a collection of the reviews he published in the early seventies, Broyard wrote that he tried to choose books for review that were "closest to [his] feelings." Lehmann-Haupt says dryly, "We began to suspect that he often picked the books according to the attractiveness of the young female novelists who had written them." Rosenthal had shamed him for voicing his disquiet about Broyard's reputation as a Don Juan, but before long Rosenthal himself changed his tune. "Maybe five or six years later," Lehmann-Haupt recalls, "Rosenthal comes up to me, jabbing me in the chest with a stiffened index finger and saying, 'The trouble with Broyard is that he writes with his cock!' I bit my tongue."

Gradually, a measure of discontent with Broyard's reviews began to make itself felt among the paper's cultural commissars. Harvey Shapiro, the editor of the *Book Review* from 1975 to 1983, recalls conversations with Rosenthal in which "he would tell me that all his friends hated Anatole's essays, and I would tell him that all my friends loved Anatole's essays, and that would be the end of the conversation." In 1984, Broyard was removed from the daily *Times* and given a column in the *Book Review.*

Mitchel Levitas, the editor of the *Book Review* from 1983 to 1989, edited Broyard's column himself. He says, "It was a tough time for him, you see, because he had come off the daily book review, where he was out there in the public eye twice a week. That was a major change in his public role." In addition to writing his column, he was put to work as an editor at the *Book Review.* The office environment was perhaps not altogether congenial to a man of his temperament. Kazin recalls, "He complained to me constantly about being on the *Book Review,* because he had to check people's quotations and such. I think he thought that he was superior to the job."

Then, too, it was an era in which the very notion of passing was beginning to seem less plangent than preposterous. Certainly Broyard's skittishness around the subject wasn't to everyone's liking. Brent Staples, who is black, was an editor at the *Book Review* at the time Broyard was there. "Anatole had it both ways," Staples says. "He would give you a kind of burlesque wink that seemed to indicate he was ready to accept the fact of your knowing that he was a black person. It was a real ambiguity, tacit and sort of recessed. He jived around and played with it a lot, but never made it express the fact that he was black." It was a game that tried Staples's patience. "When Anatole came anywhere near me, for example, his whole style, demeanor, and tone would change," he recalls. "I took that as him conveying to me, 'Yes, I am like you. But I'm relating this to you on a kind of recondite channel.' Over all, it made me angry. Here was a guy who was, for a long period of time, probably one of the two or three most important critical voices on literature in the United States. How could you, actively or passively, have this fact hidden?"

Staples pauses, then says, "You know, he turned it into a joke. And when you change something basic about yourself into a joke, it spreads, it metastasizes, and so his whole presentation of self became completely ironic. *Everything* about him was ironic."

There were some people who came to have a professional interest in achieving a measure of clarity on the topic. Not long before Broyard retired from the *Times,* in 1989, Daphne Merkin, as an editor at Harcourt Brace Jovanovich, gave him an advance of a hundred thousand dollars for his memoirs. (The completed portion was ultimately published, as *Kafka Was the Rage,* by Crown.) Merkin learned that "he was, in some ways, opaque to himself," and her disquiet grew when the early chapters arrived. "I said, 'Anatole, there's something odd here. Within the memoir, you have your family moving to a black neighborhood in Brooklyn. I find that strange— unless they're black.' I said, 'You can do many things if you're writing a memoir. But if you squelch stuff that seems to be crucial about you, and pretend it doesn't exist . . .'" She observes that he was much attached to aspects of his childhood, but "in a clouded way."

· · ·

When Broyard retired from the *Times,* he was nearly sixty-nine. To Sandy, it was a source of some anguish that their children still did not know the truth about him. Yet what was that truth? Broyard was a critic—a critic who specialized in European and American fiction. And what was race but a European and American fiction? If he was passing for white, perhaps he understood that the alternative was passing for black. "But if some people are light enough to live like white, mother, why should there be such a fuss?" a girl asks her mother in "Near-White," a 1931 story by the Harlem Renaissance author Claude McKay. "Why should they live colored when they could be happier living white?" Why, indeed? One could concede that the passing of Anatole Broyard involved dishonesty; but is it so very clear that the dishonesty was mostly Broyard's?

To pass is to sin against authenticity, and "authenticity" is among the founding lies of the modern age. The philosopher Charles Taylor summarizes its ideology thus: "There is a certain way of being human that is *my* way. I am called upon to live my life in this way, and not in imitation of anyone else's life. But the notion gives a new importance to being true to myself. If I am not, I miss the point of my life; I miss what being human is for *me*." And the Romantic fallacy of authenticity is only compounded when it is collectivized: when the putative real me gives way to the real us. You can say that Anatole Broyard was (by any juridical reckoning) "really" a Negro, without conceding that a Negro is a thing you can really be. The vagaries of racial identity were increased by what anthropologists call the rule of "hypodescent"—the one-drop rule. When those of mixed ancestry—and the majority of blacks are of mixed ancestry—disappear into the white majority, they are traditionally accused of running from their "blackness." Yet why isn't the alternative a matter of running from their "whiteness"? To emphasize these perversities, however, is a distraction from a larger perversity. You can't get race "right" by refining the boundary conditions.

The act of razoring out your contributor's note may be quixotic, but it is not mad. The mistake is to assume that birth certificates and biographical sketches and all the other documents generated by the modern bureaucratic state reveal an anterior truth—that they are merely signs of an independently existing identity. But in fact they constitute it. The social meaning of race is established by these identity papers—by tracts and treatises and certificates and pamphlets and all the other verbal artifacts that proclaim race to be real and, by that proclamation, make it so.

So here is a man who passed for white because he wanted to be a writer and he did not want to be a Negro writer. It is a crass disjunction, but it is not his crassness or his disjunction. His perception was perfectly correct. He *would* have had to be a Negro writer, which was something he did not want to be. In his terms, he did not want to write about black love, black passion, black suffering, black joy; he wanted to write about love and passion and suffering and joy. We give lip service to the idea of the writer who happens to be black, but had anyone, in the postwar era, ever seen such a thing?

Broyard's friend Richard A. Shweder, an anthropologist and a theorist of culture, says, "I think he believed that reality is constituted by style," and ascribed to Broyard a "deeply romantic view of the intimate connection between style and reality." Broyard passed not because he thought that race wasn't important but because he knew that it was. The durable social facts of race were beyond reason, and, like Paul Broyard's furniture, their strength came at the expense of style. Anatole Broyard lived in a world where race had, indeed, become a trope for indelibility, for permanence. "All I *have* to do," a black folk saying has it, "is stay black and die."

Broyard was a connoisseur of the liminal—of crossing over and, in the familiar phrase, getting over. But the ideologies of modernity have a kicker, which is that they permit no exit. Racial recusal is a forlorn hope. In a system where whiteness is the default, racelessness is never a possibility. You cannot opt out; you can only opt in. In a scathing review of a now forgotten black author, Broyard announced that it was time to reconsider the assumption of many black writers that " 'whitey' will never let you forget you're black." For his part, he wasn't taking any chances. At a certain point, he seems to have decided that all he had to do was stay white and die.

. . .

In 1989, Broyard resolved that he and his wife would change their life once more. With both their children grown, they could do what they pleased. And what they pleased—what he pleased, anyway—was to move to Cambridge, Massachusetts. They would be near Harvard, and so part of an intellectual community. He had a vision of walking through Harvard Square, bumping into people like the sociologist Daniel Bell, and having conversations about ideas in the street. Besides, his close friend Michael Miller was living in the area. Anne Bernays, also a Cambridge resident, says, "I remember his calling several times and asking me about neighborhoods. It was important for him to get that right. I think he was a little disappointed when he moved that it wasn't to a fancy neighborhood like Brattle or Channing Street. He was on Wendell Street, where there's a tennis court across the street and an apartment building and the houses are fairly close together." It wasn't a matter of passing so much as of positioning.

Sandy says that they had another the-children-must-be-told conversation shortly before the move. "We were driving to Michael's fiftieth-birthday party—I used to plan to bring up the subject in a place where he couldn't walk out. I brought it up then because at that point our son was out of college and our daughter had just graduated, and my feeling was that they just absolutely needed to know, as adults." She pauses. "And we had words. He would just bring down this gate." Sandy surmises, again, that he may have wanted to protect them from what he had experienced as a child. "Also," she says, "I think he needed still to protect himself." The day after they moved into their house on Wendell Street, Broyard learned that he had prostate cancer, and that it was inoperable.

Broyard spent much of the time before his death, fourteen months later, making a study of the literature of illness and death, and publishing a number of essays on the subject. Despite the occasion, they were imbued with an almost dandyish, even jokey sense of incongruity: "My urologist, who is quite famous, wanted to cut off my testicles. . . . Speaking as a surgeon, he said that it was the surest, quickest, neatest solution. Too neat, I said, picturing myself with no balls. I knew that such a solution would depress me, and I was sure that depression is bad medicine." He had attracted notice in 1954 with the account of his father's death from a similar cancer; now he recharged his writing career as a chronicler of his own progress toward death. He thought about calling his collection of writings on the subject "Critically Ill." It was a pun he delighted in.

Soon after the diagnosis was made, he was told that he might have "in the neighborhood of years." Eight months later, it became clear that this prognosis was too optimistic. Richard Shweder, the anthropologist, talks about a trip to France that he and his wife made with Anatole and Sandy not long before Anatole's death. One day, the two men were left alone. Shweder says, "And what did he want to do? He wanted to throw a ball. The two of us just played catch, back and forth." The moment, he believes, captures Broyard's athleticism, his love of physical grace.

Broyard spent the last five weeks of his life at the Dana Farber Cancer Institute, in Boston. In therapy sessions, the need to set things straight before the end had come up again—the need to deal with unfinished business and, most of all, with his secret. He appeared willing, if reluctant, to do so. But by now he was in almost constant pain, and the two children lived in different places, so the opportunities to have the discussion as a family were limited. "Anatole was in such physical pain that I don't think he had the wherewithal," Sandy says. "So he missed the opportunity to tell the children himself." She speaks of the expense of spirit, of psychic energy, that would have been required. The challenge would have been to explain why it had remained a secret. And no doubt the old anxieties were not easily dispelled: would it have been condemned as a Faustian bargain or understood as a case of personality overspilling, or rebelling against, the reign of category?

It pains Sandy even now that the children never had the chance to have an open discussion with their father. In the event, she felt that they needed to know before he died, and, for the first time, she took it upon herself to declare what her husband could not. It was an early afternoon, ten days before his death, when she sat down with her two children on a patch of grass across the street from the institute. "They knew there was a family secret, and they wanted to know what their father had to tell them. And I told them."

The stillness of the afternoon was undisturbed. She says carefully, "Their first reaction was relief that it was only this, and not an event or circumstance of larger proportions. Only following their father's death did they begin to feel the loss of not having known. And of having to reformulate who it was that they understood their father—and themselves—to be."

At this stage of his illness, Anatole was moving in and out of lucidity, but in his room Sandy and the children talked with humor and irony about secrets and about this particular secret. Even if Anatole could not participate in the conversation, he could at least listen to it. "The nurses said that hearing was the last sense to go," Sandy says.

It was not as she would have planned it. She says, gently, "Anatole always found his own way through things."

The writer Leslie Garis, a friend of the Broyards' from Connecticut, was in Broyard's room during the last weekend of September, 1990, and recorded much of what he said on his last day of something like sentience. He weighed perhaps seventy pounds, she guessed, and she describes his jaundice-clouded eyes as having the permanently startled look born of emaciation. He was partly lucid, mostly not. There are glimpses of his usual wit, but in a mode more aleatoric than logical. He spoke of Robert Graves, of Sheri Martinelli, of John Hawkes interpreting Miles Davis. He told Sandy that he needed to find a place to go where he could "protect his irony." As if, having been protected by irony throughout his life, it was now time to return the favor.

"I think friends are coming, so I think we ought to order some food," he announced hours before he lapsed into his final coma. "We'll want cheese and crackers, and Faust."

"Faust?" Sandy asked.

Anatole explained, "He's the kind of guy who makes the Faustian bargain, and who can be happy only when the thing is revealed."

. . .

A memorial service, held at a Congregationalist church in Connecticut, featured august figures from literary New York, colleagues
from the *Times,* and neighbors and friends from the Village and the
Vineyard. Charles Simmons told me that he was surprised at how
hard he took Broyard's death. "You felt that you were going to have
him forever, the way you feel about your own child," he said.
"There was something wrong about his dying, and that was the reason." Speaking of the memorial service, he says, marveling, "You
think that you're the close friend, you know? And then I realized
that there were twenty people ahead of me. And that his genius was
for close friends."

Indeed, six years after Broyard's death many of his friends seem
to be still mourning his loss. For them he was plainly a vital principle, a dancer and romancer, a seducer of men and women. (He considered seduction, he wrote, "the most heartfelt literature of the
self.") Sandy tells me, simply, "You felt more alive in his presence,"
and I've heard almost precisely the same words from a great many
others. They felt that he lived more intensely than other men. They
loved him—perhaps his male friends especially, or, anyway, more
volubly—and they admired him. They speak of a limber beauty, of
agelessness, of a radiance. They also speak of his excesses and his
penchant for poses. Perhaps, as the bard has it, Broyard was "much
more the better for being a little bad."

And if his presence in American fiction was pretty much limited
to other people's novels, that is no small tribute to his personal vi-
brancy. You find him reflected and refracted in the books of his
peers, like Anne Bernays (she says there is a Broyard character in
every novel she's written) and Brossard and Gaddis, of course, but
also in those of his students. His own great gift was as a feuilleton-
ist. The personal essays collected in *Men, Women and Other Anti-
climaxes* can put you in mind of *The Autocrat of the Breakfast-Table,*
by Oliver Wendell Holmes, Sr. They are brief impromptus, tonally
flawless. To read them is to feel that you are in the company of
someone who is thinking things through. The essays are often ur-

bane and sophisticated, but not unbearably so, and they can be un-expectedly moving. Literary culture still fetishizes the novel, and there he was perhaps out of step with his times. Sandy says, "In the seventies and eighties, the trend, in literature and film, was to get sparer, and the flourish of Anatole's voice was dependent on the luxuriance of his language." Richard Shweder says, "It does seem that Anatole's strength was the brief, witty remark. It was aphoristic. It was the critical review. He was brilliant in a thousand or two thousand words." Perhaps he wasn't destined to be a novelist, but what of it? Broyard was a Negro who wanted to be something other than a Negro, a critic who wanted to be something other than a critic. Broyard, you might say, wanted to be something other than Broyard. He very nearly succeeded.

Shirley Broyard Williams came to his memorial service, and many of his friends—including Alfred Kazin, who delivered one of the eulogies—remember being puzzled and then astonished as they realized that Anatole Broyard was black. For Todd and Bliss, however, meeting Aunt Shirley was, at last, a flesh-and-blood confirmation of what they had been told. Shirley is sorry that they didn't meet sooner, and she remains baffled about her brother's decision. But she isn't bitter about it; her attitude is that she has had a full and eventful life of her own—husband, kids, friends—and that if her brother wanted to keep himself aloof she respected his decision. She describes the conversations they had when they did speak: "They always had to be focused on something, like a movie, because you couldn't afford to be very intimate. There had to be something that would get in the way of the intimacy." And when she phoned him during his illness it was the same way. "He never gave that up," she says, sounding more wistful than reproachful. "He never learned how to be comfortable with me." So it has been a trying set of circumstances all around. "The hypocrisy that surrounds this issue is so thick you could chew it," Shirley says wearily.

Shirley's husband died several months before Anatole, and I think she must have found it cheering to be able to meet family members who had been sequestered from her. She says that she wants to get to know her nephew and her niece—that there's a lot of time to make up. "I've been encouraging Bliss to come and talk, and we had lunch, and she calls me on the phone. She's really responded very well. Considering that it's sort of last-minute."

Years earlier, in an essay entitled "Growing Up Irrational," Anatole Broyard wrote, "I *descended* from my mother and father. I was *extracted* from them." His parents were "a conspiracy, a plot against society," as he saw it, but also a source of profound embarrassment. "Like every great tradition, my family had to die before I could understand how much I missed them and what they meant to me. When they went into the flames at the crematorium, all my letters of introduction went with them." Now that he had a wife and family of his own, he had started to worry about whether his children's feelings about him would reprise his feelings about his parents: "Am I an embarrassment to them, or an accepted part of the human comedy? Have they joined my conspiracy, or are they just pretending? Do they understand that, after all those years of running away from home, I am still trying to get back?"

# Acknowledgments

In my early twenties, I sat in the office of William Shawn, the fabled *New Yorker* editor, who, on the basis of work I'd published elsewhere, encouraged me to write a story on a strike that was taking place at Yale. In his own inimitable manner (a manner of overpraise buffered with a homeopathic, nearly imperceptible, tincture of irony), he made me feel like a sepia William Shakespeare. That feeling lasted me all the way to the train station, by which point the conviction that I was hopelessly unequal to the task began to gain the upper hand; in any event, I never delivered the article. Still, I was a journalist before I was an academic; even as a graduate student in the seventies, I divided my energies between my studies at the University of Cambridge and a job as a London correspondent at *Time*, where I received an education of a different kind, though no less rigorous for that. When I took my first teaching position, my senior colleagues recommended that I remove any evidence of journalism, literary or otherwise, from my vita if I had any interest in tenure. These days, I think, people are less likely to regard the writing of scholarship as irreconcilable with, well, writing. A truce has been declared, if occasionally it is an uneasy one.

In contrast to literary criticism, say, writing a profile is in part an exercise in toning down your stentorian certainties; people benefit from a slightly more gingerly approach than texts. I think doing it right means trying to figure out when to get out of the way. Besides, deep down I'm no Stentor. I want to be able to rear with righteous indignation at regular intervals, but somehow it doesn't come naturally to me: I experience sadness and frustration, but despite my best efforts, these elements seldom ignite into a robust, manly emotion like outrage. I'm not always convinced that hard questions have easy answers; I prefer the exploratory to the conclusory mode. I spent my early adulthood dodging the question the militants always had at the ready, "Where you gonna be when the revolution comes?"; and I'm still not *entirely* sure of the answer. Which makes me, perhaps, a less than reassuring cicerone in these matters; maybe I'm all thumbs, but they don't always point up or down.

The profile is a genre that supposes people matter, in all their particularity—as agents and as emblems, yes, but also as themselves. This is a book of characters, for all that certain preoccupations run through it like broken capillaries. Once you start approaching people as cultural homework, you'd better hang it up. Lives don't have a "point"; admittedly, stories about them often do, but, you hope, not *too* much of one. I'll own up to having mucked about in the swampy depths of cultural theory in the course of my day job as an English teacher. Maybe that's why too much abstract theorizing on the subject makes me fidget uneasily, like a reformed alcoholic at a wine bar. I'd like to think this is a book propelled by particulars, by details, by *stuff*. It's probably never possible to ditch abstraction altogether, but you do try to get a head start before that lumbering swamp thing starts to gain on you.


This book owes its existence to two people. Tina Brown, *The New Yorker*'s boundlessly energetic and brilliantly demanding editor, believes that there *are* second acts in American life, and in effectively publishing this book on the installment plan, she has made it so. Henry Finder, my editor at the magazine, which is to say my counselor and coach, believes that acts are always there to be shaped up—though, as a devotee of reticence, he has strictly forbidden me any further effusions on his behalf. In the past few years, the magazine has sent me everywhere from the White House, where my brief was to discuss the politics of image with a slightly forlorn First Lady, to those overmiked and underlit downtown clubs where the hip-hop nation tries its hand at poetry and sometimes succeeds. Boredom has never been a peril, though whiplash might be.

Every *New Yorker* author learns what a mud-caked car feels like when it passes through a deluxe car wash—with the rivulets of hot wax, sharp jets of undercarriage rust retardant, a blast of WheelBrite, and those floppy felt anemones that flail away madly before leaving everything shiny and dry. It is indeed a privilege to be in the hands of such an attentive and rigorous editorial staff, beginning with the legendary Eleanor Gould Packard, who has parsed the syntax of nearly every sentence that has appeared in the magazine for the past fifty years; as a sworn enemy of obliquity, she is, as much as the tutelary spirits of Harold Ross and William Shawn, responsible for its discursive integrity. I'm indebted, as well, to the sensitive ministrations and unfailing good taste of Ann Goldstein, who read and redacted a majority of these profiles. On other occasions, Elizabeth Pearson-Griffiths and Mary Norris proved vigilant and tactful readers. As fact-checkers, John Dorfman, Anne Mortimer-Maddox, Elizabeth Dobell, and Adam Shatz have been scrupulous in the thankless but essential task of minimizing inaccuracy and maximizing precision. As features director at *The New Yorker,* David Kuhn was a paragon of perserverance, facilitation, and unfailing good judgment. Susan Mercandetti proved endlessly inventive at helping me to locate the subjects interviewed in these pages—at which pursuit the resourceful and unflappable Brenda Phipps, too, proved invaluable. David Remnick, the Michael Jordan of journalism, was endlessly generous with his astute editorial counsel, far above and beyond the call of collegiality; his visage appears next to the word *mensch* in my personal lexicon.

Kate Kinast, Richard Newman, and Michael Vazquez cheerfully responded to my pleas for help in my researches. Kate Medina, my editor at Random House, and her assistant Molly Stern, earned my gratitude for their forbearance and aid in shaping the format of this book. The gifted Joanne Kendall, my secretary, consistently met the crush of deadlines with good will and good cheer, expertly keying my ballpoint-pen-and-yellow-legal-pad drafts into neatly processed words; I'm also grateful to Rosalie Prosser and the staff of Alice Darling Secretarial Services for all their help. And thanks especially to my wife and daughters, Sharon Adams and Maggie and Liza Gates, for their love, patience, and toleration. Finally, I must give thanks to the people whose voices you hear in this book; all had better things to do than to speak with me but gave lavishly of their time withal, and this book is the product of their generosity.

# Index

## ABOUT THE AUTHOR

HENRY LOUIS GATES, JR., is W. E. B. Du Bois Professor of the Humanities and Chair of the Department of Afro-American Studies at Harvard University. He lives in Cambridge.

## ABOUT THE TYPE

This book was set in Galliard, a typeface designed by Matthew Carter for the Merganthaler Linotype Company in 1978. Galliard is based on the sixteenth-century typefaces of Robert Granjon.